BRAVE MEN
DARK WATERS

BRAVE MEN
DARK WATERS

The Untold Story of the Navy SEALs

ORR KELLY

Foreword by
R. Adm. C. L. ("Irish") Flynn, USN (Ret.)

Presidio

Published by Presidio Press
505 B San Marin Drive, Suite 300
Novato, CA 94945-1340

Library of Congress Cataloging-in-Publication Data

Kelly, Orr.
  Brave men . . . dark waters : the untold story of the Navy SEALs /
Orr Kelly.
        p.   cm.
  Includes bibliographical references and index.
  ISBN 0-89141-408-8
    1. United States. Navy. Sea, Air, Land Teams—History.
  2. United States—History, Naval—20th century. I. Title.
  VG87.K45 1992
  359.9—dc20   92-4385
                                                        CIP

Typography by ProImage
Printed in the United States of America

For my parents, Charles John and Edith Orr Kelly.

CONTENTS

FOREWORD

Orr Kelly's book is welcome and timely. It succeeds admirably in tracing the development of naval special operations forces from their ancestry in the combat demolition units and Underwater Demolition Teams of the Second World War, through their employment in the Korean and Southeast Asian conflicts, to their most recent experience in Grenada, Panama, and the Persian Gulf. The narrative not only follows the direct lineage from Draper Kauffman, who is universally recognized as the founder, to today's SEALs, but it also relates the important influence of units and personalities whose experiences paralleled the main line: the Scouts and Raiders; Captain Miles's Navy Group, China; and Dr. Lambertsen's seminal development of tactics and equipment in the Office of Strategic Services. Further insight comes from contrasting the American experience in underwater special operations with the different approaches of the Italian and British navies.

Much of the material was new and enlightening to me, as I believe it will be even to others who have spent a professional lifetime in naval special operations. The book's originality shows that much is owed to Orr Kelly's skillful research and interviews; it also underscores the potential returns from further research and the opening of sources which could now be declassified without risk to future operations.

The book is timely because the defense establishment has noted that special operations forces, for decades at the periphery of their parent services, possess unique capabilities and potential that will give them an essential, central place in the armed forces of the post–Cold War era. Recently assigned to the U.S. Special Operations Command, which has unique budgetary authority to provide the resources they need, naval special operations forces are being expanded on a scale unprecedented in their peacetime history and quite opposite to the overall downward trend in the size of the armed forces. Once again, as Orr Kelly aptly expresses it, naval special operations forces must answer the question, "Who are we?" Their predecessor units were created or expanded in wartime, following identification of specific operational needs to which resourceful men readily adapted themselves. In those days there was little in the way of preexisting organizations, materiel, or career considerations to fetter their adaptability Now, however, the expansion is taking place within a framework of established organizations and force structures, accompanied by long-range, expensive programs for acquisition of equipment. Unlike their predecessors, today's naval special warriors have the assurance of sustained and adequate resources, but their adaptability is programmatically constrained, and they have neither the actualities of an ongoing conflict nor the received certainties of the Cold War to guide their planning. On balance, it is probably more difficult than ever to determine the niche of operational capabilities that the expanded naval component of the U.S. Special Operations Command should fill, and toward which its development should be directed. Nevertheless, I have no doubt that naval special operations forces will find a valid answer to the question, "Who are we?" As they struggle for the answer, they could find much that is helpful and inspiring in their predecessors' experience as it is recounted in this book.

In presenting a comprehensive account of naval special forces, of failures as well as successes, and of the occasional intramural disputes over fundamental matters, Orr Kelly has given us credit for wanting the portrait done to Cromwell's taste, "warts and all." The book is all the better for this, especially since the blemishes in the record of naval special operations forces are really few, attributable to adolescence, and likely to fade as the forces mature, For now, what is needed is dispassionate commentary, not hagiography, and this book is to be commended for providing it.

R. Adm. Cathal L. ("Irish") Flynn, USN (Ret.)
The first regular U.S. Navy SEAL admiral

PREFACE

This book was written specifically to fill a gap in U.S. military history. Earlier books have described the feats of the Underwater Demolition Teams in World War II and the operations of the SEALs in Vietnam. But no single book has pulled together in one place the fascinating story of the navy's frogmen and other members of the navy's special warfare community, from the beaches of Normandy and Saipan to the brilliant deception carried out by six SEALs as the allies began their ground assault on Saddam Hussein's dug-in forces in February 1991.

One of the first stops in my research effort was the Navy Library, at the Washington Navy Yard. There, Gina Akers was especially helpful in guiding me to the unit histories of the UDT and SEAL teams and to the library's extensive collection of oral histories, most of them acquired from the Naval Institute.

My search of the paper trail also took me to the office of *Current News* at the Pentagon. Denise Brown was, as usual, most helpful in making available everything in that office's extensive collection of newspaper and magazine articles about naval special warfare.

William Arkin, of Greenpeace, also gave me access to a large selection of articles, congressional testimony, and official reports he had collected over a period of years. Although his primary interest had been in gathering information about the SEALs' training in the use of small nuclear devices—an assignment they no longer have—the material he had pulled together contained a good deal of general information about the SEALs and their activities. Similarly, Jeffrey Richelson, of the National Security Archive, let me look through the news clippings, congressional testimony, and other information he had gathered about special operations forces.

I am especially indebted to Lt. Comdr. Sankey Blanton, of Chapel Hill, North Carolina, who has made a hobby of collecting books about naval special warfare. He provided me with a detailed bibliography and loaned me a number of books, such as those describing British and Italian underwater operations during World War II, that would simply have been unavailable from any other source.

The office of the navy's chief of information, Rear Adm. Brent Baker, was, as usual, most cooperative in helping me arrange interviews with members of the naval special warfare community. Baker's predecessor, retired Rear Adm. Jimmie Finkelstein, also put in a good word for me in key places. I was assisted first by Lt. Mark Walker, until he was sent off to the Persian Gulf, and then by Lt. Dane LaJoie. I also benefited from the assistance of Comdr. J. F. Zakem, special assistant for public affairs to the secretary of the navy.

Also especially helpful were Comdr. Robert Pritchard, public affairs officer for the Naval Special Warfare Command in Coronado, California, and Lt. Ed Balaban, public affairs officer for Naval Special Warfare Group Two at Little Creek, Virginia. Before Pritchard came on the scene at Coronado, Lt. Comdr. Robert Tillman, the flag secretary, had the added duty of dealing with the press. On my first visit to Coronado in the fall of 1990, Tillman not only helped me through the usual round of interviews, but also arranged for me to make an overnight visit to the SEALs' training site at San Clemente Island. My escorts on that trip were Lt. Comdr. Richard Sisk and Chief Petty Officer Jeff Green. Green, a weapons expert, guided me in test firing all the weapons in the SEAL arsenal, with the exception of the special .50-caliber sniper rifle, and sent me away with a colorfully bruised right shoulder.

Three other public affairs officers who proved most helpful were Frank Gregory and Ken Hoffman at the Naval Coastal Systems Center in Panama City, Florida, and Gary Comerford of the Naval Investigative Service in Washington.

An important stop during my research was at the UDT/SEAL Museum near the site of the original World War II training center at Fort Pierce,

Florida. James D. Watson, the director of the museum, showed me its extensive collection of weapons and equipment used by navy frogmen over the years and shared with me some reminiscences of his distinguished service as a SEAL in Vietnam.

While time spent in libraries, museums, and research centers was an essential part of preparing this history, by far the most valuable element was the insight given me by scores of navy men in many hours of interviews. Their personal stories gave me, an outsider, some insight into what it is like to be a SEAL.

Early in my research, I arranged a series of interviews with two of the most senior SEAL officers, Rear Adm. Cathal ("Irish") Flynn, who has now retired, and Rear Adm. Irve C. ("Chuck") LeMoyne; I later met with Rear Adm. George Worthington, commander of the Naval Special Warfare Command, in Coronado. All three were helpful in providing me with access to other SEALs.

Often there was initial reluctance to meet with a writer. Much, if not most, of what SEALs do is classified. And once classified, it seems never to become unclassified. The SEALs, and the UDTs before them, have also surrounded themselves with a shield of secrecy that goes beyond the question of whether something is officially classified. Many SEALs believe that their safety so often depends on stealth that they would be better off if no one knew they even existed. Many SEALs also complain that, when they do come into the public eye, they are falsely portrayed as assassins, throat-slitters, snake-eaters, and sex fiends.

When I first called one of the early SEAL team commanders, his reaction was probably like that of many other SEALs but a bit more candid. He said he wasn't sure he wanted to talk to me and if he didn't like my book, "I'll rain on you." Later, we met and he proved most helpful.

A number of SEALs may read this book and wonder why they are not quoted, after they gave me a lengthy interview. Many will also wonder that SEALs whose adventures were at least as vivid, and as relevant to the history of the SEALs, as those included in the book are not found here. What I tried to do was to interview as many navy men, with as many diverse experiences, as possible, knowing that it would be impossible to interview as many as I would have liked. And then I have tried to winnow from those interviews the telling anecdotes and observations that help me to relate the story of the navy's frogmen.

In the course of my interviews, I developed a great admiration for these brave men. They struck me as a breed apart. They are stronger and smarter than other fighting men. They are egotistical and opinionated. They are bound together by shared experiences different from those of most people. They will do anything to help a member of the teams, or a former member, who is in trouble. And yet they also have their long-standing feuds, like members of a big but close knit family. One SEAL told me, "I don't lie, cheat, or steal, but I backbite." And he added, "If a member of the teams is down on his luck, I'll take him into my home, give him a bed, feed him, let him drink my liquor. But I might not talk to him."

For the many SEALs who agreed to interviews, talking with me was an act of trust. I have tried to return that trust by giving a true and accurate history of these special sailors although, of course, it is not the way any one individual, relying on his own background, would have told it. In several sections of the book, I have written in such a way as to give the reader as much information as possible without including data that might endanger the lives of men on operational missions.

Throughout the research and writing of this book, I benefited from the patient guidance of Robert Tate, my editor at Presidio Press, and the quiet encouragement of my wife, Mary.

Some of the conclusions I reach will be controversial within the SEAL community because the issues themselves are already controversial. Some of these conclusions may lean toward one side or the other of these contentious issues, but the conclusions are my own.

My hope is that, by bringing together in one place this account of the half century of service by the UDTs and SEALs, I will help today's and tomorrow's SEALs to know themselves better.

CHAPTER ONE
WHO ARE WE?

Shortly after midnight on the morning of 20 December 1989, Golf Platoon of SEAL Team Four, in a special tactical formation that bristled with guns, dashed up the runway of Paitilla Airfield, in a heavily populated section of Panama City, Panama. Within five minutes the SEALs, panting under as much as 110 pounds of rifles, machine guns, ammunition, radios, and other equipment, dropped to the ground about thirty yards in front of two hangars. One of them contained their target: the Lear jet belonging to Gen. Manuel Antonio Noriega.

With the city lights behind them, the seventeen SEALs made perfect targets for any ambushes hastily arranged by the small group of Panamanians defending the airfield—and they knew it.

Hugging the earth so tightly that it felt as though their buttons were making dents in the runway, they peered into the darkness with their night-vision scopes. Inside the hangars they could make out the forms of armed men crouching behind oil barrels and metal doors. It was impossible to tell how many there were or where they all were.

The SEALs couldn't hide and they couldn't retreat. They opened fire.

The Panamanians responded with a hail of bullets from their automatic rifles. That first barrage may have come from as few as two men, hiding in the darkness behind cement-filled oil drums. But it was devastating. Using disciplined fire control, the Panamanians fired low so their bullets struck the tarmac, sending pieces of shrapnel and bits of asphalt bouncing up into the bodies of the nine men in the squad—code named Golf One—on the right of the SEAL formation.

The fire was so intense that eight of the nine men in Golf One fell wounded or dead. Lt. (jg) Thomas W. ("Tom") Casey, the squad commander, shouted a frantic radio message—"We've got heavy wounded!"—as he continued to fire to protect his troops. Miraculously, he was not hit. But he did not immediately realize he was the only member of his squad alive and unwounded because several of the wounded men continued to fire until they were hit again or were unable to reload their weapons.

On the left, the eight men of Golf Two shifted their fire to cover the hard-hit men of Golf One, even though this left them exposed to fire from the hangar in front of them. Two men from Golf Two scampered over to help their comrades. Within moments, one of them fell dead with a bullet in the head.

In response to the radio calls from the platoon under fire, members of one squad of a second platoon—Bravo—dashed forward to fill in the gap between the two squads lying in front of the hangars. Their commander, Lt. (jg) John P. Connors, was hit but continued to advance. Then, as he exposed himself to fire a grenade into the hangar, he was hit again and killed.

In those few moments, SEAL Team Four lost three men dead. Another died of his wounds a short time later. Ironically, he might have been saved if there had not been a delay of an hour—the "Golden Hour"—in dispatching a medevac helicopter to evacuate the wounded SEALs. Nine more men fell to the hostile fire, some of them grievously wounded.

The combat losses at Paitilla Airfield—four dead and nine wounded—made that brief action the deadliest for the SEALs in the nearly thirty years since the Sea, Air, Land teams were formed. In a decade of fighting in Vietnam, the worst single day of combat was 7 April 1967, when three men were killed in an enemy ambush.

Operation Just Cause, the U.S. invasion of Panama, involved the largest, most varied use of SEALs since the Vietnam War. Days before the attack began, members of one SEAL team began stalking Noriega. During the assault, members of SEAL Team Two carried out a classic operation in which they swam in under enemy fire to disable a Panamanian gunboat with small mines.

The operation in Panama was the first carried out by SEALs since they had come under the control of the new, army-dominated Special Operations Command. It was also the first test of the lessons learned seven years earlier when the SEALs lost four men dead and a number more wounded in the U.S. invasion of the small Caribbean island of Grenada.

The debacle at Paitilla set off a bitter controversy within the SEAL community. Sickened by the loss of life, veterans of combat in the jungles of Vietnam angrily criticized the leadership and the planning for the assault on the airfield. They were particularly disturbed by the fact that SEALs, accustomed to working in units of no more than sixteen men, and often in clusters of two or three, were sent into combat in an assault involving more than three platoons. To them, the seizure of the airfield seemed more suitable for an army Ranger battalion than for a group of SEALs.

In a scathing letter sent up through the chain of command, one senior officer put it this way: "Our leaders sent too many troops . . . when it was absolutely unnecessary in order to achieve our objective. These leaders must be held accountable and not allowed to lead our fine young SEALs into such unwarranted and costly scenarios again. . . ."

The criticism stopped well short, however, of maligning the actions and the heroism of the enlisted men and junior officers on the ground at the airfield. Once the shooting started, they conducted themselves superbly. As one of them said, "If we had been on the other side, no one would have survived."

For the SEALs, Panama—and Paitilla in particular—was a moment of truth, forcing them to think more intensely than ever before about the role they should prepare to play in the future in the nation's defense.

Should they continue to plan and train to operate in small, elite units, as they had in Vietnam? Or was Paitilla the portent of a future in which SEALs would regularly operate in larger units, becoming maritime commandos of as many as 150 men?

Should they plan to operate within a few miles, or even yards, of the water, relying on their swimming ability and their tiny SEAL delivery vehicles? Or should they be prepared to fly or parachute deep in enemy-held territory, far from the seas?

Should they operate primarily in support of the fleet? Or should they be prepared to take on a wide variety of other assignments laid on by the "green machine," the army commanders of the Special Operations Command?

Truly, Paitilla forced the SEALs to confront their own future, to ask themselves: What makes us special? What is our true role?

In essence, they had to ask themselves: Who are we?

This was not an easy question to answer. But it was not an unfamiliar question. Ever since the early days of World War II, the SEALs and their predecessors, the fabled frogmen, have been struggling to define themselves, to answer that question: Who are we?

CHAPTER TWO
BLOODY WATERS—TARAWA
AND NORMANDY

W hen marines of the 2d Marine Division clambered into their amphibious tractors on the morning of 20 November 1943, they were already in deep trouble.

The big battlewagons of the navy's Fifth Fleet had hammered Betio, the larger of the two islands in the Tarawa atoll, until little more than the stubs of palm trees was visible above the flat surface. Still, the Japanese artillery answered back so fiercely that the transport ships carrying the marines were forced to back off from the landing beaches.

For the first wave, this meant an agonizingly long seven-mile voyage, wallowing at four knots in their amtracs—box-shaped personnel carriers with tracks like a tractor's, sealed against the seas and equipped with a propeller so they could "swim" ashore.

As the amtracs waddled up onto the beach they would speed up to fifteen miles an hour, according to the plan, and cut through the Japanese beach defenses. Then, coming quickly behind them would be thousands more marines to sweep down the little island—only two miles long and less than half a mile across at the widest.

The first wave met unexpectedly furious resistance at the shoreline despite a bombardment that the navy had promised would obliterate the defenses. That might not have been so bad except for what happened next.

As the landing ships carrying tanks and the follow-on wave of marines reached the coral reef surrounding the island, they ran aground. Instead of delivering the marines ashore with barely a drop of water on their boots, they were forced to discharge men and machines to wade ashore as best they could.

Tanks lurched off the coral shelf and groped toward shore. Many of them dropped into holes in the ocean floor and sank, drowning their crews. Many of the heavily laden marines met the same fate. Others were cut down by the murderous fire from the shore.

At one point that morning, a candid report was radioed back to Pearl Harbor: "Situation in doubt."

On that November morning, the United States had been at war with Japan for a few days short of two years. But the battle of Tarawa was also an important beginning. It was the first step in the navy's plan to hop from island to island northwest across the Pacific toward the Japanese home islands. Each island captured would provide a base from which land-based aircraft could reach out and pave the way for the next hop. A failure at Tarawa would not only deny the United States the use of a crucial airfield but also cast in doubt the whole strategy of island-hopping on to the next little Tarawa-like atoll . . . and the next . . . and the next.

Eventually, after three days of brutal combat, the marines prevailed. Of the nearly 5,000 in the Japanese garrison, only 1 officer, 16 enlisted men and 129 Korean laborers were captured alive. But the marines had lost 1,027 dead and another 2,292 wounded out of the invading force of 16,800 men. Adm. Chester Nimitz, the overall commander, flew in to find bulldozers scraping out mass graves for the thousands of dead. He likened the scene to Ypres, one of the worst battles during the bloody trench warfare of World War I.

What had gone wrong?

Before the battle, planes swept over the invasion beaches taking split-image photographs. Naval officers carefully studied the shore through powerful telescopes. A submarine circled the islands, taking soundings and photographing fortifications. Former residents of the island, fishermen, and veteran merchant seamen were sought out and interviewed. At high tide, they agreed, there should be four to five feet of water over the coral reef, plenty of room for the landing ships to carry their cargoes of men and equipment ashore.

But there was one catch: at neap tide—the time of the month when the difference between high and low tide is the least—the winds sometimes caused the level of the water to rise and fall unpredictably, often several times within a few hours. November 20 was the time of the neap tide, and the water level fell just as the second wave of marines reached the coral reef.

But what if men had actually gone in in advance of the first wave and looked at that coral barrier, measuring the depth of the water and scouting for gaps where the landing craft could skim across into the lagoon? What if they had gone in with explosives and actually cut a hole through the coral so there would be no doubt about the ability of the second wave to reach the shore intact?

Almost immediately after the battle, Adm. Richmond Kelly Turner, the amphibious fleet commander, sent out an urgent order for the creation of special teams of men trained to scout out enemy beaches, remove natural and man-made obstacles, and guide the invading forces ashore. With a whole series of island landings still to be accomplished, the need for such forces was of the highest priority.

In SEAL legend, the battle of Tarawa is counted as the date for the birth of their predecessors, the Underwater Demolition Teams.

Actually, training of such units had begun before Tarawa and a few of them had actually seen combat in the early days of World War II. To military planners, it should have been apparent at the very beginning of U.S. involvement in the war that the fighting would involve many amphibious landings and that specialized units would be needed to help get the marines and soldiers ashore.

By the time the United States entered the war, the Germans controlled almost all the European continent, from the northern tip of Norway to the Mediterranean, from the Atlantic to deep in the Soviet Union. In North Africa, Field Marshal Erwin Rommel's Afrika Korps threatened the tenuous British control of Egypt and the Suez Canal.

In the Pacific, the Japanese controlled large sections of China and had swept south to capture the Philippines, Indochina, Singapore, and the islands north of Australia.

Nowhere except in North Africa did the U.S. and its allies have even a tiny foothold. It was obvious that, if they were to come to grips with the Axis powers, they would have to land troops across many beaches against fierce opposition.

Except for a handful of marines, few in the U.S. military had much experience in amphibious operations. What they did know was not encouraging.

They were all disturbed by the memory of one of the worst disasters in recent military history: the Allies' attempt, early in World War I, to gain control of the Dardanelles, the channel which marks the boundary between Europe and Asia. Control of the waterway would permit shipping to reach the Black Sea ports of Russia, allied with Britain and France against Germany, and cut Germany off from its ally, Turkey.

The plan called for a series of coordinated amphibious landings on the Gallipoli Peninsula, which forms the European side of the channel, by forces gathered from throughout the British Empire. French forces were assigned to land on the Asian side of the channel. Advancing up both sides of the Dardanelles, the Allied forces would knock out the forts whose guns controlled shipping through the Dardanelles into the Sea of Marmara and on through the Bosporus into the Black Sea.

In the predawn darkness of 25 April 1915, some four thousand Australian and New Zealand troops, jammed together in small boats, were towed into position on the northwestern side of the peninsula. They then rowed themselves ashore. What happened to them is every amphibious planner's nightmare. The boats came ashore well to the north of where they should have been. One unit was confronted with a steep hillside, but the men succeeded in fighting their way to the top. Another unit was even less fortunate. It landed at the base of a line of almost sheer cliffs and was trapped on the beach. A third unit ran into such heavy machine-gun fire that it could not even get ashore.

During the day, thousands more troops landed on the narrow strip of sand at Anzac Cove and tried to fight their way inland. They quickly outnumbered the defending Turkish force, but the confusion resulting from landing in the wrong place, with no open routes away from the beach, left the Anzac forces at a serious disadvantage. By the end of the day there were twenty thousand men ashore, huddled in holes dug in the sand or on the sheer sides of cliffs and fighting for their lives.

For the next seven months, the Australians and New Zealanders, the British at the tip of the peninsula and the French on the Asian coast, fought bitterly to take the forts overlooking the Dardanelles. Eventually, there were ninety-five thousand men ashore and the call went out for another ninety-five thousand. Thousands were killed and wounded. All of the men suffered horribly from disease, clouds of large green flies, a slimy blanket of maggots at the bottom of their trenches, heat, shortage of water and food, and lack of medical care.

Finally, the politicians called it quits. The only real triumph of the entire operation was the surreptitious withdrawal of the landing force while in contact with the enemy. Rifles were rigged to fire sporadically. Explosive charges simulated artillery blasts. Quietly, the men rowed out to sea. The Turks were astounded to find that the beaches, littered with military equipment, held no enemy soldiers. They had all slipped silently away in the night.

The price the allies had paid for this ill-advised adventure in amphibious warfare was appalling: 265,000 casualties, including 46,000 dead. Turkish casualties probably totalled some 300,000, of which about a third were deaths.

The battle of Gallipoli was not an encouraging precedent for those planning multiple amphibious operations. But it was a perfect lesson in pitfalls to be avoided.

First, it is absolutely essential to learn as much as possible about the physical characteristics of the beach—to make a hydrographic survey. What are the tides? How steep is the beach? How firm is the sand? Will landing craft run into submerged rocks or coral reefs?

Then there is the question of the enemy's defenses. Where are his guns? How many troops does he have, and where are they? How far away in distance and time are his reserves? Has he placed obstacles in the water or on the beach that will have to be cleared? Are there mines in the beach area?

Once the landing area is chosen, the assault force must be directed to the right place at the right time. In a well-planned attack, every soldier or marine knows where he is supposed to go and what he is supposed to do. One unit takes out this pillbox, another assaults a line of foxholes. Still others move in with explosives to silence the enemy's guns. Someone has to lead the way, guiding the landing craft to their assigned targets.

And once the troops are ashore, where are they going to go? Are there cliffs along the shore, as there were at Gallipoli? Are there roads leading inland? Will the troops have to fight their way up steep, narrow, easily defended passes as they leave the beach, again as at Gallipoli?

A few of these questions can be answered by looking at maps or aerial photos or by talking to those familiar with the area. But answers to many of these critical questions can be obtained only by sending men in to look for themselves. They may have to go back to remove obstacles and return once again to lead the landing craft ashore.

One of the first Americans to become involved in the effort to solve the problem of preparing for an amphibious operation did so by happenstance. The American involvement in World War II was only a few weeks old when Gene Tunney, the former heavyweight champion, signed up as a navy recruiter. One of his first recruits as a navy physical instructor was Phil H. Bucklew, a tall, rugged, former college and professional football player. Although he could not have foreseen it then, Bucklew's decision to join the navy was the beginning of a career that was to see him on active duty in three American wars and give him a crucial role in the development of naval special warfare.

It was not long before Bucklew tired of leading reluctant sailors in calisthenics. When he heard of plans to set up a team of what were then referred to as amphibious commandos, he quickly volunteered. In May 1942, he became one of the first ten of the Scouts and Raiders.

The navy considers the Scouts and Raiders to be the direct—and earliest—forerunners of today's SEALs. But despite the original intention, the Scouts and Raiders did not become broad-based commandos like the SEALs. In most of their operations, they were limited to direct support of the amphibious force, guiding marine and army units ashore. Later a few of them served with guerrilla units behind enemy lines in China, and many were blended in with the Underwater Demolition Teams involved in the campaign against the Japanese in the Pacific. Bucklew himself remains a somewhat controversial figure because, although he later commanded SEAL and other naval special operations forces in the Pacific, his career was an unorthodox one.

Bucklew had barely settled in as one of the early Scouts and Raiders when he heard two rumors. One was that preparations were under way for a landing, later in 1942, of American troops in North Africa. The other rumor was that he and his colleagues in the first class of Scouts and Raiders were destined to be assigned as instructors rather than going overseas to practice their new trade. He managed to convince his superiors that, if he was to be an instructor, he had better go to North Africa to see what a real-life landing was like.

Altogether, the Americans put some one hundred thousand troops ashore in Operation Torch in November 1942. While one landing force approached through the Mediterranean and struck at the central North African coast near Algiers, another moved through the Atlantic toward the coast of what was then known as French Morocco. There, forces loyal to the French government set up in Vichy after the German conquest of France fought to defend their African colony. It was here that sailors who had been hurriedly trained for the task attempted to pave the way for the first American invading force of the war.

While soldiers on the troop transports prepared to land, seventeen sailors boarded a small, wooden-hulled boat and headed up the Wadi Sebou, a stream that coursed through Port Lyautey (now Kenitra, Morocco). Their task was to cut the cables anchoring a boom and antishipping net stretched across the river directly under the machine guns and cannons in a fort overlooking the river. With the way cleared, American warships would be able to fight their way up the river and protect soldiers moving in to seize the city's military airfield.

Things began to go wrong even before the small Higgins boat entered the harbor. A sudden rain squall cut what little visibility the sailors had in the dark night. And then a ground swell picked the boat up and sent it careening up the river, almost out of control. A red flare arced into the sky, and searchlights from the fort quickly made the small boat a target for the fort's 75mm guns. With the chance for a surprise approach to cut the cable gone, the Americans turned and headed for the sea, only to be battered by the waves as they left the river entrance.

The next night, the cable-cutting crew loaded their small boat with explosives and set out toward the Wadi Sebou once more. This time, they slipped into the river without detection and made their way to their target, a one-and-a-half-inch cable, supported by a chain of small boats, holding the net across the river. Moving stealthily, members of the demolition team escaped detection and clamped explosives to the cable, neatly shearing it. The small boats, dragging their anchors, drifted off to the side of the river, taking the net with them. But a smaller cable stretched above the net apparently served as an alarm. As soon as it was cut, machine guns from the fort above sought out the American craft.

Their work done, the sailors headed for the mouth of the river, zigzagging frantically to avoid the fire from the fort. At the mouth of the river, they again encountered monstrous waves that nearly ended their successful mission in disaster. But they managed to fight their way through the seas to the transport. The craft itself had taken thirteen hits, but not a man was wounded by the French gunfire.

Bucklew was not involved in that first naval demolition effort. Instead, he was aboard the USS *Leedstown* off the coast of Algiers. Bucklew later recalled his baptism of fire as German planes began a bombing run on the *Leedstown:* "They didn't come very close to us, but we had all hands topside, those not manning guns, and watched the bombs fall, but didn't really have any near misses." But while the Americans stared in fascination at the first enemy planes they had seen, a German submarine silently surfaced and sent a torpedo into the ship, sinking her.

Bucklew managed to survive this ignominious introduction to war and returned to the States to find the Scouts and Raiders training operation set up in a former casino near Fort Pierce, Florida, about sixty miles north of West Palm Beach. By early spring, he was back in Algiers and then went on to Malta, where he worked with the British in preparing for the imminent Allied invasion of Sicily.

In the spring of 1942, the British had formed a secret unit called the Combined Operations Pilotage Parties, or COPP, in preparation for the amphibious landings that lay ahead. The COPP swimmers used two-man kayaks. Special hoods encased the men's bodies, but still the little boats leaked badly in heavy seas. To avoid detection, the swimmers made their scouting trips under cover of darkness.

In preparation for the landings in Sicily, four small British subs, about 150 feet long, surfaced at different points along the coast. Then the scouts clambered out onto the deck, stepped cautiously into their tiny canoes, and quietly paddled toward shore. Their job was to check the gradient of the beach, see if there had been any changes since the most recent charts had been drafted, and look for shoals and other underwater obstructions, then paddle back out to the sub.

Bucklew and the other Americans involved suffered no losses in these scouting operations. But the British losses were devastating. Five men were lost at sea, four were captured, and two, unable to find their way back to the submarine, paddled eighty miles to the island of Malta.

Daunting as the task of crawling up on an enemy beach may have been, the job of leading the actual invasion ashore was far more formidable. Bucklew was assigned to guide the soldiers of Gen. George Patton's Seventh Army as they came ashore on the southern coast of Sicily, an unprecedented operation involving more than six U.S. divisions.

About one o'clock in the morning, with a quarter moon providing a glimmer of light across the water, Bucklew and his team of scouts climbed into a small motorboat and headed for shore. First they had to identify the proper beach, a difficult task because the flat landscape provided few visual clues. Then they made a fast pass from one end of the beach to the other, attempting to pick out landmarks at the borders of the beach. At one end, a soldier was put ashore. Then Bucklew sped to the other end and dropped another man to mark the spot. Each was equipped with a flashlight to signal his location.

Bucklew then backed off and watched for the two signals so he could center himself as the guide for the assaulting forces. As he did so, the Germans flashed on their searchlights and began pinging away at him with an 88mm gun. Fortunately the glare of the lights on the water tended to blind the gunners, making Bucklew less vulnerable than he felt.

As the landing craft surged toward the beach, Bucklew used the signals from his two flank men to guide the boats to the proper spot. But he noticed an alarming thing: enemy machine-gun fire was coming from the same spot as the signal from one of his guides.

"I was getting the flank signal with machine-gun fire coming right over it, and it [the signal] was steady. I found my sergeant on the beach the next morning and said, 'What in the hell were you doing?' He said, 'Well, the pillbox was occupied. I felt the safest thing to do was to get my back right up against it.' They were firing over his head. And he was sitting there safe with a shielded light. He was right under their fire." For his bravery, the sergeant was awarded the Silver Star.

Bucklew later recalled the Sicily landing as relatively easy. Once the soldiers were ashore, however, the operation almost collapsed in the face of a vigorous German counterattack. The Americans and the British, in a companion landing operation, may well have been saved from disaster by the fact that the sites of the landings came as a surprise to the defenders.

Two months after the conquest of Sicily, the Allied forces were ready for a landing on the mainland of Italy, the beginning of the long, bloody, frustrating struggle up the Italian boot. Again Bucklew was designated to guide the invading force. This time he chose a two-man kayak instead of a powerboat, hoping to make himself less visible. He and Ray King, his boatswain's mate, disembarked from a landing craft about three miles offshore and paddled in.

Behind them, a row of British destroyers began the bombardment of the German positions. But the British ships lacked radar and modern fire-control instruments. So instead of aiming upward and sending their shells arcing high into the sky and back down onto the target, they aimed low and skipped the shells across the water like flat stones, right over the tiny kayak. "A shell coming at you in that salvo looks like a big ball of fire, and it looks like it's going to hit you right on the nose. It either goes over or it doesn't. . . ." Bucklew recalled.

The fire from the naval guns was expected, if not exactly welcomed, by the two men in their flimsy craft. What they had not counted on was the sudden explosion of fire from another British ship carrying fifty rocket launchers.

"They went over our heads—the rockets have a tremendous roar—and they went overhead with a swish, swish, swish, and we didn't know what it was," Bucklew says.

Unlike Tarawa, where the problem was getting ashore, the problem for the army troops at Salerno was staying ashore once they had established a beachhead. The Germans had put their 88mm guns on tracks and hidden them in caves. The guns popped out, fired, and then slipped back into the caves, safe from the navy guns. The German defense was so vigorous that the army commander suggested a withdrawal. But the navy commander feared that an attempt to extract the soldiers from the beach would be even worse than leaving them there. It would be too much to hope for a repeat of the successful withdrawal at Gallipoli. Instead, he recommended a continued naval bombardment, which went on for three days of such intense fire that it burned out the guns on one cruiser. Finally the Americans secured their foothold on the Italian mainland and began their painful march to the north.

Months before, in January of 1943, the Army had begun to experiment with clearing man-made beach obstacles at Fort Pierce. On 6 June, Adm. Ernest J. King, the chief of naval operations, gave the order for the training of Naval Demolition Units. By coincidence, his order was issued exactly a year before the Allied forces landed at Normandy against the most formidable array of beach defenses ever erected. This was also five months before Tarawa, and Washington's concern seemed to be focused more on the problem of dealing with the obstacles Hitler might place along the French coast than with the island-hopping campaign in the Pacific.

Picked to lead this new effort was a young naval reserve officer named Draper L. Kauffman, one of the most colorful figures in the history of naval special warfare. A very slender man who stood just about six feet tall, Kauffman had graduated from the U.S. Naval Academy in 1933. In those depression years, the navy seized on any excuse to deny commissions to those completing the course at Annapolis. Of the 432 graduates in Kauffman's class, only 216 received commissions. Even though Kauffman's father was a senior officer, he was screened out because of his poor eyesight. But by the time of Pearl Harbor, Kauffman had managed to see more of war through his thick Coke-bottle glasses than his classmates who had been granted commissions.

Using his naval background, he went to work for a steamship line and was assigned to work in Europe early in 1939. He spent two months in the company's offices in England, two in France and two in Germany. He twice attended speeches by Adolf Hitler and, even though he couldn't understand German, found him thoroughly frightening. In mid-1939, he returned home convinced not only that war was imminent, but that the West would lose. Shortly after war broke out in September, he signed up as a member of an American volunteer ambulance corps. When the Germans attacked France on 10 May 1940, he was attached as an ambulance driver to an elite French unit operating in the no-man's-land between the Maginot and Siegfried lines.

The next two weeks were filled with horror. Kauffman learned three lessons from that experience: he gained a great and lasting respect for the infantry; he understood how a man can throw down his rifle and run away; and he vowed that if he ever got into combat again, he would again want to be in a volunteer outfit.

As the German juggernaut rolled westward, the French hospital closest to the front lines was overrun, leaving the French wounded without adequate care. A French general asked Kauffman if he would drive his ambulance back through both French and German lines and try to get the most seriously wounded to the hospital. Kauffman and a German-speaking lieutenant set off, ringing the bell on the ambulance frantically. The scene was like a pastoral painting, with cows grazing peacefully in the fields. Suddenly they saw a movement at the side of the road up ahead. Kauffman and his aide jumped out with hands over their heads, shouting "Kamerad!" When he thought about it later, the scene seemed like something out of a grade-B movie. But at the time, it was deadly serious. The German soldiers permitted them to continue on to the hospital, from which they had helped evacuate the wounded only three days before. But then they were made prisoners.

Because he was an American, Kauffman was eventually released and worked his way, over a period of a month and a half, down to Lisbon, across the South Atlantic to Brazil, up to Boston—and back to Scotland as a volunteer in the British navy. This was nearly a year and a half before the United States entered the war.

In a sense, Kauffman seemed to go out of his way to look for trouble. But trouble also came looking for him. While he was in a British naval school, a German bomb fell nearby and British army experts moved in to disarm it. As they worked, the bomb went off, killing the army crew. The next morning, a call went out for volunteers for bomb disposal. It was only after Kauffman had volunteered that he went out and took a sobering look at the hole in the ground where the army experts had been atomized.

Kauffman worked throughout the German blitz against Britain in the winter of 1940–41 and into the spring of 1941. Much of the work was unglamorous manual labor—digging as deep as thirty feet in the ground and shoring up the earth around the bomb before beginning the delicate business of disarming it.

The British quickly learned that the German bomb fuzes were numbered and that the numbers told what kind of fuze it was. A number ending in *1* was an antidisturbance fuze. A *7* meant a time fuze. A *4* was antiwithdrawal, and *5* was a straightforward arming fuze. The numbers remained a reliable guide because the Germans needed them to disarm bombs when their planes crashed at home.

But two other devices seriously complicated the task of the disarmament experts.

One was a two-thousand–pound mine dropped by parachute. If the mine came down on land instead of water, it was supposed to go off seventeen seconds later. But sometimes the fuzes jammed and the experts were called in. If in tinkering with the mine, the bomb-disposal man started it ticking again, he had something less than seventeen seconds to get away. The first mine Kauffman saw and successfully disarmed came down in Liverpool about Christmas time. He found it in a house of ill repute, sitting in an overstuffed chair draped in Christmas streamers.

The other threat was the German acoustic fuze. It was designed to react to any noise and begin ticking. The rule the bomb disposal crews worked out was to wait ten to twelve seconds after making any sound lasting more than half a second. Thus, if a man was trying to remove a screw, he would turn it a quarter turn, check his watch, turn it another quarter turn, and so on. On 2 January 1941, Kauffman was working on an acoustic fuze when his hand slipped and he heard the fuze begin to tick. He ran and was far enough away to survive, although the blast of the bomb hurled him through the air. His British commander awarded him a certificate for setting a new record in the one-hundred-meter dash.

After the blitz ended in May 1941, Kauffman returned to the United States and finally received his navy commission. His eyesight had not improved, but his experience was too valuable to waste. He was assigned to set up an American bomb-disposal school. But before he could get the school organized, the Japanese struck Pearl Harbor. A week later, he was in Hawaii disposing of unexploded bombs. One bomb had landed just outside an ammunition depot at Schofield Barracks. Kauffman, with no experience with Japanese ordnance, approached it with extreme care, fearful of an ingenious device that might quickly take his life.

"It turned out that I couldn't have set that bomb off if I'd had a sledge hammer," he later recalled. "There was no way. The fuze was completely faulty. So the risk was absolutely zero. . . ."

In spite of Kauffman's modest appraisal of the danger, he was awarded the Navy Cross for his work at Pearl Harbor.

Kauffman finally organized his bomb-disposal school at the Washington Navy Yard in January 1942. Except for Kauffman, who had been assigned to set up the school, the class was made up entirely of volunteers, all of them bachelors. For the next year and a half, Kauffman turned out bomb-disposal experts, first at the navy yard and then at American University, in northwest Washington. Much of the training involved digging deep holes. The final exam required nearly thirty hours of hard work, a foolproof way to find out if a man would become careless with fatigue.

This reliance on physical stress as a way of testing a man's capability and screening out those who don't measure up remains an important part of the training of the navy's SEALs to this day. Today's SEALs are also experts on using explosives and, if need be, disarming enemy munitions. So there is a direct link back to the bomb-disposal experts Kauffman trained half a century ago.

In May of 1943, Kauffman was called back from his honeymoon to set up a school to train the first Naval Comabt Demolition Units, generally considered the direct ancestors of the SEALs. In a hurried meeting in Washington, he was shown pictures of obstacles being built on the beaches of France and told to "put a stop to that." With his orders came a document permitting him to travel wherever he had to and to assemble the men and equipment he needed.

On 6 June 1943, the same day that Admiral King issued his authorizing order, Kauffman set up shop at Fort Pierce, a short distance from the old casino occupied by the Scouts and Raiders. The first volunteers came mostly from the Seabees, the legendary navy construction battalions, with officers raided from the bomb-disposal school.

Training began with a one-week ordeal that is still known as Hell Week and that quickly eliminated 40 percent of the class. The survivors were proud of their accomplishment, but they joked that "Hell Week separated the men from the boys; the men had sense enough to quit and left us with the boys." That humorous assessment reflected a more serious concern, one that has continued to nag at those responsible for selecting members of the Underwater Demolition Teams and the SEALs. Since no one knows just what it takes for a man to excel as a SEAL, how can one be sure that men who might make superior SEALs are not being screened out by the contrived hardships of Hell Week?

The trainees at Fort Pierce spent much of their time in rubber boats and in the mud, and they ran miles every day. But surprisingly, little attention was paid to swimming. The assumption was that they would paddle ashore as part of an amphibious operation and do their demolition work in relatively shallow water while army demolition experts took over at the high-water mark.

Although men of the Underwater Demolition Teams later prided themselves on their nickname of the Naked Warriors, the trainees at Fort Pierce were anything but naked. They did their work dressed in soggy fatigues, with heavy boondocker shoes on their feet and awkward metal helmets on their heads. Much of their training was done at night.

The men quickly became adept at handling high explosives. Those who couldn't overcome their fear of being blown to kingdom come were sent off to other assignments. They were probably the smart ones. As the UDT men later realized, they and their explosives-filled rubber boats were disasters waiting to happen.

Although Kauffman was probably the nation's expert at disarming bombs and mines, the demolition men had a good deal to learn about handling explosives safely, placing them on obstacles at the edge of the sea, wiring the whole complex together, and making it all blow up at the same moment.

One breakthrough was the brainchild of a man named George Kistiakowsky, an irrepressible scientist who loved to careen around the compound at the controls of a tank and who quickly earned the nickname of the Mad Russian. It was his idea to stuff blocks of tetryl, a powerful explosive that comes in the form of a yellow powder, into floatable rubber tubes. Packing eight two-and-a-half–pound packages of tetryl into a section of tube created a twenty-pound length of explosive hose that could be towed by a swimmer, manipulated in the water, and wrapped around an obstacle. Later, much longer explosive-filled tubes, based on Kistiakowsky's original concept, were used for clearing obstacles and blasting trenches on the ocean floor.

Kistiakowsky was a favorite in the training compound until he disappeared one night. Shortly after the war ended, Kauffman saw a picture of Kistiakowsky with Robert Oppenheimer and learned he had been spirited away to work on the first atom bomb. Kistiakowsky later went on to serve as science adviser to President Eisenhower.

Kauffman and his men worked hard not only at training but at developing workable tactics. Still Kauffman couldn't rid himself of a nagging worry. He couldn't picture his men paddling ashore in their explosives-laden rubber boats, groping around in the dark, and successfully destroying the enemy's beach defenses. He had the un easy feeling that they were really trying to prepare for an impossible mission.

Despite his misgivings, the first six men of the Eleventh Naval Combat Demolition Unit were sent to England early in November 1943 to begin preparing for the Normandy invasion.

A few weeks later, Bucklew and four members of the Scouts and Raiders, still a separate unit, also arrived in England and began stealthy reconnaissance operations along the Normandy coast. In what was quickly recognized as a classic breach of the most basic security rules, an admiral thoughtlessly permitted Bucklew and his men to see the plans for Overlord, the code name for the Allied invasion of France. When it was realized that these men would actually be crawling up on the enemy's beaches months before the invasion and were therefore in serious danger of capture, they were sent to a special school to teach them how to resist interrogation and to escape, if captured.

Operating from small rubber boats at night, Bucklew and his men took soundings of the water depth all along the planned invasion beaches. Bucklew even crawled ashore one night and brought back a bucketful of sand so army experts could test it to determine how well it would support tanks and other heavy vehicles as they came ashore. Perhaps more important, Bucklew also studied the nighttime silhouette of the French coast so he would be able to guide the invading force as it approached the Normandy beaches for one of the most crucial battles of the European war.

The six graduates of Kauffman's academy who arrived in England early in November of 1943 made up a Naval Combat Demolition Unit. These units were later enlarged into thirteen-man gap-assault teams. In contrast, the Underwater Demolition Teams being formed in the Pacific were much larger, consisting of about eighty enlisted men and sixteen officers—smaller than, but roughly comparable to, an army infantry company.

Those first demolitioneers were among the initial victims of the great secrecy surrounding plans for the invasion. No one knew who they were, what they were supposed to do, or even where they were expected to eat and sleep. This was in contrast to the situation in the Pacific, where Admiral Turner gave his personal high-level attention to the welfare of the Underwater Demolition Teams. Not until early April, just two months before the Normandy invasion, did the navy men get together with the army engineers to plan the clearance of beach obstacles. And it was well into May before two lieutenant commanders—with no experience in demolition work, but enough rank to gain access to needed intelligence—were sent to England to take command of the units assigned to clear the obstacles at the two American beaches, Omaha and Utah.

The intelligence was ominous.

Field Marshal Rommel himself had visited the potential invasion beaches and sketched out formidable defenses in which steel posts were driven deep into the sand, connected with barbed wire, and reinforced by mortar and machine-gun emplacements. To further strengthen the defenses, the posts were topped by platter-shaped teller mines that would go off on contact.

Even more worrisome were the huge metal structures that had been spotted hidden near beaches all along the French coast. These so-called Belgian gates were steel latticework barriers, ten feet square and propped up by heavy steel braces. Although they weighed three tons, they were designed to be manhandled far out onto the sand at low tide to block access to a beach.

Word of these formidable defenses worked its way down to the navy demolition teams early enough for them to build their own Belgian gates and then try to destroy them. The trick was not only to blow up the structure but to prevent littering the beach with a tangle of steel that would remain as much a problem as the original obstacle. A young lieutenant named Carl P. Hagensen came up with the solution: a waterproof canvas bag filled with plastic explosive and fitted with a cord at one end and a hook at the other so that it could be quickly attached to an obstacle.

Bucklew, who did not like loud noises, was impressed by the practice explosions conducted in a sandy area near Plymouth on the south coast of England. In the States, training usually involved a charge of half a pound, on rare occasions a full pound. In England, the demolition men used twenty-pound charges, enough to "blow that steel for half a mile." In those tests, the sausage-shaped packages of explosives designed by Hagensen worked perfectly. Attached to the braces of a Belgian gate, they caused the big frontal latticework to fall flat on the beach. By the time of the invasion, ten thousand Hagensen packs were ready for use, and they soon became popular with the Underwater Demolition Teams in the Pacific.

In the weeks before the invasion, every available man was flown from Fort Pierce to England, while other sailors were simply drafted into the demolition teams and hastily trained. As the training ended in late May, the men were organized into thirteen-man gap-assault teams, one for each of the eight gaps planned for the beach code-named Utah and one for each of the eight gaps in the two halves of Omaha Beach. Working in tandem with them were twenty-six–man teams of army engineers whose job was to take care of the obstacles above the high-water mark while the navy worked on those closer to the water or actually submerged.

Long before dawn on 6 June, Bucklew was in a big landing craft in the van of the armada churning across the channel. About fifteen miles off the French coast, his small boat was launched, and he set off on a now-familiar assignment—to lead the troops to the proper landing zone on Omaha Beach. With his little boat stripped of most of its armament, his gasoline engine pushed him along at about fifteen knots, which meant a run of an hour or a little less.

Bucklew had gone only about three miles when war suddenly erupted far down the coast to his right, about ten miles away. The sound of powerful explosions echoed across the choppy seas, and flares lighted up the sky. Bucklew had a terrible feeling that he had missed the time and the place of the landing and that the troops had gone in at the wrong spot on their own. But that was impossible. If he had gone only three of the fifteen miles to the beach, he couldn't be that far off course. Then he recalled that army Rangers were scheduled to scale a cliff some distance away from the actual site of the landing, and he recognized the sounds of conflict as part of that diversionary operation.

Still he did not feel really comfortable that he was heading for the right spot until he saw the steeple of the church at the French town of Vierville, centered behind Omaha Beach. Not only had the steeple been pointed out in intelligence briefings, but Bucklew had seen it himself in his earlier visits to the landing beaches.

Everything seemed to be going precisely according to plan. In the hours before the landing, waves of bombers swept over the Nazi defenses, dropping thousands of pounds of explosives. Then navy guns took up the task of paving the way for the landing force. Bucklew watched in awe as the salvos from the battleships, looking like huge balls of fire, passed overhead three at a time. The gap-assault teams approached the beaches in one-hundred-foot-long tank landing craft, each carrying a thirteen-man navy unit, a twenty-six–man army team, two tanks, and a tank fitted with a bulldozer blade. Each landing craft towed behind it a fifty-foot boat filled with explosives and other equipment. Watching the gunfire display, it was easy to believe the assurance many of the men had received that they would find nothing alive on the invasion beaches.

The demolition men also had the added comfort, under the plan, of forming the second wave of the assault rather than going in first to take out the obstacles. First would come Sherman tanks that had been fitted with large, waterproof canvas girdles which permitted them to swim ashore. With the tanks would come infantrymen to clean out the few snipers who might survive the ferocious bombardment. Two minutes later, just as the low tide turned, the gap-assault teams would step ashore. They would race the incoming tide up the beach, doing most of their work on sand not yet covered by water.

The plan and the reality turned out to be two quite different things. The bomber crews, anxious not to hit the Americans, dropped their bombs slightly inland. Many of the navy shells also passed over the positions commanding the beaches and plowed the French farmland, digging long furrows eight feet deep and ten feet wide. The result was that many of the German guns, carefully positioned and sighted to cover the approaches to the beaches from the most advantageous angles, survived and greeted the approaching landing craft with withering fire.

The current along the coast also played havoc with the plan. Many of the gap-assault teams drifted off course and landed in the wrong places, finding themselves the first on the beach rather than following tanks and infantry ashore. Many of the men were killed or wounded before they ever set foot on French soil, either cut down by machine-gun bullets or swallowed up in the blast when their own landing craft were hit by enemy shellfire.

A few of the teams were able to work their way among the obstacles, placing their explosives and linking them together with primacord, a thin, explosive-filled cord that served a dual purpose. It carried the fire to the charge, much like the fuze on a firecracker. And it also gave an extra bang, to set off the explosive. Quickly the men ran for shelter, popped off a purple flare to warn of the impending blast, and then set off the explosion. In some cases, the explosions had to be delayed because infantry had taken shelter among the obstacles, too frightened to move on up the beach. The sailors ran among them, urging them to move, and setting fuzes timed to go off in two minutes. The GIs moved.

According to plan, the gap-assault teams were to land on Omaha Beach at 6:33 A.M. They had twenty-seven minutes to clear sixteen fifty-foot-wide gaps to permit the bulk of the D-day assault force to come ashore. But by noon, only five of the gaps had been successfully opened, and several of them had been partially blocked again by sunken landing craft and shattered tanks.

All through the afternoon, the demolition men followed the retreating tide, fighting to open the remaining gaps. Often, they were handicapped by lack of explosives because of the loss of some of their landing craft. The small mines that the Germans had attached to the obstacles were salvaged to eke out enough explosive power to blast the remaining barriers. At several points, the defenders seemed to hold their fire until a series of obstacles was almost ready to blow. Then they would set it off prematurely with gunfire. In one crew, five men were killed and six more were wounded by such a tactic.

By evening, when the tide turned once more, thirteen of the planned sixteen gaps had been cleared and marked, and the Americans had a firm foothold on Hitler's "Fortress Europa." But the cost had been hideous. 6 June 1944 is remembered as by far the worst single day in the history of naval special warfare. Of the 175 navy men involved in the assault on Omaha Beach, 31 died and 60 more were wounded, a casualty rate of 52 percent.

Twelve miles to the northwest, the remaining gap-assault teams came ashore with the second American landing force on Utah Beach. Here the line of obstacles along the beach was incomplete, a much less formidable gauntlet than that arrayed at Omaha Beach. Within an hour and a half, the demolition men cleared seven hundred yards of beach. Then they waited for the tide to recede and opened up another nine-hundred–yard gap. Four of the sailors were killed and eleven wounded when an 88mm shell fell among them, a much smaller casualty toll than that suffered by their colleagues a few miles away.

As the army fought its way inland—with a few of the more adventurous navy demolition men tagging along—preparations were nearing completion for the next major battle in the Pacific, the invasion of Saipan.

CHAPTER THREE
FROM SAIPAN TO TOKYO BAY

I n the Pacific events moved swiftly toward a different kind of battle, but one as important, in its way, as Normandy.

Even before Tarawa, the Fifth Amphibious Force had set up a training site at Waimanalo, on the coast of Oahu west of Honolulu. Gathered there were not only men who had been trained at Fort Pierce but also soldiers and marines assigned to develop the tactics for paving the way for the amphibious operations that lay ahead in the American advance across the Pacific.

Their first test in combat came in Operation Flintlock, the attack on Kwajalein on 31 January 1944. This operation, coming little more than two months after the near-disaster at Tarawa, was very much an experiment as far as the newly formed Underwater Demolition Teams were concerned.

Kwajalein, fortunately, was an almost ideal site for the fledgling UDTs to work out their tactics and test their innovative devices. The atoll lies in the Marshall Islands about halfway between Hawaii and the Philippines and is surrounded by a cluster of small islands. The original American plan had been to advance step-by-step toward Kwajalein itself by taking the outlying islands. But navy intelligence experts, analyzing Japanese radio transmissions, learned that the bulk of the Japanese forces had been moved to the outlying islands, leaving Kwajalein relatively lightly defended. Instead of hacking away at the heavily defended outer islands, U.S. commanders decided instead to cut straight through to the heart of the enemy complex.

The attack consisted of two spearheads, one aimed at Kwajalein and the other at the nearby twin islands of Roi-Namur. Two Underwater Demolition Teams, hastily formed with a nucleus of Scouts and Raiders veterans, were on hand.

Team One was assigned to support the army's 7th Division in its assault on Kwajalein.

Team Two accompanied the 4th Marine Division in the attack on Roi-Namur. The training given and the tactics followed showed the strong Fort Pierce influence. Accompanied by marine scouts, the team members set out in rubber boats with outboard motors for a nighttime reconnaissance of the invasion beaches. They were in full combat uniform, and all wore life vests. They were under strict orders—drawn directly from the rules at Pierce—that if any of the men went into the water, they were to be attached to the boat by a lifeline. Although they were hampered by darkness and the choppy water, the recon teams reported back that the beaches were suitable for landing, and they turned out to be right.

As dawn broke, the team prepared for a major experiment. They had brought with them a promising new secret weapon: small wooden landing craft converted into remote-controlled floating bombs. These Stingrays, as they were called, were designed to speed in toward enemy defenses where they would be exploded by radio, clearing a path for the following troop craft. They were one possible answer to the difficulty the marines had had getting ashore at Tarawa.

The first Stingray was aimed at a pier jutting out from the center of the beach at Roi-Namur. Filled with five tons of dynamite, it sped off toward the beach, disappearing into the smoke hanging heavy in the air. First the arming signal was sent. And then as the seconds ticked off, the *Fire* signal was flashed. The sound of ten thousand pounds of explosives detonating should have been loud enough to be clearly audible, even over the sounds of the naval bombardment. The men in the control amtrac exchanged puzzled glances. Suddenly, the Stingray emerged from the haze and went into a tight turn, directly into the path of the landing craft carrying the first wave of marines.

Three of the UDT men pulled alongside the errant drone in a small boat and two of them jumped aboard just in time to cut the wires to the arming device, which was within moments of setting off the explosion.

One more Stingray was prepared for action. It had barely headed toward the beach when it turned in a tight circle and rammed the boat from which it was supposedly being controlled. Fortunately, it did not go off.

When Team One tried their little fleet of Stingrays at Kwajalein, they had even less success. Of three drones launched, one promptly sank, and the motors on the other two conked out, leaving them wallowing in the waves. Although the Stingrays still seemed like a good idea—if they had only worked—the concept was abandoned, and they were never used again in the Pacific war.

This was one major lesson of Kwajalein: the task of destroying enemy underwater defenses and other obstacles would have to be done by men, not by push-button warfare.

The other major lesson was learned by Team One in two reconnaissance operations before the Kwajalein landing. Although they had planned to make a nighttime survey of the beaches, Admiral Turner ordered two daylight approaches, at the morning and evening high tides. He was worried about a log wall under construction by the Japanese and the possibility of other surprises, perhaps hidden by the water off the invasion beaches.

True to Fort Pierce doctrine, the UDT men began their reconnaissance dressed in full combat gear. But the danger of ripping out the bottom of their boat on the hidden coral heads forced them to stay too far off shore to be sure of the condition of the beaches. Two men— Ens. Lewis F. Luehrs and Chief Bill Acheson, a Seabee—made an historic decision. They peeled off their heavy combat uniforms and stripped down to swim trunks hidden underneath. They spent about forty-five minutes in the water and came back with crucial information. They were able to sketch out the Japanese gun emplacements and the log barricade. Even more importantly, they reported that the coral heads would prevent the landing of small boats but that amtracs could make their way to the beach. They also assured the army commanders that there were no mined obstacles lying beneath the water.

Even to most members of the demolition teams, the fact that two men had swum in close to an enemy beach in the daytime and returned safely must have seemed like a lucky aberration, not a blueprint for the future. But the use of swimmers for daytime reconnaissance made a lot of sense—if they could survive and report back safely. Less than three weeks after the successful assault on Kwajalein, veterans of that operation set up a new Naval Combat Demolition Training and Experimental Base on Maui, one of the Hawaiian islands; training began early in April 1944.

One of the first teams to arrive was UDT Seven, commanded by Lt. (jg) A. B. Onderdonk. As they debarked after a rough passage from Pearl Harbor, they found that the mess hall had burned down. During the entire month and a half they remained there in training, there were no mess hall or galley facilities available. Food was prepared in fifty-five–gallon GI trash cans and ladled out into mess kits in the open air. When the wind blew, the food became liberally coated with sand. The eighty men and sixteen officers of UDT Seven felt as though they had arrived in a different world—as, in many ways, they had. An anonymous team historian later described the scene at Maui:

> From the very first it was apparent the training program here was not integrated or coordinated in any way to that of Fort Pierce. In fact, the general impression created by the very meager training staff at Maui, consisting of one officer and five enlisted men, was that much of the Fort Pierce training had best be forgotten. While Maui training was intended to be specific and detailed for the needs of amphibious warfare in the Pacific, much of the basis of the training program was at complete variance and new and different from that of Fort Pierce. Major points of difference can be summed up as follows:
>   1—Emphasis on developing strong swimmers.
>   2—Minimizing the use of rubber boats.
>   3—Conducting training operations while in the water without life belts—a violation of a Fort Pierce order.
>   4—Working in the water or on the beach wearing swim trunks and swim shoes as compared to the combat greens, field shoes, and helmets required at Fort Pierce.
>   5—The use of face masks.

The completely different atmosphere at Maui came as a particular shock to Draper Kauffman, who had set up and commanded the training facility at Fort Pierce. Not one to be sidelined in a training command while a war was on, Kauffman had arranged through friends to have messages sent up through the chain of command requesting his assignment to combat units in both England and the Pacific. His ploy worked, and he was in command of UDT Five when it sailed for Maui—although the fact that the messages coming in from commanders in both the Atlantic and Pacific were identical was a cause of some embarrassment.

Shortly after his arrival, Kauffman was called to Oahu by Admiral Turner and shown what he later recognized as a chart of the island of Saipan. He suffered two quick shocks. One was the realization that his men would have to swim a mile in to the beaches and a mile back again—much more demanding than the four-hundred–yard swims that were part of the training at Fort Pierce.

The second shock came when Turner told him: "Now, the first and most important thing is reconnaissance for depth of water, and I'm thinking of having you go in and recon around eight."

It never occurred to Kauffman that Turner meant eight in the morning. So he replied, "Well, Admiral, it depends on the phase of the moon."

"Moon? What the hell has that got to do with it? Obviously, by eight o'clock, I mean 0800," Turner replied.

Kauffman gasped: "In broad daylight? Onto somebody else's beach in broad daylight, Admiral?"

The decision to send the swimmers in during the daytime was just the opposite of the practice of the British COPP swimmers, who used the cover of darkness, but suffered because of the difficulty of working at night.

As soon as Kauffman got back to Maui, he instituted a new training requirement: a one-mile swim before breakfast each morning. Realistically, he should have required a two-mile swim. But he personally hated that early morning swim—and he figured that, if his men made it in to the beach at Saipan, they'd muster the strength to swim back out again.

Kauffman also quickly realized something that had been apparent to Turner and other veterans of the Kwajalein operation: daytime reconnaissance of an enemy beach could only be done successfully if the swimmers had overwhelming naval gunfire support to suppress enemy fire. On his next visit to Oahu, Kauffman sought out Turner again.

"What I would really like is to borrow, just for a weekend, a couple of battleships and cruisers and destroyers," Kauffman told him.

Turner, who was not known for a placid disposition, thundered, "What in hell would you like to borrow my battleships and cruisers and destroyers for?"

"Well, sir," Kauffman replied, "you speak of this very heavy fire support, these guns firing directly over us, and I would guess that this would be a very unusual experience, to be swimming in with eight- and sixteen-inch guns firing almost flat trajectory right over your head."

Perhaps it helped that Kauffman's father was, at the time, COMCRUDESPAC—commander of cruisers and destroyers in the Pacific. Turner agreed to loan Kauffman his father's ships. It is some measure of the naval might the U.S. had mustered in the Pacific in the two years since much of its fleet went to the bottom at Pearl Harbor that, the next weekend, two battleships, three cruisers, and a squadron of destroyers arrived off the coast of Maui to give the swimmers a feel for what it was like to approach the beach under heavy gunfire. It was the same lesson Bucklew had learned the hard way off the coast of Sicily.

All of this activity at Maui was part of the preparation for a new phase of the war. On 17 February 1944, less than three weeks after Kwajalein, the men of UDT One had done the beach reconnaissance— again in swim trunks—for the marine landing on Eniwetok, directly to the west of Kwajalein. This successful landing was the final battle of the "atoll war" in which the United States worked its way north and west, taking the flat little islands of the central Pacific. Next to come was the movement toward the larger islands of the Marianas, where strong defenses had long been in place and where caves and rocky hills added to the man-made defenses.

A key target in this new phase was the island of Saipan. Except for the symbolic raid on Tokyo in 1942, in which Jimmy Doolittle led a flight of B-25 bombers from the deck of the USS *Hornet,* the Japanese home islands had remained immune from Allied attack. The capture of Saipan would bring Tokyo and other major cities of Japan within range of the new B-29s of the Twentieth Air Force. For both sides, the battle for Saipan would be one of the most crucial of the Pacific war.

On 30 May 1944, Underwater Demolition Teams Five, Six, and Seven left Hawaii on three destroyers to begin reconnaissance of the Saipan shoreline. The men found themselves jammed into tiny spaces deep down in the ship's hold with bunks stacked four deep. Under the bunks and in any spare space, they stored their tetryl, which was not supposed to explode but was highly flammable. Their explosive fuzes were carefully stored away in metal lockers.

Three days before they left Pearl Harbor, Turner put Kauffman in charge of the three teams. Kauffman was a worried man. He still had grave reservations about Turner's plan to send them in to survey the enemy beaches in daytime, and he feared a terrible loss of life. One order he issued on the way across the Pacific indicates his state of mind: all his sailors were required to memorize the chain of command so that, no matter how many were picked off, they would still know who was in charge.

Even as their crowded old four-stack destroyers sailed westward, the sailors were still trying to work out the best way to chart the contours of a beach while under enemy fire. One plan called for the men, working in two-man teams, to carry slates and pencils capable of writing underwater and to use them to note the estimated depth of the water and plot the location of coral heads, mines and man-made obstacles. Another, more ingenious, plan called for the men to paint stripes on their bodies, with a solid line every foot and a striped line each half-foot. This way they could quickly estimate the depth of the water.

Supply officers puzzled over the strange orders they received from these UDTs, whose role in the invasion was a closely guarded secret. They demanded fifty-five miles of fishing line. Then they wanted dozens of empty four-inch–diameter milk cans welded end-to-end. Oddest of all was the insatiable demand for condoms.

To the team members, this all made sense. The fish line would be knotted every twenty-five feet and attached to buoys. The milk cans would serve as reels for the line. Counting the knots in the line, painted swimmers would be able to signal both their depth and their position to officers in rubber boats bobbing a short distance off shore. And the condoms? They were used to protect watches, fuzes, and other equipment from the salt water.

As the beach reconnaissance began on the morning before the invasion, scheduled for 15 June, Teams Five and Seven each took separate beaches. Team Six remained on its destroyer, ready to replace the losses Kauffman fully expected. Turner, true to his word about gunfire support, lined up four battleships, six cruisers, and sixteen destroyers to plaster the Japanese defenses. When the swimmers closed to within seventy-five yards of the beach, the ships, fearful of hitting the men in the water, aimed further inland. Waves of carrier aircraft were supposed to swoop in at that moment to make strafing runs just above the water line, but they failed to show up.

Despite the lack of air cover, the teams swam to within fifty feet of the beach, close enough to see the Japanese standing up in their trenches and firing at them. They returned with information that changed the basic plan for the operation. If the tanks took the planned route, they reported, they would be drowned in deep water. But another route was feasible. This meant shifting the tanks from one flank of the infantry assault over to the other side, a major last-minute change in the operation.

All of the fears about heavy losses proved groundless. Of some two hundred men in the water, a number were wounded, but only one was killed. No one had realized how hard it is to hit a target as small as a man's head bobbing up and down in the surf, especially since the swimmers would dive under the surface, come up for a breath at a different place, and dive again. The low casualty rate was not for lack of trying on the part of the Japanese. The swimmers were fascinated to see bullets drifting down through the water like autumn leaves.

When the time for the landing came the next morning, Kauffman was in the lead boat, marking the channel with buoys for the tanks following closely behind. Later he visited the beach, wearing swim trunks, canvas shoes, and a face mask, his body still showing the depth-marking paint lines. A startled marine looked up from his foxhole and exclaimed, "We don't even have the beachhead yet, and the so-and-so tourists have already arrived."

The UDT operation at Saipan was very much a matter of on-the-job training. Although the fishing-line method of measurement was used in later operations, many of the UDT men found it awkward and no more accurate than swimmers making their own estimates. And while slates and waterproof pencils are still used today, members of Team Seven, under fierce enemy fire at Saipan, found themselves too busy to do much writing.

One practice which had worked fine in the peaceful waters off Maui quickly proved to be a major hazard while under enemy fire. At Maui, the landing craft that had brought the men in close to the shore circled slowly. Then when the time came to pick them up, the boat would stop beside each man while he was helped aboard. The coxswains of the waiting boats quickly learned to career about in unpredictable high-speed maneuvers. That made the waiting boats somewhat safer, but how could they pick up the swimmers without stopping? The first solution was for a man in the boat to throw a lifebuoy attached to a line to the swimmer as the boat sped past. Then he could be pulled aboard. A better method was soon devised: A rubber boat was attached to the side of the landing craft and a man crouched in the smaller boat holding one end of a line with loops at both ends. As the boat sped toward the swimmer, he held one loop over the side. The man in the water thrust his arm through the loop—and suddenly found himself in the rubber boat. The sudden jolt could easily dislocate a man's shoulder, so the double-loop was soon modified to give it some elasticity. That method is still used to recover swimmers after they have completed their missions.

Other precedents were also set at Saipan. After the operation, Turner ordered medals for the swimmers who had actually swum up onto the enemy beaches: the Silver Star for the officers, the Bronze Star for the enlisted men. Kauffman argued that they should all get the same medal, a Bronze Star, or share in a unit citation. But a lieutenant commander can only go so far in arguing with a three-star admiral. Turner won that argument, and that same pattern was followed throughout the war.

Kauffman was more successful in another argument. The battle for control of the island became a long and bloody one, with more casualties than had been suffered at Tarawa. Ground commanders looked for more troops to throw into the battle and spotted the UDT men, the equivalent of about two infantry companies. But Kauffman argued that his men were too valuable to be used as infantry, for which they had no training. Some, he noted, had never even fired a rifle. He won that argument. But the temptation to use SEALs in tasks for which they are not suited persists to this day, and it is a risk from which their relatively low-ranking commanders have a difficult time protecting them.

Saipan was an exception to many of the other island landings in that it did not require the demolition of underwater obstacles before the landing itself. But on the night of the invasion, Kauffman's men were called upon to enlarge the landing area where supplies were being brought ashore. They worked until 10 P.M., placing 105,000 pounds of explosives in twenty-pound packs to blow a channel three hundred feet long, forty feet wide and six feet deep.

In the last hour, the Japanese zeroed in with mortar fire, and the men worked with the fear that a mortar round might trigger a premature explosion. In the eagerness to get the job done and blow the channel, no one remembered to warn the task-force commander. Suddenly a wall of black water erupted far into the sky and then began spreading out, coating many of the ships with the black residue from the thousands of pounds of powder. Kauffman was not to see anything comparable until, after the war, he witnessed the test of an atomic bomb at Bikini.

Despite the success of daylight operations by the frogmen at Saipan, the fear of going onto an enemy beach in broad daylight did not disappear. At Guam, where the invasion came on 21 July, Team Three worked for four nights without making any progress. Finally they were ordered to go in the daytime to blast the beach obstacles. James R. ("Jim") Chittum, a chief petty officer, recalls his reaction: "I can remember what I thought of that goddamn idea. I thought somebody had sold the goddamn farm. There was no way in the world we were going to get by with it." But in the next four days, they took out some six hundred obstacles with the loss of only one man.

For many of the men of the Underwater Demolition Teams, the war involved long periods of training or rest at Maui or at camps set up in the western Pacific, interspersed with a few days or just hours of intense physical activity and terrible danger. And sometimes there was the frustration of standing by in reserve while other teams did the dangerous work. Team Six, for example, was the reserve force at Saipan and again at Guam. In both cases, the team was called upon after the initial invasion to blast coral heads and expand the landing area. The days of boredom ended for the men of Team Six in September, when they went in before the assault on the little island of Peleliu. A team historian later chronicled the operation:

> This operation, conducted three days prior to the assault, was accomplished under heavy machine gun and sniper fire. The data assembled showed the areas were strewn with large coral boulders which would prevent the passage of tanks, DUKW's [an amphibious vehicle] and other vehicular equipment. Furthermore, the enemy had erected lines of heavily braced posts near the shore abreast of the beaches. Finally it was reported that heavy machine guns effectively covered the area. On the following two days, although constantly exposed to enemy fire, the operating platoons blasted the large coral boulders just off the beaches. On the second night eight picked units proceeded to within 50 yards of the enemy's rifle pits and machine guns to place over 1,000 demolition charges which successfully cleaned out the obstacles on the beaches. A fortuitous combination of good fire support, coolness and battle-wisdom and good luck enabled the team to accomplish this whole operation without a casualty.

Normally the work of the UDTs was pretty well finished when the marines or soldiers had secured their beachhead. But on the twelfth day of the battle for Peleliu, when the marines had driven the enemy to the northern end of the island, Teams Six and Eight were assigned a dangerous task. The Japanese still controlled neighboring Negesebus island and, at night, slipped supplies across to troops holding out on Peleliu. The two islands were connected by a causeway, but if marines tried to cross it, they would be exposed to concentrated artillery fire. The UDT swimmers were asked to swim the length of the strait dividing the two islands to see if tanks and other vehicles could ford the strait rather than feeding themselves into the gunfire concentrated on the causeway.

Thirteen men set out to swim up the strait, a total of three miles in water no more than four feet deep. Ships could not approach closely enough to shell the Japanese on both sides of the strait, so the only protection the swimmers had was a few strafing runs by navy fighters. They swam in as close to the causeway as they could until machine gun fire forced them to stop, then swam back out to sea. The mission was a complete success. Not only were they able to pinpoint a safe route across the strait for the tanks, but all of the swimmers returned unharmed.

The attack on Peleliu reflected a major decision in the strategy for carrying out the war against Japan. The navy favored a direct approach toward the home islands, employing both naval and air power. The successful capture of Saipan and its airfield was part of that strategy. Gen. Douglas MacArthur, who was in command of forces in the southwest Pacific area, favored a different strategy built around the recapture of the Philippine Islands. MacArthur, who had fled from the Philippines by PT boat and B-17 bomber to escape the invading Japanese, had vowed to return.

By agreeing to the attack on Peleliu, which guarded the eastern approaches to the Philippines, the admirals were taking what seemed to them a detour on the route to Tokyo.

While the forces engaged in the navy strategy had been moving west and north across the central Pacific, MacArthur's forces were moving from Australia through the New Hebrides toward the Philippines. With him was a young navy lieutenant named Francis Riley ("Frank") Kaine.

Kaine had been recruited early in the war by Kauffman. First he went through Kauffman's bomb-disposal school in Washington, and then he accompanied him to Fort Pierce as a member of the first class in underwater demolition training. By one of the happenstances of war, Kaine and a small group of swimmers found themselves under MacArthur's command in Australia rather than with the other UDT men in Hawaii. The soldiers wondered what to make of these sailors, until Kaine told them. He stood up in front of a thousand members of the army's 32d Division and explained how he and his small group of swimmers could scout out invasion beaches and help them avoid the fate of the marines at Tarawa.

"I guess we were convincing," Kaine recalled later, "because from then on, every landing they had, they had some of our units in it."

Kaine himself became known as "MacArthur's frogman." The preparation for each landing saw a strange scene where MacArthur would gather with his generals and admirals and then they would all listen carefully as Lieutenant Junior Grade Kaine advised them about the condition of the invasion beaches.

Kaine's men were divided into six five-man units, and they took turns, each team going on every third mission. Kaine directed thirty-six UDT operations and participated in a third of them himself. The campaigns in which he was involved sound like a roll call of the war in the southwest Pacific: the Admiralty Islands; a triple play at Aitape, Tanahmerah Bay and Hollandia; Biak and Numfoor in the Dutch Schouten Islands; Halmahera; Leyte; Mindoro; Lingayen Gulf; Palawan; and, finally, Sarawak and Brunei Bay in Borneo.

The two branches of the UDT family came together at Leyte Gulf for the return to the Philippines. Teams Six, Eight and Ten took part in the difficult survey of potential landing beaches on Leyte prior to the landing on 20 October 1944. The teams went in at three o'clock in the afternoon following a typhoon that had not only muddied the water but also prevented the sweeping of mines close to the shore. This meant they had support from only four destroyers standing more than a mile offshore. Team Eight suffered heavily, with six men wounded by enemy fire. One man later died of his wounds.

The day after the invasion, representatives of the team were sent ashore to witness the famous scene in which MacArthur fulfilled his promise: "I shall return."

Although there was much heavy fighting ahead to complete the liberation of the Philippines and to dig out the Japanese remaining further south in Borneo, the attention of the UDT commanders shifted focus in late 1944 toward the battles lying ahead for the islands guarding the approaches to the Japanese homeland. The number of men in training was expanded dramatically, and several of the teams that had borne much of the burden of the island-hopping campaign were called back to pass on their knowledge to the new men.

Despite the vital role the UDTs played in the amphibious war, their existence and purpose remained shrouded in secrecy, at least from the folks back home. Ernie Pyle, the legendary war correspondent who lost his life on Ie Shima, often argued with Kauffman, trying to get his okay to tell the dramatic story of the Naked Warriors. Kauffman always refused, arguing that the less the Japanese knew about the swimmers, the safer they were. It was not until the war ended that Kauffman collaborated on an article about the UDTs which appeared in the *Saturday Evening Post*. Kauffman's insistence on secrecy began a tradition, even an obsession, that has continued with today's SEALs.

On 16 February 1945, Teams Twelve, Thirteen, Fourteen, and Fifteen arrived off the tiny island of Iwo Jima, which the Japanese had turned into a rocky, almost indestructible fortress. All four of the teams had been trained by the veterans of UDT Seven but only two, Teams Fourteen and Fifteen, had seen action—in the Battle of Lingayen Gulf a short time before. Team Fourteen, made up of veterans of the Atlantic and Pacific fleets, was the first team drawn directly from the fleets. Among them, the men could count participation in thirty-three landing operations.

As the size and importance of the underwater demolition command grew, it was placed under a senior officer, Capt. B. Hall ("Red") Hanlon, Commander UDT, Amphibious Forces, Pacific Fleet. Kauffman served as his chief staff officer.

Despite the bloody reputation Iwo Jima earned during the marines' battle to dislodge the Japanese defenders, the swimmers who surveyed the invasion beaches suffered few casualties and even the UDT officers who guided the first waves of the marine landing teams escaped without serious injury.

For the UDT men, Iwo seemed almost to serve as on-the-job training for the bigger operation a month and a half later at Okinawa. They had even escaped the pounding by Japanese kamikaze planes that had begun during the Philippine operation to make life so perilous for anyone at sea. Then tragedy struck.

The men of UDT Fifteen were safely back aboard their destroyer, the USS *Blessman,* on the night before the Iwo invasion when a Japanese Betty bomber, following the ship's luminescent wake, dropped two bombs. One fell into the water alongside the ship. The other plunged directly into the mess hall, which was filled with men. Eighteen members of UDT Fifteen were killed, as was a marine observer attached to the team. Twenty-three others were wounded or burned. The blast and fire aboard the *Blessman* was the worst disaster suffered by the teams in the Pacific war. The losses from that one bomb were second only to those suffered at Omaha Beach.

The memory of this shattering loss hung over the teams as they went through last-minute training and then embarked for the assault on Okinawa—by far the largest operation in the history of UDT. Involved were Team Seven, reorganized after training many of the new teams; Teams Twelve, Thirteen, and Fourteen, veterans of Iwo Jima; and untested Teams Eleven, Sixteen, Seventeen, and Nineteen. Together they would put nearly a thousand men into the water, both on the real invasion beaches and on those where the commanders wanted the Japanese to expect a landing.

First at Iwo, and even more at Okinawa, the swimmers faced a new and potentially deadly enemy, cold. In the warm waters further south, cold had not been a problem, and most of the training had been done in relatively warm waters off Hawaii and the island of Ulithi. Perhaps the water at Okinawa did not seem all that cold. It still registered about seventy degrees Fahrenheit, reasonably comfortable to a recreational swimmer. But scientists now know that when the water temperature drops below about seventy-five degrees, it sucks away warmth two hundred times faster than air. A man immersed in water below seventy degrees without protection for a few hours is in danger of death.

The swimmers who went into the waters off Okinawa long before the days of the wet or dry suit had no effective protection against this new enemy. Their legs doubled up with cramps so painful that they couldn't tread water. One man wore the top of a pair of white long johns, but all that did was single him out as a target for the Japanese gunners. The UDT men, forced to remain in the water for hours, found themselves drained of warmth and energy. And the first thing to go was their power to grip and to manipulate their fingers. Even holding a slate and noting the contours of the beach or tying a fuze in place were almost impossible.

Aside from the cold, the biggest challenge at Okinawa was an array of sharpened poles, some with explosives attached, stuck into the reef about forty yards out from the high-water mark. Kauffman sent in two teams—Eleven and Sixteen—to blast the poles. More than 160 men swam toward the beaches, each carrying three to five packs of explosives. Overhead whistled the shells from three battleships and a number of smaller ships. Carrier aircraft hammered the Japanese positions with machine guns and bombs. The men swam underwater from one obstacle to the next, surfacing behind each post long enough for a breath of air before diving down to attach a pack of explosives and connect the primacord. It was a long, dangerous mission, placing hundreds of charges on the obstacles. Finally the swimmers backed off and waited as the trigger men set off the blast.

Half the beach erupted in flame and smoke. But when the smoke cleared, most of the posts remained on the half of the beach for which Team Sixteen was responsible. Members of Team Eleven had noticed members of the other team swimming away from the beach while they were still struggling to place explosives on the posts in their sector. It was not until later that they learned that the members of Team Sixteen, shocked by the death of one of their members, had broken and failed to carry out their mission. It was the most serious failure of a team in the history of navy special warfare.

"It had been badly done," Kauffman later recalled. "The next day I really made a group of enemies because I refused to send back the team that had botched the job to fix it. Naturally, they wanted very much to go in, but I didn't dare take a chance because this was almost our last opportunity. I sent my best team back in and they did a very fine job."

Sympathy for the members of Team Sixteen quickly evaporated when the men of Team Eleven were told they had to go back in the next morning—the day before the invasion—to destroy the remaining obstacles. It would be their third straight day under Japanese fire, and this time the Japanese would be prepared for them. The men worked until 2:00 A.M. preparing a thousand charges and checking all their equipment. When everything was in order, most of them sat up the rest of the night, drinking coffee and smoking. A few went to sleep and were excused from responding to general quarters while kamikaze planes made their early-morning attacks.

The anonymous historian of UDT Eleven reported:

In this operation over 1,000 charges were carried to the obstacles, all were placed and some 50 or more others were salvaged from the previous day's work and used. It is estimated over 1,000 obstacles were demolished in this operation. Combined with the previous day's results, it appeared that UDT 11 had cleared some 1,300 yards of beach of nearly 1,400 obstacles.

On the day of the invasion, members of UDT Eleven led wave after wave of amtracs, which could swim ashore. But when the landing craft carrying the first wave of tanks reached the reef, the commander insisted he wouldn't send his tanks into the water until he had specific information on the water depths between him and the beach. Gunner's Mate First Class S. C. Conrad gave the army officer a withering look, jumped into the surf, and waded ashore, signalling for the tanks to follow him.

Despite the failure to blow the beach obstacles, five officers of UDT Sixteen received the Silver Star and fifteen men were awarded the Bronze Star following the Okinawa operation. But the team, one of three recruited from the Pacific amphibious command, was sent back to Oceanside, California, and remained there on stateside duty as UDT Eleven and the other teams prepared for the invasion of Japan.

The plan called for at least thirty teams—some three thousand men—to pave the way for the landings. Kauffman, who had dropped from his normal 175 pounds to a scrawny 126, was deeply worried. He had been given a temporary promotion to captain and responsibility for preparing for the landing on Kyushu, the southernmost of the main Japanese islands. He concluded the teams would be lucky if they lost only two-thirds of their people. Therefore each area had ten teams assigned, with yet three teams to go in first, then be relieved by three more teams, with three more teams prepared to replace the second wave. The last team would remain in reserve.

The Japanese had used frogmen in the very early days of the war to clear a British minefield at Hong Kong. But despite several false alarms, the UDT men were never confronted by Japanese swimmers. That might well have changed during the invasion. After the war, it was learned that four thousand men had been gathered at the Yokosuka naval base for training as combat swimmers. One of their assignments involved a variation on the kamikaze attacks. The men were trained to remain under the water in diving bells and then to swim up to attack landing craft with ten-kilogram explosives, enough to sink a ship and kill the swimmer.

Kauffman was home in Washington on two weeks' leave when the United States bombed Hiroshima and then Nagasaki. Within days the war was over, and the plans for the great invasion were laid aside.

By VJ-day—14 August 1945—one part of the pattern that was to form today's SEALs was apparent. The UDT man was the Naked Warrior, wearing a jock strap, button-fly cotton trunks, sneakers, and a face mask. Strapped to his leg was a hunting knife. Only in the late stages of the war did he even wear swim fins. He had no breathing apparatus, and his ability to operate under water was limited by the length of time he could hold his breath, seldom more than two minutes.

At the same time, other parts of the pattern were beginning to take shape. The scene shifts to an oddball navy operation in the hills of China and to an Office of Strategic Services unit under British command in Burma.

CHAPTER FOUR
A DIFFERENT BREED—COMMANDOS FROM THE SEA

While today's SEALs continue to treasure the image of World War II's Naked Warrior, their origins can also be found in two quite different places: in a Philadelphia medical school and behind enemy lines in China. More than a year before Pearl Harbor, Christian J. Lambertsen, a twenty-three-year-old student at the University of Pennsylvania Medical School, had developed a remarkably sophisticated self-contained breathing system that would permit swimmers to operate underwater for long periods of time.

Although the LARU—Lambertsen amphibious respiratory unit—was the result of his studies in human physiology, Lambertsen was not some ivory-tower scientist. With the war already underway in Europe, he quickly understood the military advantages of his system. He could imagine one or two swimmers moving silently and invisibly through the water to sink an enemy battleship. Nothing could be more efficient.

With the development of this system, the U.S. Navy was in a position to take its place in the front ranks of countries with the ability to send combat swimmers against the enemy. Brimming with enthusiasm, Lambertsen arranged to demonstrate his device for the navy. In those days, the navy's only divers were in the salvage corps. They wore the familiar bulky suit and hard helmet, tethered to the surface by an air hose, communications lines, and safety rope. Lambertsen was told to make his case to the officers in charge of navy diving and they watched his demonstration with interest. But then they told him politely that the navy had no use for such a device.

Although the navy failed to recognize the fact, a race to exploit the skills of combat swimmers was already very much underway. Instead of taking its place in the lead, the U.S. Navy simply dropped out of the race.

The concept of having men swim underwater for military purposes was not, of course, a new one. When their city was under siege by Athens in 414 B.C., the citizens of Syracuse, on the east coast of the island of Sicily, built palisades to impale enemy ships. The Athenians foreshadowed the appearance of the UDTs by having swimmers dive down to cut off the pilings supporting the defense works. Syracuse also used swimmers, sending them out to try to damage the ships threatening their city. Similarly, when Alexander the Great besieged Tyre, swimmers were sent out to cut the anchor ropes of his ships.

All of these swimmers seem to have done their work without any source of air in addition to their own ability to hold their breath. But there were very early efforts to provide men with air from the surface so they could stay under longer. According to legend, Alexander himself went to the bottom of the sea in some sort of diving bell and remained there for a full day.

More than eighteen hundred years later, Leonardo da Vinci sketched plans for a self-contained underwater breathing device that would permit a swimmer to sneak up on a ship underwater and drill holes in its bottom. But then, horrified by the thought of the death toll from such an attack, he changed his plan so his swimmer would be linked to the surface by an air hose attached to a visible platform that would alert those on a ship to the danger of attack. This self-defeating concept apparently never got beyond the sketch stage.

In World War II, the Italians were clearly the leaders in the use of combat swimmers. The reason is obvious: Italy could not hope to match the British navy, ship for ship or gun for gun. But by attacking stealthily and attaching mines to ships supposedly safe in harbor, they might be able to change the balance of naval power.

Using both manned torpedoes and swimmers with underwater breathing devices, they did just that. Men riding torpedoes sank three ships, including a battleship, in the harbor at Alexandria, Egypt. And combat swimmers, working out of a wrecked ship in neutral Spanish waters, made frequent forays against British ships in harbor at Gibraltar.

Lt. Lionel Crabb, a British officer, was sent to Gibraltar in 1942 to attempt to stop the Italian raids. A twofold defense was devised. At the entrance to the harbor, sailors dropped explosive charges into the water, hoping to kill the Italians or force them to surface. Crabb and a small group of hastily trained swimmers formed the second line of defense, searching the bottoms of ships in the harbor on the chance that the Italians had gotten through. If they found a mine, they had to pry it loose, hoping it had not been booby-trapped.

Crabb went on to become a legendary frogman, whose exploits were chronicled in a number of articles and books. Then in 1956, he disappeared while apparently attempting to examine the bottom of a Soviet cruiser then on a courtesy visit to Portsmouth, England. Theories of what happened abound. One is that he simply drowned. Another is that he was detected and killed by the Russians. Still another holds that he was captured by the crew of the ship and sent to Moscow. And carrying the conspiracy theory to the extreme, he may have been sent on a secret mission that called for him to be captured and then to penetrate the Soviet combat-swimmer teams.

In the early days at Gibraltar, the equipment used by the British swimmers was far more primitive than that available to the Italians. They wore swimming trunks and overalls instead of wet suits. And for breathing underwater, they used the almost totally unsuitable Davis submarine escape apparatus, which had been designed to help crew members breathe underwater long enough to escape from a sunken submarine and reach the surface. It was not designed to enable a combat swimmer to remain underwater doing strenuous labor.

The British, who had almost totally neglected research in this field, were desperate to find better equipment for their combat swimmers. By chance, one of Lambertsen's teachers, a professor of physiology, was a British citizen, and he heard of the Royal Navy's frantic search for something better. He arranged a meeting with Lambertsen, then serving his residency, the final phase of his training as a doctor. As a resident, Lambertsen had no office of his own, and certainly no place suitable to entertain officials of a foreign government. So he and his visitors took to meeting in the hospital's maternity waiting room, quietly discussing military secrets while the others in the room waited anxiously for word from the delivery room. Between their visits, Lambertsen often borrowed a sewing machine used to repair caps and gowns from the operating rooms and sewed together prototype breathing devices from canvas.

The British were quick learners, developing their own manned torpedoes, called chariots, ridden by swimmers equipped with breathing devices based on Lambertsen's invention. Although at first the British lagged behind the Italians, they made remarkable advances during the war. Much of their effort was focused on finding ways to get at the small but formidable German navy, particularly battleships such as the *Bismarck* and *Tirpitz,* which the Germans kept in well-protected ports at home or in Norway where they always posed the threat of a sudden raid on Allied shipping.

Those days in the hospital in Philadelphia were frustrating ones for Lambertsen, who held a commission in the army reserve. He was confident that the United States could have been ahead of the British and perhaps even the Italians in this stealthy form of warfare. But the American navy was not even in the game and showed little interest in getting into it. Opportunities to advance beyond breath-holding slipped by. Instructors at the underwater demolition school at Fort Pierce did experiment with an early-model underwater breathing device and found it so inadequate that they put the idea of such systems out of their minds. They also tried swim fins, but they, too, were rejected because the navy men used the wrong stroke and quickly got leg cramps.

Watching the U.S. Navy slip further behind, Lambertsen turned instead to a new organization with which he had come in contact while working with the British. His proposal for the development of a combat swimmer corps was eagerly adopted by the Office of Strategic Services, an innovative, fast-moving outfit that combined intelligence-gathering with guerrilla operations behind enemy lines.

Lambertsen was called to active duty as an army officer and put in charge of equipping and training about one hundred of what the OSS called operational swimmers. Unlike the navy's UDT men, who worked close to the water's surface in the daylight with the support of massive naval gunfire and air strikes, Lambertsen trained his swimmers to operate under the water at night by stealth. Their job was to sneak in and sink enemy ships; to gather intelligence reports from agents; to deposit agents from the sea on hostile shores and pick them up again.

First, they needed a way to breathe underwater. Lambertsen's device fitted into the stealth pattern perfectly. It permitted the men to breathe pure oxygen, and then it filtered the exhaled carbon dioxide to provide a new supply of oxygen. For the combat swimmer, the Lambertsen device had the great advantage of operating without releasing a telltale stream of bubbles.

Training of the OSS swimmers was done at Camp Pendleton and Catalina Island in California, and at Nassau in the Bahamas where they worked with the British. The OSS swimmers were organized into three teams of about thirty men each. With the preparations for the advance toward Japan taking shape, one of the units was quickly dispatched to Maui and became a part of UDT Ten in June 1944. They took with them all their equipment, including the LARU breathing devices, but the officers in charge at Maui, already seasoned veterans of the landings at Kwajalein, Eniwetok, and Saipan, were unimpressed. The one thing they did quickly adopt was the use of swim fins, after the OSS men showed them how to use the fins with a relaxed motion from the knee rather than the rigid-legged kick most swimmers are taught.

When Lambertsen learned that his highly trained swimmers had simply been blended in with the UDT surface swimmers, he accepted the news philosophically.

"This was not unintelligent," he says. "Someone is unlikely to use his stealth weapon when his cruisers are back in shape."

Lambertsen and his OSS men hoped to put their skills to use in the South Pacific, but there again they were rebuffed, just as Lambertsen had been in his first approach to the navy. The problem was General MacArthur, who refused to permit the OSS, with its unconventional and unorthodox methods, to operate under his command.

The OSS men—who had come originally from the army, marines, and Coast Guard, as well as the navy—were sent on to Southeast Asia and attached to the British Fourteenth Army on the Arakan coast of Burma. Again Lambertsen suffered a period of frustration. Japanese targets were ruled out of bounds, and the team was involved in only one operation, the preliminary reconnaissance of an island before a British landing.

While the Americans remained on the sidelines, a forty-man group of British frogmen, known as the Sea Reconnaissance Unit, and trained, incidentally, in southern California, led the million-man Fourteenth Army in its crossing of the Irrawaddy River in February 1945. Earl Mountbatten of Burma called the Irrawaddy operation "the largest and most difficult river crossing I have ever heard of."

Instead of using their stealthy techniques against the enemy, the OSS men spent most of their time in training and development work. But Lambertsen drove his men as hard as if they had been slated for immediate combat. In a letter of commendation, Lt. Comdr. Derek A. Lee, a British naval officer who was Lambertsen's superior, wrote:

> He is a keen officer, continually looking for improvements to keep up the efficiency of the men. This concern is often interpreted by officers and men as an attempt to push them beyond their limits and through his keenness he appears at times to have little regard for personal feeling. He is an extremely hard worker, and willing and able to lay his hand to any and all work. He met with my entire satisfaction.

Lambertsen spent only about a year and a half on active duty with the OSS, but in that short period of time he was responsible for a remarkable list of developments in both equipment and tactics for combat swimmers. He is credited with:

1. Improving his underwater swimming unit and devising tactics for its use in combat
2. Inventing a speaking device built into the face mask that permitted two-way voice communication between divers at ranges up to seventy-five yards (For distances up to a half mile, Lambertsen's men used a tiny cylinder of ammonia gas. When a brief jet of gas was released, it made a hissing noise, like the crackle of radio static. A swimmer could send a coded message by releasing a series of tiny jets of gas.)
3. Developing an underwater compass that enabled a swimmer to find his way over long distances under the water at night
4. Devising a neutral-buoyancy container that permitted a swimmer to tow as much as thirty pounds of explosives or equipment underwater for long distances

"These all occurred in operations, in the field," Lambertsen says. "Wherever we were, we just went ahead and made these things."

He also worked with the OSS in the development of the limpet mine, which takes its name from a shellfish that clings to rocks or timbers. The limpet mine comes with a powerful built-in magnet, which holds it fast to the steel hull of a ship until a timer sets off the explosive.

Lambertsen also found time to work with the British to devise tactics for use of their underwater X-craft.

At the same time that Lambertsen and his OSS swimmers were whiling away the final months of the war, Phil Bucklew was back in the States, about to embark on one of the strangest adventures in a venturesome life. About Christmas of 1944, he was called to Washington and briefed on a secret guerrilla operation in which a U.S. Navy officer was running his own little war behind the enemy lines in China.

Bucklew's new assignment was to join up with the guerrillas under the direction of Capt. Milton E. Miles. Then he was instructed to make his way to the coast and personally eyeball the beaches on which Allied troops would land if the decision was made to establish a beachhead in China in preparation for the assault on the Japanese home islands. Bucklew had been on the scene for the landings in North Africa, Sicily, Italy, and Normandy. No one was better qualified to size up the chances for making a successful landing on the coast of China.

The trip to China was an adventure in itself. Posing as a courier, Bucklew flew to Egypt, spent twenty-four hours in Cairo, then flew on to Calcutta. From there, he flew over the Hump across Burma into southern China, where he was introduced to what Draper Kauffman called "this weird but wonderful operation going on behind the Japanese lines in China."

This operation was the creation of Miles, who was then in his early forties. While at Annapolis, his classmates had given him the nickname "Mary," for a silent-screen star named Mary Miles Minter. The incongruous nickname stuck, so it was Mary Miles who was called in by the chief of naval operations shortly after the United States entered the war. He was then a commander and looked forward to a wartime command at sea. But he had also lived in China. Instead of the coveted command at sea, he received an unusual verbal order:

> You are to go to China and set up some bases as soon as you can. The main idea is to prepare the China coast in any way you can for U.S. Navy landings in three or four years. In the mean-

time, do whatever you can to help the navy and to heckle the Japanese.

By the time Bucklew arrived, Miles had been in China for two and a half years. He had formed a working alliance with a Chinese warlord and set up a thriving training camp for Chinese guerrillas. Named Happy Valley, the camp was near K'un-ming, far south in China outside the area of Japanese occupation. Bucklew found some eighty American sailors, soldiers and marines assigned to the U.S. Naval Group, China. He also found that Miles had acquired still another name. The Chinese had dubbed him *Mei Shen-tung,* literally, "Winter Plum Blossom Mister."

For a visitor from the outside world, used to the rigid discipline of the navy, with its sharp line between officers and enlisted men, Happy Valley must have been a shock. No one wore a uniform or insignia of rank. Saluting was forbidden. The officers and men mixed casually in the mess hall. The Americans worked to make themselves as inconspicuous as possible, practicing to walk with a bouncing gait like that of the Chinese coolies, to carry their gear on long poles balanced on their shoulders, to squat rather than sit in chairs, and to eat native food with chopsticks.

From Happy Valley, Miles oversaw a network of naval units and raiding groups scattered widely across central and southern China, many of them operating in areas occupied by the Japanese.

Of particular interest to Bucklew was the intelligence net Miles had established along the Chinese coast, beginning just below Shanghai and extending more than eight hundred miles south to Hong Kong and up the Pearl River to Canton. Equipped with binoculars and small radios, coastal watchers kept track of Japanese shipping moving in and out of Chinese ports and provided frequent weather reports. Because of the general west-to-east movement of major weather systems, these reports provided crucial warning to American commanders in the Pacific of what to expect in a day or two.

Valuable as these "eyes" along the coast were, neither the Americans nor the Chinese observers were experts in amphibious operations. Bucklew, who had not only scouted enemy shores but actually led amphibious forces ashore, was assigned to provide that expertise. From K'un-ming, Bucklew set out on foot with a band of guerrillas led by a tough, aggressive Chinese who wore black coolie pajamas, a derby hat, and a Luger on each hip.

Bucklew dressed in a coolie suit and a big hat, with two grenades and a .45-cal. pistol concealed under his baggy suit. The Chinese almost refused to take him because he was so tall, so obviously not a coolie. This strange-looking apparition later served as the model for the character Big Stoop in the *Terry and the Pirates* comic strip. Worried about being discovered and painfully afflicted with shin splints, Bucklew still saw the humor in the situation.

"We would be walking along and would pass coolies coming head-on, with their minds a hundred miles away," Bucklew later recalled. "As we would pass one another, I would be looking back at them from under my big straw hat to see if they had detected me, and they would be looking back at me, saying, 'What was that?' because I was so out of proportion in size to them."

Twice they had narrow escapes from the Japanese. Once, when the Japanese learned an American was in the area, Bucklew's guides smuggled him from one village to another until the enemy patrol moved on.

The other brush with the Japanese was even closer. As a patrol approached, Bucklew hurriedly burrowed into a small haystack. While he cautiously peered out through the hay, he saw his guides sit down around the stack, weapons at the ready. To Bucklew, it must have seemed obvious to the Japanese that something was hidden in the haystack. And it was obvious to him that, if any shooting started, that's where most of the bullets would go. After a tense few moments the patrol moved on, and Bucklew began to breathe again.

Finally the little group reached the coast. Bucklew was reminded of Salerno, where the Allied landing force was almost pushed back into the sea.

"I recommended strongly against an amphibious landing for the simple reason that there were no exits," Bucklew says. "The mountains came up to the shoreline. It was a lot like Salerno in that sense. Within three to five miles of the hoped-for landing beaches was a very rugged, mountainous terrain with no roadways whatsoever. It would have been a case of landing and being bogged down on a limited sand strip."

To his relief, Bucklew's recommendation was accepted, and the decision was made to advance directly toward Japan rather than take a position on the Chinese mainland. But Bucklew was given another assignment that he found even more personally threatening.

He was sent down to the coast near the port of Amoy to spy on the Japanese. He was not the first American there; a marine working for Miles had rented a little house, hired a cook, and settled down in a village across the harbor from Amoy. Every day, he spent hours on a point of land where he could see not only the city of Amoy but the port and its entrance. On one occasion, he watched as the Japanese carefully camouflaged a destroyer with trees. In response to his radioed report, three bombers showed up. They hit the airfield, fuel dumps, and a small freighter but couldn't see the destroyer until the marine radioed directions. Then they hit it, too.

Bucklew's assignment went well beyond observing and passing information along. He had been ordered to prepare for a daring commando raid on the Japanese base in an attempt to acquire a book containing one of the few Japanese codes the Americans had not already broken. The more Bucklew saw, the less he liked the idea, and he was immensely relieved when the raid was called off.

"I am grateful to this day that we never got that far," he later recalled. "They had a sixteen-inch gun, and that's a lot of firepower against sampans. I was very much relieved, I truly was . . . because I really couldn't see that operation."

When the war ended there was a frantic rush for the exits. Everyone wanted to go home, and most were gone within a few months, Bucklew among them. He returned to civilian life and became an assistant to Lou Little, the head football coach at Columbia University in New York.

Lambertsen and his team were on a ship headed toward Japan when the war ended.

"The teams were discharged immediately," Lambertsen recalls. "That meant all the training of the first operational swimmers, the beginnings of the SEAL teams, was gone. I was the only one left. So I pulled a dirty trick."

He commandeered a truck and scurried around Washington gathering up equipment and documents. No one seemed to ask what right a captain in the army medical corps had to all this stuff. He signed receipts for everything he got and sped off. Then he delivered it to those he thought would want to know how to operate underwater: the chief of army engineers, the salvage section of the navy, the commandant of the Coast Guard. Thus Lambertsen salted away a kind of combat-swimmer time capsule, to be opened when the nation once again felt the need for men with these rare skills.

CHAPTER FIVE
NEW HORIZONS—AND WAR IN KOREA

Within a few months of the end of the war, the navy's UDT force had shrunk to a tiny shadow of its wartime strength. Officers with stars in their eyes quickly moved on to the "real navy." Those who remained in the Underwater Demolition Teams had little or no hope of making commander, to say nothing of admiral.

The result was a lean, mean, highly innovative force led by remarkably independent-minded officers, less concerned than most with fitness reports and promotions. Although they could not foresee the changes that lay ahead, they were setting the stage for the transition, years later, from UDTs to SEALs.

One officer stands out in those early days. Although they were to return later, Frank Kaine—"MacArthur's frogman"—and Phil Bucklew had both left the navy. But Francis Douglas Fane, known to his friends as "Red," and later, after his hair had turned nearly white, as "Doug," remained in the navy and took charge on the East Coast.

Even then, Fane seemed an old-timer to the young sailors. Born in Scotland in 1909, he had gone to sea in the midtwenties as a merchant crewman. By the time World War II started, he had his papers as a ship's master. Enlisting in the navy a year before the American entry into the war, he was assigned to an ammunition ship. Someone in the navy bureaucracy had a twisted sense of humor. Ammunition ships were named after volcanoes. Fane's was the *Mauna Loa*.

On one occasion, in the Pacific, the ammo ship was alongside the battleship USS *Pennsylvania.* Cans containing bags of powder were being transferred to the battleship and then rolled across the deck to a hatchway. Suddenly, friction caused a spark within one of the cans, and it began to burn. The sailor rolling it jumped overboard, and the other crewmen ran. Fane turned a fire hose on the can and washed it over the side, but it hung up on a protrusion on the side of the ship. While the other sailors stood dumbstruck, Fane jumped down and kicked the smoldering can into the sea.

About that time, Fane decided that he had had enough of life aboard an ammo ship—not because of the danger but because he sought the experience of combat. He decided to sign up as a member of the UDT although, because of the secrecy surrounding the program, he knew little about what they actually did except that it involved especially hazardous duty and the use of explosives.

One thing he did know is that it involved swimming, and that posed a problem. Not only did he not know how to swim, but while fascinated by the sea, he feared its forces. Fane theorized that his fear of the water stemmed from something that had happened two months before he was born. His father went for a swim off a rocky shore in England and was lost at sea. Perhaps his mother's distress transferred itself to her infant while he was still in the womb.

While on leave in Chicago, Fane prevailed on a Red Cross instructor to give him a crash course in swimming, and within a couple of weeks, he had learned to propel himself through the water well enough to qualify for UDT training at Fort Pierce. When the war ended, he had just been assigned as commanding officer of UDT Thirteen as it prepared for the invasion of Japan.

By that time, Fane, using an unorthodox sideways stroke, had conquered his fear of the water and become a strong swimmer. He had learned to work his way through crashing breakers by diving under the big waves and letting the undertow carry him out beyond the breaker line. He had even become a bit of a show-off, running into the water on a public beach and swimming far out to sea as a frantic lifeguard whistled for him to return.

It seemed obvious to Fane that it was of great advantage to a UDT swimmer to be able to remain under water as long as possible. He began to experiment with breath-holding and found that, by taking a series of deep breaths—by hyperventilating—he could load his tissues with oxygen, reduce carbon dioxide retention, and substantially increase the time he could remain under water.

Soon he had all his men trained to remain underwater for four or five minutes. One of his men became so skillful at holding his breath that he could swim three lengths of a swimming pool without surfacing for air. Fane himself could hold his breath long enough to dive down a hundred feet and swim under a submerged submarine from one side to the other, a particularly dangerous trick because the current can suck a swimmer up and hold him against the vessel's bottom. Fane believes that years later, when he suffered a heart attack, he survived because he automatically sucked in oxygen in the moments before he lost consciousness.

Learning to hold one's breath and swim under water for five minutes or so was an impressive feat of physical stamina but, militarily, it still gave the swimmer only a short time underwater before he had to surface for air. Surely there had to be a better way.

At this point, Fane heard of Lambertsen, who had returned to the University of Pennsylvania Medical School but retained his wartime interest in underwater breathing. Fane found Lambertsen working with the army, teaching the soldiers how to swim under a river's surface to mine bridges and small boats and to infiltrate behind enemy lines. Fane arranged for Lambertsen to come to Little Creek, Virginia, to work with him on the development of devices that would permit swimmers to work underwater for long periods of time and still move about freely, unlike the hard-hat diver with his permanent connection to the surface.

Lambertsen's LARU—Lambertsen amphibious respiratory unit—was basically the same device he had invented before the war and that was used by the OSS combat swimmers. It consisted of a small bottle of oxygen, a container of soda lime, and a rebreathing bag. At the beginning of a dive, the swimmer released a small amount of oxygen into the rebreathing bag. As he breathed, the air he exhaled was channeled through the soda lime, which filtered the carbon out of the carbon dioxide and returned purified oxygen to the rebreathing bag. The system was truly self-contained, and it gave off neither bubbles nor sound. But it did have serious limits. If water got into the soda-lime canister, a choking "caustic cocktail" could bubble up into the diver's face mask. If the lines got clogged, the diver suddenly found himself without oxygen and in danger of death. If, on the other hand, he ventured too deep and forced too much oxygen into his system, he might be suddenly and unpredictably thrown into a violent convulsion.

Men cannot live for long without oxygen, but too much oxygen can also be lethal. When too much oxygen is forced into a person's body, it destroys red cells, attacks the neurosensory tissues of the eyes, and eats away at the tissues of the nervous system. If the person is not treated immediately, oxygen poisoning can result in permanent damage or death.

If combat swimmers were to use the LARU routinely in their work, someone would have to calculate its limits: How deep could a diver go and how long could he stay without succumbing to oxygen toxicity? Fane and Lambertsen agreed there was only one way to find out: send divers down into a tank with windows in the sides and see what happened when the men stayed at various depths for varying periods of time.

Fane volunteered. Donning the LARU, he dove down to the bottom of the tank and swam placidly around, totally unconnected to the surface. Suddenly the observers were shocked to see him go into violent convulsions, his face distorted horribly, his arms and legs and body jerking uncontrollably. His pulse raced at more than 140 beats a minute. Then he relaxed into unconsciousness. Divers quickly brought him to the surface. The treatment was simple: he was allowed to breathe air until he regained consciousness, a process that took half an hour or less.

Fane survived without lasting ill effects. And surprisingly, he described the whole experience as rather pleasant, with no consciousness of the convulsions that had so alarmed those observing the experiment.

Gradually Fane and Lambertsen, with the help of other volunteers, worked out a set of rules. They concluded that, breathing pure oxygen, a swimmer could work at a depth of 25 feet for seventy-five minutes. But if he went down to 40 feet, he could only work for ten minutes. This means a diver on oxygen must constantly monitor the time he remains at various depths.

Even after safe limits had been worked out, another puzzler remained: Did those limits apply to all divers, or were there differences among individuals that might cause a person to go into convulsions even though all the rules were followed? The navy has worked out an elaborate procedure in which those who want to become combat divers are tested in the same recompression chamber that is used to treat those suffering from the bends. The air pressure in the chamber can be increased to simulate breathing deep under the water. In the test, the divers are taken to a pressure equivalent to that at 60 feet, where they breathe oxygen for thirty minutes. Then they are taken down to 112 feet for five minutes before returning to the surface. In this test the diver is at rest, so he can breathe oxygen longer at a greater depth than if he were working.

The navy uses an acronym for the symptoms of oxygen poisoning: VENTID. It stands for Vision (blurred or tunnel); Ears (ringing); Nausea; Twitching (usually facial muscles); Irritability; and Dizziness. If the person being tested shows any of these symptoms, he is moved into another section of the chamber where he breathes air until he recovers.

The only trouble with this test, which is required of everyone who wants to become a SEAL, is that Lambertsen and the navy's own doctors have concluded that it is totally unreliable. A trainee who fails the test might well have performed superbly as a SEAL. Someone who passes the test might suddenly go into convulsions during a dive. Illogically, the navy washes out a trainee who fails the test, but if a man becomes a SEAL and later succumbs to oxygen toxicity, he will be allowed to remain a SEAL.

Lambertsen himself had a chilling brush with death from oxygen poisoning when he broke two fundamental rules. He went swimming alone, without a swim buddy. And he carelessly drifted far deeper than he should have. Fortunately he had thought through what to do if he got into trouble on such a dive.

"As the process of muscle-jerking began," he says, "I hit the oxygen valve. That filled the bag, and that carried me to the surface unconscious."

Those years immediately after World War II were a period of rapid technological development in underwater breathing; but suddenly, much of the progress in military systems stopped. This is how Lambertsen recalls what happened:

Things began to go bad when the French came over and commercialized the Aqua-lung—what people now think of as SCUBA. There are many SCUBAs. It is a term I devised: self-contained underwater breathing apparatus. Most people think it is all air— take a breath and blow it away. That has very little military usefulness. And yet it was so easy that Fane got so happy with the ease of doing things that way that he just more or less rolled over and had his people use it. They became a bunch of skin diver types. That's when that long, nearly fifteen-year period of almost stagnation began. And it was largely because they went from a rapidly advancing technical system to where they were satisfied to train large numbers of people with open-circuit apparatus.

People were too comfortable. The system worked as a breathing apparatus but it was not effective operationally. It made bubbles. It was too heavy. Certainly from the standpoint of detection, surface detection, sonar and radar detection, those big tanks and all the rest of that just were not sensible.

The Aqua-lung was made more attractive to the frogmen by the fact that they often had to make do with LARU devices left over from World War II. The rubber face masks were cracked and the webbing was rotted. Too often, water leaked into a soda-lime canister, creating a caustic cocktail. Undeservedly, the term *LARU* became almost a dirty word, and the old devices were finally consigned to a bonfire.

The ease of operation of the Aqua-lung was its greatest appeal. Preparing for a mission was a matter of a few minutes: check the air volume and controls, strap on the tanks, and go. Since the tanks were filled with air, there was no threat of a caustic cocktail and no worry about convulsions from oxygen toxicity if a diver went too deep or stayed too long. By contrast, even the oxygen and mixed-gas breathing devices in use today require at least half an hour of tinkering and adjustment, and the swimmer must still keep careful track of his depth and the time of his excursions to lower levels. But a swimmer using an Aqua-lung on a combat mission would, in effect, write his own death warrant in a stream of bubbles.

About the time the French air-tank system came into use, Fane moved to the West Coast and then to the command of a unit based in Japan. Kaine, returning to active duty, became deputy to Comdr. David G. Saunders and later succeeded him as commander of Underwater Demolition Unit Two on the East Coast. Fane took with him his enthusiasm for the air-tank system, and the California swimmers used them almost exclusively. Kaine, on the other hand, liked the bubble-free oxygen system, especially for sneaking up and attaching mines to ships. But money was in short supply, and the rapid development that Fane and Lambertsen had fostered in the period immediately after the war petered out.

It was only much later, after the creation of the SEALs, that attention was again directed toward the development of advanced versions of the bubble-free underwater breathing device Lambertsen had invented so many years earlier. On most operations, today's SEALs use a similar device known as the Mark XV. To Lambertsen, it is in some ways inferior to the devices his OSS men used in World War II. One problem is that it has an intricate electronic monitoring system to feed in additional oxygen as the diver uses it up. Even the most experienced divers find themselves devoting at least half an hour to adjusting and testing the system before they are ready to dive.

Lambertsen also worries that most of the devices used by the SEALs require the swimmer to grip a mouthpiece in his teeth. This makes it impossible for him to talk. The OSS divers, on the other hand, used a full face mask that left the mouth free to communicate. While today's SEALs, taught to swim silently with their mouths immobilized by a breathing device, say they don't really need to communicate with each other except by taps on the shoulder and hand signals, Lambertsen insists there are many occasions when combat swimmers would be better off if they could talk to each other, and that they could do so without detection.

The difference between the East and West coasts over the matter of underwater breathing devices reflected the extent to which the UDT units on the two coasts were free to—and actually did—go their own ways. Although they have grown somewhat closer together in recent years, differences between the East- and West-Coast SEAL teams persist to this day. The differences involve preferences in equipment, style of operating, relationships with frogmen in other nations, and even the way they socialize. The East Coasters, in the resort and farming region of coastal Virginia, tend to party together. The West Coasters, a few minutes from the freeways connecting the vast urban area of southern California, are more apt to take off by themselves to the hot spots of nearby San Diego and Tijuana or up the coast a hundred miles to Los Angeles.

While work on the underwater breathing devices lagged, a good deal of innovation was under way in other areas. It all tended to expand the traditional role of the UDTs, moving toward the creation of the SEALs.

As early as 1949, Fane brought in an army warrant officer, a combat infantryman, to drill his sailors in infiltration and the use of weapons. And he began thinking of ways in which the UDT men could not only survey and clear beaches for the amphibious force, but actually carry out commando raids ashore. But as Fane conceived of these operations, they would be confined within narrow, very carefully defined boundaries.

The key to the success of such operations, Fane realized, was secrecy and stealth. He carried out pioneering experiments with both helicopters and small submersibles as a means of getting his men in and out quickly and safely. He preferred helicopters to parachutes because the helicopter provided a means not only for delivering a man to the target but for retrieving him as well.

He felt his men should work close to the water, not far from the high-water mark that was the boundary of their responsibility in World War II. And he wanted to limit the role of his men to surreptitious attacks using explosives.

"It is all right to go in and mine something, but get your ass away before it blows," Fane says. "I didn't think it was our business to be shooting people. The marines are trained to do that. They know one end of a rifle from the other. I felt any land assault should be done by trained troops with heavy weapons. I told my men, 'You start shooting at people, they're going to shoot back. Let the guys that are trained to do it, do it.' Use the marines and let them get their ass shot off."

Kaine focused his attention on another problem. A strong swimmer, under favorable conditions, can cover about one nautical mile in an hour. If he's swimming against a one-knot current, he will never get where he wants to go. If he is swimming against a stronger current or fighting a crosscurrent, who knows where he will end up?

One development was a skim boat, capable of carrying a two-hundred–pound man at speeds up to forty knots. It was equipped with antennae like those of a praying mantis. The sensors felt the waves just in front of the craft and adjusted the hydrofoils so it skimmed the surface of the water. But the one-man skim boat proved not to be suitable for the UDTs, who worked in two-man teams.

For swimming underwater, the swimmers experimented with a device called the Aqua Ho motor. It looked like a three-tank Aqua-lung, but the middle tank had batteries and a shrouded propeller, permitting it to travel at three or four knots for as long as forty minutes. Kaine says:

It was a beauty. It was just a great, great thing. But whoever was in the power seat for buying equipment for the UDTs just didn't want it. I haven't any idea what happened to the thing. Most of the equipment that was developed in those times was pretty good, but you have a hard time, when you're an operator, selling to nonoperators. It was very hard to convince them that a thing was a necessity, especially if it looked like a toy. And most of the things you operate with underwater look like toys; they look like fun. The Aqua Ho motor looked like fun. They don't see the practicality in things.

Our problem many times is that people cannot understand the incompressibility of water. Oftentimes you look for speed, but you don't really need a lot of speed to improve yourself thousands of percent underwater. A good strong swimmer maybe can swim one knot for a limited time. A piece of equipment that can move three knots for forty minutes is a tremendous improvement underwater. If you get up over speeds of three, four, five, six knots without protective hooding, you lose your equipment. Your face mask will come off, so you just can't go really fast. But any improvement, even half a knot, is a jump underwater.

One of the serious problems faced by the sailors as they thought about becoming commandos and making surreptitious forays into enemy territory was how to get back out again safely. An imaginative inventor came along with an ingenious answer to the question. His name was Robert E. Fulton, Jr., and inventiveness ran in his family. Fulton says that, according to family tradition, he is descended from the inventor of the steamboat, although he is not sure of the relationship.

The younger Fulton is now in his eighties, but his mind still spins out new ideas at a mile a minute. Often he will awake in the middle of the night, pick up a notebook, and, in the darkness, write down an idea that has come to him in his sleep. What is unusual about Fulton is that his ideas make good sense in the light of the morning.

One brilliant idea came to him as he was flying in his private plane over the Rockies. He looked down at the rugged, snow-covered mountains and wondered how anyone could rescue him if he happened to crash and survived the impact. His idea is the sky hook, and this is the way it works:

A rescue plane drops a small package to a person on the ground or in the water. The person may be the survivor of a wreck, an espionage agent, or a frogman who has just completed a mission. In the package, the man on the ground finds a pair of coveralls with a built-in parachute harness, a balloon, a helium canister for filling the balloon, a long nylon rope, and a battery pack.

The man dons the coveralls, blows up the balloon, and sends it aloft with one end of the nylon line. He fastens the other end of the line to his harness and then attaches a wire from the battery pack, which fits into a pocket on the leg of his coveralls, to a wire running up the nylon line and connected to a series of tiny strobe lights.

On the nose of the recovery plane is a large V-shaped device. The pilot, attracted by the flashing strobe lights, aims for the line just below the balloon, and flies so the line is caught by the device on the front of the plane. The line is then pulled up by a winch in the belly of the plane.

As the line is captured by the plane, the man is lifted from the ground. Fulton calculated that the man's first motion would be quite gentle and almost straight up, even though the plane is traveling forward at 120 to 150 knots. Only after the man has risen well above trees and other obstacles does he begin to move forward at the same speed as the plane. The winch then lifts him up into the plane.

Fulton lives in the rolling hills near Newtown, Connecticut. He calls his place Flying Ridge, and it has its own small grass landing strip, where he keeps the two planes he uses for most of his travels. Near his home he has established a small factory that provides sky hook equipment for the military and for intelligence agencies. How often, and under what circumstances, his device has been used, even he does not know.

Once, he received an urgent call from a contact at the Central Intelligence Agency, who wanted to know if his device could be used at high altitude. Because the air is thinner the higher one goes from sea level, the speed at which a person is whisked into the air would increase. Fulton quickly set up a series of experiments and determined that such a pickup was perfectly feasible. Only much later did he learn the reason for the sudden concern about a high-altitude pickup: Tibet was being overrun by China, and thought was being given to ways that the Dalai Lama might be rescued. One idea under consideration was to use the sky hook to whisk him off a Tibetan mountaintop. As it turned out, he managed to escape by more prosaic means.

On another occasion, during the early testing of the sky hook, Fulton was asked to try to rescue a scientist who had fallen seriously ill while working on a floating ice island in the North Atlantic. He agreed, but the sick man refused to be picked up, and a few days later, he died. The man's family wanted his body recovered, so Fulton arranged to use the sky hook for the purpose. Flying in a converted B-17 bomber, Fulton and his crew found the ice island covered with fog, but they dropped the harness and balloon and radioed instructions to those on the ground.

As the pilot came around again, he saw the balloon floating just above the fog bank, and he aimed for it. Since the men down below couldn't see the plane, they lay on the ground to avoid being struck. As they watched, the dead man rose slowly from the ground and then disappeared up into the clouds. A few minutes later, the sound of the plane could be heard overhead again. And then, just at the point where the dead man had risen, a case of vodka, suspended from a parachute, descended to the ground.

To the UDT men—and later to the SEALs—the sky hook looked like an ideal addition to their bag of tricks to be used in commando operations. In the next few years, more than a hundred pickups were made by the sky hook, many of them involving UDT men or SEALs. The young sailors, having learned to jump from an airplane, clamored for the reverse thrill: the distinction of being snatched from the earth up into a plane. It was a fast and thrilling ride. And it could be dangerous.

On 24 June 1964, the navy scheduled a demonstration of the sky hook near Little Creek. Two pickups were planned, one from the beach and one from a rubber boat floating just offshore in the Chesapeake Bay. Charged with arranging for the test was a young SEAL officer, Lt. (jg) Irve C. ("Chuck") LeMoyne. Scheduled for the pickup were a veteran petty officer who had already had a ride on the sky hook and LeMoyne himself.

LeMoyne recalls a crowd of sailors lining the dunes, shouting at him, "Hey, Mr. LeMoyne. Me next! I want on that!" Almost at the last minute, LeMoyne decided his plan wasn't really fair. The enlisted man had already been picked up, and LeMoyne figured that he, as air operations officer of the team, would have plenty of chances in the future. He gave the cherished assignment to two other SEALs.

As the jealous sailors watched from the dunes, the first volunteer donned his coveralls, inflated the balloon, and was whisked into the sky by a twin-engined RC-45J aircraft. It was a flawless performance.

Then Photographer's Mate Third Class James Earl Fox prepared for his pickup from a rubber boat. The plane roared overhead once more, and Fox floated off into the sky at the end of the nylon line. LeMoyne observed the pickup from a boat. A photographer in a chase plane flew nearby recording the entire pickup. Another photographer peered down through the belly of the plane, capturing the scene as the winch pulled Fox up inside the plane.

Suddenly there was a loud pop, the line parted, and Fox fell away toward the surface of the bay, some seven hundred feet below. A nearby fishing boat sped to the scene and pulled the sailor from the water. He was probably already dead. Despite mouth-to-mouth and mechanical resuscitation and heart massage, he could not be revived.

Fulton, deeply concerned, hurried down to examine the sky hook to determine what had gone wrong. He found that the winch had not been turned off as Fox came into the plane but had continued to turn until it snapped the nylon line. He recommended insertion of a device to prevent that from happening in the future and improved training of the air crewmen operating the system.

Despite the accident, training with the Fulton system continued. Maynard Weyers, who was then a lieutenant, has a vivid recollection of a night pickup off the coast of Coronado, California, on 20 October 1965. Two two-man teams of SEALs swam ashore, carried out a simulated attack near the roadway that runs along the shore south of the amphibious base at Coronado, and then swam out to rubber boats dropped from a circling plane. There, they went through the familiar ritual of donning the coveralls with the built-in harness and sending the balloons aloft.

As they bobbed in the choppy waves, Weyers could see the other team sitting in their little boat. Suddenly they disappeared, wafted aloft by the sky hook. And then Weyers noticed smoke coming from the nylon line. He called over to Fulton, who was in another boat nearby. Although the inventor assured them the line was okay, Weyers and his partner insisted on a new one.

Weyers, who was to be the top man in the two-man pickup, sat in the front of the boat, which was bouncing in a strong wind. Just as the plane approached, he fell into the water. As he struggled to climb back in, the line went taut and he zoomed up into the night. The shock of the pickup tore the battery out of his coveralls, and he grasped it to keep it from falling on Boatswain's Mate Second Class Jerome D. Cozart, his partner, who was hanging below him.

Weyers reached up and felt the nylon line connecting them to the plane. With the weight of the two men, it was stretched so tight it felt no thicker than a thread.

Because the plane had only enough power to reel the men in slowly, it took twenty-one minutes before they were finally helped up into the cabin of the plane. The pilot thoughtfully flew up and down the coast near San Diego so his dangling passengers could enjoy the lights along the shore.

Shortly afterward the navy decided, wisely, that there was little to be gained by having SEALs practice being whisked into the air by sky hook. As LeMoyne explains, it took no skill to be picked up. And the air crews, who needed practice to become adept at their end of the operation, could pick up dummies just as well as live men.

Whether, and under what circumstances, the SEALs or others have used the sky hook in actual operations is a closely guarded secret. But it is no secret that the air force has a fleet of planes specially equipped with the sky hook system and that Fulton's little factory continues to produce the packages that are dropped to the person to be picked up. Experiments have also been conducted with an advanced version of the sky hook capable of picking up as many as six men at a time.

Fulton and Fane first met in the early 1950s, when Fulton was working on his sky hook at El Centro, California. A friend told Fulton he ought to look up Fane, who was then at Coronado. "He doesn't have any money, but he has a lot of interesting problems," the friend said.

A few days later, Fulton hopped in his plane for the short flight over to Coronado. He found Fane in an office with pictures on the walls of the original steamboat built by Fulton's ancestor. Fulton soon realized that Fane knew more about the earlier Fulton than he did. The feisty Scot sailor and the erudite inventor hit it off immediately, and Fulton set to work at once on one of Fane's most serious problems.

The problem was how to recover a group of swimmers quickly after they had finished a beach surveillance mission. The UDT units were still using the system developed during World War II in which a swimmer thrusts his arm through a loop held out to him as the recovery boat speeds past. The system was slow, and it permitted the recovery of only one man at a time. If the pickup failed, the boat would have to turn around and run the gauntlet of enemy fire once more.

Fulton's inventive mind quickly came up with a maritime version of his sky hook. As he sketched out the system to Fane, the swimmers would gather in two clusters. As the recovery boat sped past, the crew would drop a rubber sled close to each group of men, with a line connecting the two sleds. Then the boat would make a fast turn and aim for the middle of the line between the two sleds. A snare on the front of the boat would capture the line and lead it up over the bow to a winch, which would then reel the two sleds, with their loads of swimmers, onto a platform at the stern of the boat.

Fulton tested the system first with his own sons in Long Island Sound and then worked with the navy to perfect it in tests in the Virgin Islands, where the teams went for winter training, and in Puget Sound. The navy was so enthusiastic about the system that special boats were built, designed to be carried as part of the gear that accompanied the teams as they traveled with the fleet. But there were others in the navy who resented these special teams with all their special equipment.

Just before they were ready to deploy, the sea sled boats were assigned to other navy units, and the teams were told to keep on using the old rope sling method of recovery, which is still in use today. No one ever gave Fulton a sound explanation of what had happened, but the result, as he puts it, was that "the whole thing went down the drain." Such is the lack of institutional memory in the SEAL community that few of today's SEALs have ever even heard of the Fulton sea sled system, which, if it had survived the navy's trial by bureaucracy, might have made their lives a good deal easier.

The enthusiasm for experimentation in the period after World War II led those involved in naval special warfare up some strange pathways. At the end of the war, Phil Bucklew had returned to civilian life as an assistant football coach at Columbia University. But he was back in the navy in the early fifties, adding his energy to the free-flowing experimentation that would later give shape to the SEALs.

In June 1951 he set up shop in an old brig at the East Coast amphibious base at Little Creek as commander of a top secret outfit, separate from the Underwater Demolition Teams, known as Beach Jumper Unit II. Over the next few years, they built up a squadron of a dozen boats, with 30 officers and 220 enlisted men. The boats bulged with the latest high-tech electronics of that era.

"We had distributed among our twelve-boat squadron the electronics equivalent of a cruiser and worked it into a team effort by which we did intercept, monitoring and jamming," Bucklew recalls.

Using their electronic equipment and a twenty-foot balloon carrying radar reflectors—they called it a kytoon—they could simulate an entire fleet. If that wasn't enough to confuse the enemy, they would set off explosions, as many as fifty at a time, to create the sound of a massive barrage by naval guns.

This was a large step beyond what the men of the UDTs had done inadvertently in World War II, when the approach of their flotilla of small boats sometimes caused the Japanese to react as though a full-scale invasion were underway, thus revealing their hidden gun positions.

Many of the electronic surveillance techniques developed by the Beach Jumpers were later transferred to a fleet of slow-moving converted merchant ships. These cruised the waters off the coasts of potential foes, listening to their communications and plotting the locations and frequencies of radar installations. They continued operating until 1968, when the North Koreans seized one of the ships, the USS *Pueblo,* and her eighty-three–man crew as she was going about her electronic snooping off the Korean coast.

The North Koreans held the ship and its crew for almost a year. A proposed rescue attempt by the SEALs was rejected as too risky.

Bucklew's Beach Jumpers and the UDT men also carried out another mission familiar to today's SEALs: simulated attacks on U.S. Navy ships to teach the crews how to defend themselves against combat swimmers. The swimmers are still amazed at how quickly the sailors aboard ship forget the very real threat from this source. They worry about the enemy's big guns and airplanes and forget the lone man in the water with a limpet mine.

John Raynolds served a tour of duty in the UDT in the early fifties and is now the chief executive officer of Outward Bound, an organization that teaches people to expand their capabilities by putting them into unfamiliar situations in the wilderness or in big cities. He still recalls with a glow of satisfaction the night he was one of a group of swimmers attacking ships in San Diego harbor with smoke bombs.

"I had a great success one time because I sank the *Bon Homme Richard,* one of our great carriers," Raynolds says. "They got most of the other swimmers. They dropped concussion firecrackers in, and the swimmers were supposed to surface. I swam in from a different direction and managed to get a smoke bomb on the *Bon Homme Richard.* The captain was livid—sunk by one man swimming in."

The water—on the surface or just under it—was the milieu of the Underwater Demolition Teams during World War II and in the years immediately afterward. But they soon began looking up toward the skies.

This was the beginning of the expansion that was to result in the air operations at which the SEALs later became so skilled.

During the Korean War, Raynolds was assigned to UDT Five in Japan. Also there was William H. ("Bill") Hamilton, Jr., a 1949 graduate of the Naval Academy who had become a protégé of Fane. While waiting for assignments in the war zone, the frogmen began to talk among themselves about how they might expand their horizons if they could use helicopters to drop swimmers in the sea and recover them again.

As early as 1947, Fane had carried out experiments with the helicopters of that era and had demonstrated that it was possible to insert and recover swimmers from a hovering chopper. But by the time of the Korean War those early experiments had been forgotten by most of those involved in UDT operations.

Before joining the UDTs, Hamilton had served as a carrier aviator and had a number of friends in the aviation community. He slipped over to the nearby Atsugi airfield and asked the marine helicopter pilots if they would mind dropping some frogmen into the ocean and trying to pick them up again. Raynolds explains how they did it:

> We wanted to determine how fast the helicopter could fly and still have the swimmer enter the water in workable condition. We kept increasing the speed. People would skip like a stone across the water. That was a little too fast. In the first group of tests, we had all our gear on: swim fins, masks, knives, explosives. When we hit the water, naturally it tore everything off. So we made a pack of equipment, with a flotation bladder. The guy had a knife on his leg, that was about it. He'd go in holding his nose and his ass. We'd drop equipment at the same time in a flotation device.
>
> We spent a lot of time developing that technique. How high should the helicopter be? How fast should it go so the swimmer hit the water in a reasonable fashion? What kind of angles should the person take? Most of the momentum was forward rather than down. We were flying about twenty feet at twenty-five to thirty knots. We developed a pretty good technique for getting a person into the water.
>
> Then we had this idea of picking them up. We were already trained in boat pickup. The swimmer puts his arm up, the guy catches him with the rubber loop, flips him into the boat like a fish. Well, we figured we'd get a rubber loop on a ladder. We'll

attach the ladder with bungee springs to the helicopter so it has some spring in it. The chopper will come along dragging this loop. The guy will do his thing, climb up the ladder into the helicopter.

It was a disaster. Just as he was going to get the loop, it would hit a wave and bounce over him. Or he'd get the loop and he'd get about halfway up the ladder and the next man would hit the loop and it would fire the fellow who was on the ladder right off, like a bow and arrow. We tried for a long time to find ways to make it work. We never really did get a way that would work except having the ladder just hang there and have the guy climb up.

That was the first concept of UDT getting airborne. We were also talking with the Korean air force about getting our people jump training. And some of our people did jump out of Korean airplanes, mostly because they wanted to get the little Korean wings. Then somebody broke a leg, and we weren't allowed to do it any more. That dropping people from helicopters was the genesis of what became the SEAL teams.

Later the SEALs improved on the methods of dropping men into the water, or onto land, from a helicopter. One technique involves letting down several thick nylon ropes from a hovering helicopter. Wearing heavy welder's gloves, the SEALs grasp the ropes with their hands and slide quickly to the surface. This is a distinct improvement on an earlier method, borrowed from mountain climbers, in which the rope is cinched around the man's body and he rappels down it to the surface. Using only their hands to control the speed of descent, a squad of SEALs can drop to the surface from thirty-five or forty feet in a few seconds.

Another method is used to drop a string of swimmers rapidly from a moving helicopter. Holding their bodies rigid, so as to present as little resistance as possible when they hit the water, the men jump, one after the other, as the chopper buzzes the drop zone. The trick, the SEALs found, is to match the speed of the helicopter to its altitude: ten knots at ten feet, twenty knots at twenty feet, thirty knots at thirty feet, and forty knots at forty feet. The forward momentum helps the man to retain the exact body position needed for safe entry into the water. Although a fast drop from a relatively high altitude can be made safely, SEALs normally prefer to drop from ten feet at ten knots.

Although the techniques for dropping men safely have become routine for the SEALs, a practical way to retrieve men from the water with a moving helicopter has remained elusive.

The fact that the frogmen found time for long days of experimentation with helicopters is an indication of the extent to which the Korean War was a period when they were again searching for their proper role, again asking the question, "Who are we?"

Except for Inchon, where MacArthur brought his forces ashore in a massive amphibious landing behind enemy lines after the North Koreans had come within a hair's breadth of overrunning all of South Korea, there were few operations of the kind in which the frogmen had made their reputation during World War II. And since North Korea had only a small navy, there was little opportunity for underwater ship-attack operations. Instead, the UDT men found themselves involved in explosive ordnance disposal—mine clearing. After the landing at Inchon, many mines remained in the harbor, and the UDT men were assigned to help remove them.

The mines were designed to pop to the surface when they sensed the magnetism given off by the metal hull of a passing ship. They were studded with pressure-sensitive horns designed to set off the mine on contact with the ship. The mine clearing was carried out in the depths of the harsh Korean winter, but the frogmen had only primitive diving suits, which were supposed to keep them dry and relatively warm. The suits were made of green latex, and they were bulky, awkward things with the loose material cinched in front with a metal clasp and with a flutter valve to let the air out. They almost always leaked, so the swimmer ended up cold and wet with his legs weighted down by sea water.

Because the mines were magnetic, the swimmers used only equipment made of materials such as aluminum that would not be attracted by the mine and perhaps set it off. Raynolds recalls:

It wasn't terribly deep, thirty or forty feet of water. The mines had been spotted by some other means. We had a chart, and we knew roughly where they were. So we went down and just looked for them, by feel, really, because the visibility was poor. It was cold as hell, and we had a big fire going on the beach. It was the dead of winter, maybe ten above zero. We'd go down in these stupid dry suits to locate these mines and then buoy them. Then we would attach lines to them and a wooden-hulled sweeper would come and tow them out of the harbor and detonate them. It was hairy. They had nodules sticking out of them, which you don't want to touch because they go boom.

The big thing was frostbite of the face. We'd really get catatonic because of the cold. When you're young—twenty-three or twenty-two or twenty-one—you don't think of the consequences that much. But make a wrong move and poof!

As they searched for a role, the UDT men began to experiment more and more with commando-type operations, either on their own or with Korean guerrilla groups. On several occasions, frogmen swam or rowed their rubber boats ashore behind enemy lines to disrupt North Korean operations by blowing up railroad tunnels.

Whether such raids were worth the risk was questioned even within the UDT community. Even though he had encouraged his men to prepare for commando-type operations, Fane was one of the critics of the attacks on tunnels.

"You don't blow up a tunnel," he says. "That just makes it bigger. A tunnel is already blown up. The coolies go in, they get a lot of nice rocks for ballast. They fix the rail in the night, and the trains go through. These are the fallacies of these glory boys. If you use a little logic, you see how inefficient such operations are."

Sometimes on their own, and sometimes working with the Central Intelligence Agency, they inserted guerrilla units far behind enemy lines and then supported them in their operations. Although still in the navy, Bucklew spent two and a half years working with the Central Intelligence Agency in Korea. Fane also operated against North Korea, launching Korean guerrilla units from the sea and then maintaining contact with them. This was in early 1952, more than a year after the United States and its allies had been driven out of North Korea by a massive attack by Chinese forces across the China-Korea border.

"We landed North Koreans, who had been trained in the south as guerrillas, on the east coast of Korea up within sixty miles of [the Soviet port at] Vladivostok, using the techniques of the UDT," Fane says. "We landed upwards of fifty a night for a couple of nights, from rubber boats, at two or three in the morning. We'd lie in the rocks while the Chinese passed by twenty or thirty feet away and wait until the coast was clear. They advanced some thirty or forty miles into the mountains, and I went over on a C-47 and dropped rice and explosives for them."

One of the most ambitious assignments given to the frogmen was to destroy the North Koreans' fishing nets. A blockade by the United Nations forces had severely cut the flow of supplies into the north. But fishermen working near the shore brought in a harvest of a million tons of fish a year, a major source of food for the North Korean military.

UDT Five made the first foray in Operation Fishnet in the summer of 1952 near the North Korean port city of Wonsan. Twice they hacked away at the nets without attracting the attention of soldiers on shore. But on the third operation, they were spotted by soldiers who fired at them with machine guns while they were in the water, attempting to cut holes in the nets with their knives.

Protected by the combined firepower of a transport ship, a South Korean patrol boat, and their own landing boats, the men managed to escape without casualties. But no longer could the effort to destroy the nets be kept a secret.

Two months were allowed to pass. Then in September, members of UDT Three sailed far north of Wonsan, to within fifteen miles of the Manchurian border. There they rode their small assault boats, with muffled motors, into a cove. Quietly they slipped into their smaller rubber boats and rowed in toward shore. One boat went in too close. The men were startled to hear the sound of a soldier's footsteps crossing a wooden bridge almost overhead. They waited until he passed and then cautiously paddled back out a short distance.

Other members of the team had located a portion of the huge net and radioed the code name of the target: "Key West." The net was about three hundred feet across, supported by cork, pieces of wood, and clusters of glass balls. At one end, a large line anchored the net to the shore. Soldiers ashore had built a large bonfire to warm themselves against the chill of the September night. The light from the fire was a godsend to the frogmen, helping them to see what they were doing, while against the darkness of the sea, they could not be seen.

The frogmen quickly set about destroying the net by dragging sections of it up onto their rubber boats, cutting out a portion and dropping it into the sea. Another group attacked the anchor line. But what appeared at first to be a heavy manila rope was, in fact, a steel cable encased in hemp. The men waited while bolt cutters were brought from the landing craft. But the cable was too tough. Again, they waited while explosives were brought in. Just as they finished rigging the demo charge, shots rang out from the shore. The men clambered into their landing craft and sped out to sea.

They listened for the sound of the explosion but heard nothing. Then, just as they began to worry that something had gone wrong, they heard the *whump, whump* of the two charges going off.

Operation Fishnet made a slight dent in North Korea's food supply, and plans were made for a renewed assault on the nets at the height of the fishing season in 1953. But before it could begin, an armistice ended the fighting on 27 July 1953.

By the beginning of the 1960s, with the Korean War and many years of experimentation behind them, the navy's frogmen had vastly expanded their horizons. They had learned how to operate for long periods of time under the water. They had become competent commandos, and they had added the third dimension of the air to the areas in which they felt free to operate. While the navy still had a strong need for the beach reconnaissance and obstacle removal work traditionally done by the Underwater Demolition Teams, the outline of something new was rapidly becoming visible.

CHAPTER SIX
BIRTH OF THE SEALs

The annual winter deployment of the East Coast Underwater Demolition Teams to St. Thomas in the Virgin Islands was an almost idyllic experience, with long days of swimming and long nights of drinking and, often, romance. But, after a while, it could also be rather boring.

The winter of 1960–61 was little different from previous deployments despite the dramatic happenings on the world stage. In November 1960, John F. Kennedy was elected president. On 20 January 1961, he took office. On 17 April 1961, American-trained Cuban exiles landed in Cuba in an attempt to overthrow Fidel Castro and suffered a disastrous defeat at the Bay of Pigs.

One of the many lessons from the Bay of Pigs was that the U.S. had difficulty carrying out an operation that was too big to be kept secret but smaller than an all-out commitment of U.S. forces.

On 25 May 1961, President Kennedy addressed a joint session of Congress in what he described as his "second State of the Union message." It was one of the most important speeches of his presidency. In it, he set the goal of putting an American on the moon before the end of the decade and called for a major restructuring of the nation's military to build up conventional forces and move the country away from sole reliance on "massive retaliation" with nuclear weapons. Two paragraphs pinpointed the gap exposed by the Bay of Pigs.

"I am directing the secretary of defense to expand rapidly and sub-stantially, in cooperation with our allies, the orientation of existing forces for the conduct of non-nuclear war, paramilitary operations and sub-limited, or unconventional wars," the president said. "In addition, our special forces and unconventional warfare units will be increased and reoriented. . . ."

Kennedy backed up his words with a separate message in which he ordered the Pentagon to take more than one hundred million dollars from other programs to beef up the military's special operations forces.

Bill Hamilton, by then a lieutenant commander and the command-ing officer of UDT-21, was in St. Thomas when he heard the president's words, and they immediately caught his interest. Fane had since re-tired, but Hamilton recalled their thoughts of an expanded role for the frogmen.

"It occurred to me that this was what Doug Fane and I had been looking for for years," Hamilton recalls. "I saw it as a great opportu-nity."

With other officers in the team, he set about writing a letter to the chief of naval operations proposing the creation of a new naval unit that would not be tied as tightly to the amphibious force as the UDT had always been. It would, in effect, be a naval commando force capable of operations not only at sea but on land and in the air as well. It would be prepared to work with the navy's aviators, submariners, and all of the surface fleet.

Even before the letter reached Washington, the admirals had already sensed which way the wind was blowing. Vice Adm. Ulysses S. G. Sharp, deputy CNO for plans and policy, summed up the navy's thinking in a memo shortly before the president's speech. He noted that the navy had done little to increase its emphasis on counterguerrilla warfare and warned, "Since this type of operation is held in such high regard in high places, we had better get going."

Actually, the navy, under prodding from the CNO, Adm. Arleigh A. Burke, who was himself being vigorously prodded by President Kennedy, had begun giving serious thought to its role in this new kind of warfare. At the beginning of May, the navy's Unconventional Activities Committee recommended the formation of a unit on each coast to be the focal point for navy involvement in guerrilla and counterguerrilla operations. The SEAL acronym—a contraction of SEA, AIR, LAND—was used by this committee for the first time in a memo dated 29 April

1961. But the role of these new units was still vague: ". . . an all-around, universal capability."

Hamilton's memo obviously fell on fertile soil. Capt. Harry S. ("Sandy") Warren, who headed a special operations section for Burke, showed up in Little Creek, where UDT-21 had returned from its winter in St. Thomas. "We're going to cut orders on you," Warren said. Within days, Hamilton found himself in the Pentagon, with a $4.3 million budget and a yeoman as his one-man staff, charged with preparing for the creation of two SEAL teams, one on each coast.

Navy records from the time reflect the uneasiness which many officers felt about this new venture. It would take money and manpower from other parts of the navy. And it would run counter to the long traditions of a blue-water navy that had plenty of work to do out on the open seas without getting into messy guerrilla operations or venturing up muddy inland rivers.

In later years, after they had proved their worth in just such operations, the SEALs treasured two critical quotes from the navy brass. In the early 1960s, the vice CNO, Adm. Horacio Rivero, had sent out a memo decreeing that the navy should not become involved in any shallow-river, muddy warfare. And Adm. James Holloway, an aviator who was later to become CNO himself, snapped, when someone broached the subject of funds for SEALs, "If it doesn't have airplanes, I don't want to hear about it." In fairness, it should be noted that Rivero later became a strong supporter of the navy's muddy-water operations in Vietnam, and that Holloway had, at the time he made his comment, a full-time job making the navy's case for continued construction of supercarriers.

One ruling that Rivero made in the early days of the SEALs did stick, however. When the suggestion was made that the SEALs wear black berets like the jaunty green berets of the army Special Forces, he was adamant: "We call them white hats in the navy. I don't know any black berets and I want that term wiped out."

Hamilton never sensed any lack of support from on high. Both Arleigh Burke and his successor as CNO, Adm. George Anderson, continued to push the program. More surprisingly, he also received strong backing from Vice Adm. Charles D. Griffin, an assistant CNO and a destroyer sailor whose surface forces would be expected to bear most of the cost, in money and manpower, of setting up the two commando teams. One obvious solution was quickly ruled out. Existing UDT units could not simply be converted into SEAL teams because the amphibious force still needed its frogmen. Although the first SEALs would come from the UDTs, they would have to be replaced by new trainees.

"The amphibious force had to continue to have the support of the UDTs. That meant this would be a new organization with new bodies, new billets, new money, new equipment and a new mission," Hamilton recalls.

Much of Hamilton's time in the latter half of 1961 was devoted to questions such as, How big should the SEAL teams be? How should they be armed? What should their training be like, and where should it be conducted? What kind of boats, weapons, and other equipment should they have?

A basic decision followed the UDT model. There would be one team on each coast: one at Little Creek and the other at Coronado. They would have fifty enlisted men and ten officers, with a lieutenant as commander. This guaranteed a youthful organization but it also meant that the low-ranking SEAL officers would have relatively little clout with the navy bureaucracy—the same problem that had bedeviled Kauffman and the other UDT officers of World War II. Following the UDT precedent, it was decided that each of the teams would conduct its own training. This meant each team was free to develop its own individual culture and that, in many subtle ways, East Coast and West Coast SEALs would be somewhat different from each other, as well as rivals.

Well before the creation of the SEAL teams was actually authorized, Little Creek was moving rapidly ahead. One reason was its proximity to Washington. Hamilton, who had come from Little Creek, tended to rely on the UDT teams there to help work out the structure of the new teams. Another reason was that Lt. Roy Boehm, a mustang who had come up through the ranks as an enlisted man before earning his commission, was executive officer of Hamilton's old team, UDT-21, and he sensed the changes on the horizon. At least half a year before the SEALs became operational, he had placed men in specialized schools learning such untraditional skills as hand-to-hand combat, cracking safes, and breaking locks.

The SEALs were formally authorized in December 1961 and commissioned in January 1962. Lt. John Callahan was named as first commanding officer of SEAL Team Two, but he was delayed in reaching Little Creek, so Boehm was named as acting commanding officer awaiting his arrival. The creation of the new teams was considered so important that they were given a high presidential priority for both men and equipment. But Boehm moved so fast that he soon found himself in trouble with his more stodgy superiors.

His men needed new underwater breathing devices, so he bought them on the open market and then—even worse—modified them without going through all the required paperwork. A formal inquiry was triggered.

Then he bought so-called HALO (high-altitude, low-opening) parachutes so his men could practice surreptitious entry into enemy-controlled territory. The parachutes, too, needed modification. And another inquiry began.

The biggest fuss came when he went out on the open market and bought 132 of the new AR-15 rifles. The AR-15 was a lightweight automatic that evolved into the M-16 rifle, which became the standard for American infantry. But at that time, no one else used it, and the military had no support system or spare parts for the new rifle. Actually, Hamilton had arranged for the AR-15 to be issued to the SEALs. But Boehm had moved faster than the paperwork, and he was in trouble once more.

J. H. ("Hoot") Andrews, a senior petty officer and highly competent storekeeper who had been drafted away from the submarine service to take charge of acquiring equipment for the new team, recalls, "I told Roy, 'This is serious!' I thought he was going to jail on that one."

Boehm might well have been court-martialed had it not been for a visit to Little Creek by President Kennedy. The president fell into conversation with A. D. Clark, a member of the team who was displaying their new equipment, including the new lightweight rifle. The president asked how the men liked the rifle and in typical SEAL fashion, Clark told him, "As far as I'm concerned, you can take all the rest of this garbage and jam it. This is what we want. And my boss is about to get a court-martial for open-purchasing this."

A few days later, Clark received an autographed photo from President Kennedy. And, as if by magic, the troubles that threatened Boehm disappeared.

Boehm had arranged for half of the new rifles to be sent to the new West Coast team, where Lt. David Del Giudice, former executive officer of UDT Twelve, was the first commanding officer. Del Giudice, a veteran

UDT officer, was in on much of the early planning for the new SEAL teams. He became heavily involved in the preparations in the latter part of 1961 but found much still to be done. When he took over as commanding officer, all he had was a small office in the UDT head-quarters on the Strand south of Coronado, on the edge of the beach just across the street from the Pacific amphibious headquarters. He found an old warehouse on the amphibious base and took it over as his headquarters. Then he requisitioned an old building that had been used by the base fire department for drying hoses. The SEALs converted it into a parachute loft.

One of Del Giudice's concerns was to determine the various types of weapons the SEALs should carry. He was surprised later when he visited the Pentagon and came across a list of the weapons that Mary Miles's guerrilla units had used behind the Japanese lines in China nearly twenty years earlier. Although the weapons themselves were differ-ent, the firepower was similar to what the SEALs had settled on. "He invented and we reinvented," Del Giudice says.

Despite the powerful support they had from the president and top navy officials, the SEALs were not exactly rolling in money. It wasn't like the hand-to-mouth existence of the UDTs, but those were still lean days.

"I won't say we lived out of salvage, but we certainly used salvage to the maximum amount allowed by the rules," Del Giudice says. The SEALs closely monitored the salvage depots, where surplus material was collected, and made sure they got first crack at anything they could use. An old compressor, for example, would be signed out of salvage, modified, and then used to fill SCUBA bottles.

The East Coast SEALs already had a venerable tradition of carry-ing their raids on salvaged goods to the extreme. Henry S. ("Bud") Thrift, who served as air-operations officer for both UDT Twenty-one, and SEAL Team Two in the midsixties and early seventies, recalls that the men were so eager to parachute that they would go out on their own time to practice jumping. But the navy could not afford very many chutes. This meant a man had to take time after each jump to repack his chute. If he had several chutes, he could get in more jumps in the time the plane was available.

"We couldn't buy parachutes; we didn't have any money," Thrift says. "We would go to salvage—the place in supply where things [go] that are out of date, or not good, or have done their tour, or were turned in to be sold as scrap or destroyed. We would get parachutes out of salvage, their ten-year life expectancy over, and repair 'em. And that's what we were free-falling with."

The SEALs also complained that the chutes provided by the navy were the standard military version that was difficult to steer. They decided to make modifications on their own.

William ("Bill") Bruhmuller, a plank owner, or original member, of SEAL Team Two, was introduced to the use of salvaged chutes as a member of an underwater demolition team in the late fifties.

"We would take these chutes and mark them with a Magic Marker, take scissors and cut it out, whatever modifications we wanted to make," Bruhmuller says. Cutting holes in seven of the twenty-eight gores in a typical circular military chute made it into a reasonable copy of the more sophisticated chutes then coming into use by sport jumpers. The modifications permitted a forward speed of four or five knots and made the chutes steerable.

But cutting the holes and then carefully hemming them on a sewing machine was a time-consuming process. The frogmen soon realized that if they marked the hole and then ran a hot soldering iron down the line, they could cut out a section of the chute and anneal the nylon at the same time.

"We could get four or five jumps before they started tearing," Thrift says.

"What did we know?" Bruhmuller says. "We could have killed ourselves. But we didn't—at least not because of that. We still followed the basic procedures and tried to be as safe as we could be, with a salvaged parachute."

Even with the modifications, the chutes used by the SEALs in those early days were a far cry from the flying mattress chutes they use today. It is now possible to jump from a high-flying plane and land fifty miles away. Jumping over England, flying across the Channel and coming down in France is not considered a serious challenge.

The forward speed of today's chutes is also much higher, as much as twenty-five miles an hour—so fast that, as Thrift says, "you can kill yourself even on a good landing if you're not careful." But SEALs are trained to land safely by spilling air from the chute to halt the forward momentum just before they touch down.

By the time the SEAL teams were formed in 1962, many of the UDT members had a good deal of experience in jumping, although much of it had been done on their own time and at their own expense. Their first jumps were done in the classic pattern developed by the army's paratroops. The jumpers lined up in the plane, marched in lock step to the door, turned, grasped the sides of the door and thrust themselves into space. A static line automatically opened each chute as soon as the jumper was clear of the plane. After the first few jumps, this began to seem pretty tame to the frogmen. Soon they made a game of the departure from the plane. Bud Thrift tells how they dove out the door and tried to slap the engine nacelle before falling away from the plane.

Then came the challenge of the free-fall, in which the chutist delays opening his chute for many thousands of feet. Added to this was the challenge of jumping in a group into the vast expanse of earth and sky revealed when the huge rear door of a C-130 transport plane is opened—much more frightening than shuffling up to the small side door, where the long drop is visible only at the last moment.

Many of the SEALs found a night jump less intimidating than a day jump. But jumping in a group at night posed its special problems: How do you keep track of each other? One solution was for the jumpers to spray themselves with patches of fluorescent paint. But the paint loses its glow after about ten minutes. Then someone suggested using the paint just before the jump. That was not a good idea; suddenly released from a pressurized can at ten thousand feet, the paint coated not only the jumpers but everything else in the plane.

For the SEALs, one of the most critical questions was how to land safely in the water. Members of navy air crews are, of course, taught how to parachute into the water from a disabled plane. But an air crew member is weighted down only by his survival vest and a life raft, which dangles below him. A SEAL, on the other hand, may be encumbered by hundreds of pounds of gear: swim fins, underwater breathing system, weapons, ammunition, radios, raft, food, and water. He may even have to carry a special device for disposing of human waste so he will leave no trace of his visit to enemy territory. When a heavily-muscled SEAL, weighing about 180 pounds, steps out into the night at five hundred feet above the water, the weight of his equipment, added to that of his body, may well total four hundred pounds.

Bill Bruhmuller was one of a team of SEALs assigned to the naval air test center at Patuxent River Naval Air Station in Maryland. Day after day—and night after night—they parachuted into Chesapeake Bay, learning when and how to release the equipment package dangling below the chutist, how to release the chute at the right moment, and how to find the equipment package and get everything into a rubber boat. The biggest problem, particularly at night, Bruhmuller found, was how to get rid of the chute and avoid being dragged through the water. Even in the daytime, it is difficult to estimate the distance to the surface and safely release the chute just before splashing in. At night it is virtually impossible. Bruhmuller and the other members of the team found that if a jumper enters the water with the chute still attached, he should grasp the harness and roll onto his back as quickly as possible so he can reach the chute-release buttons. Being dragged facedown can be fatal.

The test team also worked out the guidelines for weather conditions. It is possible, they found, to jump safely into heavy seas, but the wind speed is critical. Normally, they concluded, a jump should not be made if the wind speed is greater than fifteen knots. On a critical mission, the jump might still go ahead with winds up to eighteen knots.

As the SEALs gradually acquired more and more skill as parachutists, they formed their own parachute demonstration teams—the Leap Frogs on the West Coast and the Chuting Stars, which has since been disbanded, on the East.

The chutists found that, no matter how high they jumped or what kind of spectacular displays they put on by trailing smoke as they fell, the spectators were unimpressed if the SEALs didn't land right in front of them. Thus, they began to stress "relative work," in which the men jump from relatively low altitudes and maneuver their chutes so close they actually touch.

In one maneuver, called stacking, one chutist sits on the top of another man's canopy. In another, called the biplane, one chutist swings in and stands on the other man's shoulders, with the two chutes appearing joined together.

Pierre Ponson, a retired command master chief and veteran member of the Chuting Stars, says the two maneuvers are quite safe, but the transition from one to the other must be done very carefully and at sufficient altitude to allow for problems.

Such a problem occurred on 16 September 1980 during a demonstration at Lakehurst, New Jersey. Ponson said he had just landed when he heard a shout and looked up. Two men were trying to transition from a stack to a biplane when the upper man inadvertently cut loose from his chute. He grabbed at the other man's chute, and it collapsed.

Both men, Hull Technicians Third Class Paul P. Kelly and Richard Doheny, fell about four hundred feet to the ground and were killed.

When the two first SEAL teams were formed, their training was adapted directly from the training of the World War II UDT members at Fort Pierce and Maui. Of course the training has been extensively modified to take into account the new missions of the SEALs. In making the modifications, the navy borrowed heavily and unabashedly from the training course developed by the army's green beret Special Forces. Training for all would-be SEALs is now conducted at a single training center in Coronado, but the course is basically the same as those developed separately by the two original teams.

Before a man becomes a full-fledged SEAL, he goes through a rigorous six-month course, followed by another six months of on-the-job training with a team. This full year of training is the toughest, most demanding required of any military unit in the world. It is not unusual for half of those who begin the six-month course to drop out before they finish. In the midseventies, one class set a record. Thirty-seven men were there at the start, and none of them finished.

Even before the trainee begins the course, he undergoes four to six weeks of physical training and indoctrination. The six-month course itself is broken down into three phases.

The first phase is nine weeks long, continuing the physical conditioning. The pace of the regular two-mile swims in the surf and the four-mile runs along the beach is steadily increased. While guests at the stately old Hotel del Coronado sip their after-dinner drinks, cold, wet SEAL trainees practice riding in through the crashing surf in rubber boats to land on a cluster of rocks just south of the hotel. One trick is to clamber onto the rocks in the moment between breakers and then use the rock itself for shelter as the next wave comes crashing in. A man caught between wave and rock can easily break an arm or leg.

During that first phase, a man endures a level of physical activity he has never experienced before unless he has participated in the decathlon. The men run in soft and hard sand and on hard surfaces in boots or tennis shoes. They are constantly wet. They suffer from inflamed tendons, twisted knees, and falls on the obstacle course.

The biggest problem is the stress fracture, a hairline crack in a bone. The trainees are particularly susceptible to such fractures because they are at an age, in their late teens or early twenties, when their bones are still not mature.

"Running on sand does all kinds of crazy things to the body," says Lt. Scott Flinn, a physician who monitors the health of the trainees. "A stress fracture is most common in the tibia [the shinbone] or the femur [or thighbone, the large leg bone above the knee] and the foot. It is very painful and it can be severe. It can go to a complete fracture. A man will be running down the beach and the bone will snap and come popping through his leg in a compound fracture."

Despite the pain, trainees are so reluctant to be dropped from training or "rolled back" to another class that they sometimes keep going until a bone snaps.

The sixth week of the first phase of training is a hallowed SEAL tradition: Hell Week. The nonstop ordeal of running, swimming, rowing, and wallowing in the mud is limited only by the instructors' fiendish imaginations.

"Hell Week is a completely different thing [from the earlier training]," Flinn says. "It is interesting to see it from the medical standpoint. The goal there is to push the student further than he thought his limits were and make him realize he can do more than he thought. We encounter a lot of medical injuries, problems along the way that would normally hold them back."

Each day during Hell Week, the students are examined one by one. Often they are given antibiotics and pain medicine and released to continue the ordeal with ailments that would normally send them to the sick bay.

"We see trauma, broken bones. We see severe infections like pneumonia and abscesses. Little cuts get infected. We let them go until they're ready to break and then pull them out. If they're holding up their boat crew, we may have to pull them out, but generally we don't have to," Flinn says.

A key part of the Hell Week ordeal is deliberately contrived sleep deprivation. The men are scheduled for two hours of sleep each night, but they seldom get more than forty-five minutes to an hour of intermittent sleep, often in the sand or mud or even in the surf. One instructor used to delight in gathering the trainees in a circle on the sand after hours of strenuous activity and turning on a radio with soft music. Just as they began to drift off, he would shout, "Okay, on your feet. Into the water."

Hell Week usually begins on Sunday. By Tuesday night, Flinn says, the men are running on autopilot, and it is not uncommon for them to begin to hallucinate. They will see men or strange animals rising up out of the sea, firmly convinced that they exist.

In the early days at Fort Pierce, Hell Week was the first week, and it was a quick and dirty way of screening out those who might not finish the course. Today when a trainee goes into Hell Week, he has had a couple of months to build his stamina. This change recognizes that Hell Week, for all its physical demands, is basically a test of a man's mental and emotional makeup rather than his physical condition. He learns what it takes to keep going when his own internal fuel gauge screams "empty!" The test thus takes into account that the demands upon a SEAL are basically different from those on most other military men. A soldier who tires can always sit beside the road. But a SEAL who locks out of a submarine on a mission has to keep going until the job is done. And he must continue to use his head no matter how tired he is. On a combat mission, a SEAL may well find his fingers so cold he can't use them and have to find some other way to finish his task.

SEALs are all volunteers and, at any time, they can volunteer back out again. Most of those who drop out—or are dropped because of a physical problem, like a broken bone—do so in the grueling first weeks of training or during Hell Week. Until recently, there was a bell in the courtyard of the training center in Coronado. If a man wanted out, all he had to do was ring the bell. Or, if the bell wasn't handy, he could simply say, "I DOR (Drop on Request)." In early 1990, several important changes were made. The bell was removed because of the fear in the navy's training command that its presence might intimidate a man into doing something dangerous against his better judgment. And now if a man wants to quit, he is counseled by several layers of petty and commissioned officers to make sure he really wants to drop out.

Officials at the training base say the changes are a reasonable way of avoiding injury, on the one hand, or needlessly losing men who could, if they continued, become valuable members of the SEAL community. Privately, many SEALs complain that the training has been softened under unrelenting pressure from higher naval authorities to cut down the failure rate at a time when the demand for SEALs is growing.

The men who make it through Hell Week are given a few days of light duty to recuperate from their ordeal. In the final three weeks of the first phase, they learn the basic UDT skills: how to survey a beach and prepare a chart of its contours.

The second phase lasts for another nine weeks and concentrates on working with explosives, reconnaissance, land navigation, small-unit tactics, patrolling techniques, rappelling, and the use of SEALs' weapons.

For the final four weeks of that phase, the men fly to San Clemente, a rocky, brush-covered island about sixty miles off the California coast, where they learn to use the arsenal of weapons favored by the SEALs, practice with explosives, and swim.

Until recently, when new masonry buildings were erected, the SEAL encampment was a rough collection of Korean War–era one-story wooden buildings set in a cove below the island airstrip. One, no fancier than the others, was called the Hell Box—named for the electrical device used to set off an explosive—and served as the headquarters for the instructors.

For the officer-trainees, the period on the island is probably more demanding than any of the other phases. They are required not only to go through all the training given to the enlisted men, but also to act as officers. If there is a night exercise in which the men have to work their way through "enemy" positions set up by the instructors, the officers have to not only plan the operation but lead their men and give orders. This means they are up earlier and get to bed later than the other trainees.

For several nights, the instructors stress fire control. Unlike soldiers, who are taught to fight and shoot, the SEALs are taught how to avoid fighting and how to avoid shooting. They are warned not to give away their positions by shooting back when they hear or see gunfire. The shooting may simply be "reconnaissance by fire," in which troops shoot randomly to see if there is any response. The students learn that they can often crawl right through the enemy position in the dark if they keep quiet and maintain strict discipline.

"I've walked away from more firefights than I've gotten into," says Warrant Officer George Hudak, one of the few Vietnam veterans remaining as an instructor. He tells about one night in the Plain of Reeds in Vietnam. "We saw a little fire. We said, 'We'll move this way.' We saw another. 'Move this way.' Before I knew it, there were about 150 fires around us. We walked right through a base camp. I was scared to death one of my guys would panic and we'd have to start shooting.

"Too many people get this gunslinger attitude. Every time someone shoots, they want to dump their load. I tell them they should assess the situation. Is this guy really shooting at me? The only time you want to shoot is if you have him. Then shoot. But if not, why shoot? You can only fire so long. You've got seven men. How many does he have? You have five or six minutes of firepower. If you dump your load and come hauling ass out of there, you could run into another situation and not have anything left to shoot."

After the trainees learn this lesson so well that they are reluctant to shoot at all, they are suddenly confronted with an ambush in which the instructors pop off a flare that leaves them feeling naked and exposed. Now they must locate the enemy guns, aim accurately, and lay down covering fire that will permit them to extricate themselves from their predicament. In each case, whether it is working their way through an enemy position or responding to an ambush, the officers are expected to tell their men what to do and make sure they do it right.

Perhaps the most demanding test is on the firing range. One three-man unit lies on the ground, protected by a section of telephone pole. Behind and to the right of them, another unit takes advantage of similar scant shelter. Then they both fire live ammunition from their M-16 rifles at an imaginary enemy. At a shouted order from the officer in charge of the first group, the men cease fire, stand, turn, and dash back to drop down behind another log. The other three men continue their covering fire with the bullets passing a few feet from the men who are pulling back. It is as close as a man can come to being in a firefight without actually being shot at, and it is frightening. It is no wonder that some officers forget to stop shooting so their voices can be heard, or are too frightened to shout above the din of the gunfire.

Hudak teaches them to use claymore mines with thirty-second fuzes, plus smoke and tear gas. "Smoke yourself to get out of there," he tells them. "Make 'em pay to kill you."

Although the exercise ends when the men have pulled back to the bottom of the firing range, in actual combat the goal would be to continue their withdrawal out into the nearby ocean. "That's our lifesaver right there," says Lt. Comdr. Richard ("Rick") Sisk, pointing to the ocean. "That's why we take water so seriously. Not just because it is a way to get in. If things go bad, we're going to be heading for the water. Not many people will follow you at night into the water."

While veteran SEALs complain about what they see as a softening of the training, they agree that the preparation for small-unit combat given at San Clemente represents a marked improvement over what was provided a few years ago. In the four weeks at San Clemente, the men learn tactics that, in the past, they would not have learned until they had been in a SEAL team for many months.

On the firing range, the trainees get a chance to shoot hundreds of rounds from the special weapons in the SEAL arsenal. They are introduced to the old .45-cal. pistol. But the SEALs soon learn to prefer the Heckler & Koch P-9S or the simple Sig Sauer P-226 9mm pistol. Because its only safety feature is a double-action trigger, the Sig Sauer is not issued to regular military units.

Another favorite, especially among counterterror units, is the H & K MP-5 submachine gun, good for shooting quickly and accurately. It operates so smoothly that a man can fire off its thirty-round magazine with one hand. A bigger machine gun is the M-60, a slimmed-down version of a standard infantry weapon used by the Germans during World War II. The eighteen-pound model used by the SEALs makes a big, booming sound. With a tracer every five rounds, it is easy to walk a stream of bullets right into the target, even firing from the hip. Together, these two weapons take the place of the Stoner, an automatic weapon favored by Vietnam War–era SEALs but no longer in use.

Other weapons include a twelve-gauge, pump-action shotgun with a powerful kick; the 60mm mortar; the Gale McMillan 86 sniper rifle; and the big .50-cal. sniper rifle, developed for the SEALs and used to take out heavy targets such as generators, trucks, and aircraft. The SEALs also use a special navy version of the standard M-16 infantry rifle, with drainage holes and a Teflon coating to protect it from moisture, and the M-14 rifle, capable of hitting targets at seven hundred yards.

The work at San Clemente also includes intensive instruction in the use of explosives. Today's SEALs favor a plastic explosive designated C-4 and a similar material called C-5. The C-4 comes in a twenty-pound pack. Inside are eight two-and-a-half–pound canvas sleeves, called socks, that can be taken out and shaped around an object or cut to a size suitable for the target. The explosive itself is relatively insensitive. It can be cut, molded into various shapes, and even dropped without going off.

In preparation for a blast, a SEAL wraps a length of explosive cord, called det cord, around the block of C-4 several times. The det cord is also relatively benign—until it is set off. Then it burns at the rate of twenty-six thousand feet—four and one-half miles—per second. This gives it a high level of what explosives experts call *brisance*, a sharp shattering or crushing effect, which sets off the C-4 with a bang.

After preparing an explosive, the SEAL has to get far enough away to be safe from the blast. One method is to place a timer on the explosive. When the time comes, the timer sets off a very sensitive blasting cap which, in turn, ignites the det cord. Another method involves attaching a fuze cord to the blasting cap and then reeling out a length of cord. The fuze cord is similar to the det cord but much slower burning. It burns at the rate of a foot every forty seconds. Thus, if a SEAL lays out a ten-foot length of cord, crimps on a fuze igniter, and sets it off, he has a little more than six minutes to get away.

A third method, used for large explosions such as beach clearance projects, uses an electrical wire to carry a spark from a hell box to the detonating cap. The hell box creates a current of electricity by means of a plunger, a squeeze mechanism, or a crank.

One of the lessons taught to today's SEALs is just the opposite of what the World War II frogmen did. When in doubt, they overloaded the coral reefs or obstacles they wanted to get out of the way. But Hudak stresses how much can be done with a small amount of explosives.

At first, when given an assignment, many trainees are inclined to load themselves up with as much as forty pounds of explosives.

"With two pounds, you can destroy a building or screw it up so it can't be used," Hudak tells them. "With two pounds, you've got five or six charges, if you know what you're doing."

In this way, the training is focused squarely on the kind of work SEALs might be expected to do, moving surreptitiously behind enemy lines, perhaps for days, carrying everything they need to sustain themselves and to fight effectively. They are taught, for example, how to use readily available materials to make explosives. Just outside the cove where the SEAL encampment is located is a small rocky island, called Bird Island, covered with a thick layer of white guano, deposited there by generations of sea birds. Mix the dung with diesel oil and presto: you have an excellent, homemade explosive.

In the past the island had another meaning for SEALs during their stay at San Clemente. While the instructors got the fires going, trainees were sent out with rubber boats to dive for abalone, the succulent shellfish that once covered the California coast in great abundance but has now become a rare treat.

Everything the SEALs do is closely related to the water. It is only a short swim from the camp to the rocky border of the neighboring navy air strip. There the SEALs practice crawling up out of the water for an assault on the field. Only after a man, lying flat on his belly, has peeked over the edge of the runway does he realize how big and formidable a target even a small airstrip can be.

If the trainees dive down just a few yards from shore, they find metal tetrahedrons, underwater obstacles that look like giant jacks of the kind that little girls play with. These provide excellent training in the techniques for attaching explosives to similar obstacles during actual landings, just as the UDT men of World War II did.

The water near the encampment also provides the setting for one of the most arduous challenges of SEAL training: the five and a-half-mile swim. The swim is done on the surface, with the man clad in a tight-fitting helmet, face mask, wet-suit top, gloves, swim fins and booties. If the water temperature is below sixty degrees, he must wear the pants of the wet suit as well, although many SEALs think that is more trouble than it is worth.

It is probably impossible to swim out into the Pacific off the California coast without giving at least a passing thought to what might lie hidden beneath the surface, such as a man-eating great white shark.

Several years ago, when Capt. Theodore Grabowsky was a young officer assigned as an instructor, he was accompanying the swimmers in a power boat. On one side of his craft was lashed a small rubber boat so a swimmer who got in trouble could be pulled from the water quickly.

Suddenly two of the swimmers shouted that they had seen a shark. Grabowsky had his coxswain pull up beside the swimmers, but with the rubber boat on the side away from them, and then began an interrogation.

"How big was the shark? Do you see it now? Put your head in the water and see if you can see it."

Grabowsky knew that if he took the two swimmers out of the water, there would never be an end to shark-sightings. He also knew that, if there really was a shark there and one of the men was bitten, he would be in big trouble. Failing to see the shark again, the swim buddies remained in the water and completed the swim. When they finally struggled up onto the shore, they were so tired and so happy to have finished the swim that they didn't even remonstrate with Grabowsky for leaving them in the water as possible shark bait.

Although SEALs often see sharks and other large marine creatures, in the nearly half-century that UDT men and SEALs have spent swimming on and under the world's waters in the line of duty, none of them has been attacked by a shark. The only exception was one SEAL on his day off, out swimming with his girl friend in the Virgin Islands, who was attacked and killed by a black tip shark.

Far more dangerous is hypothermia, a condition in which the body temperature drops to dangerous levels. Dr. Flinn says that in the winter, when the water temperature is in the fifties, the doctors at the training center see one or two cases of hypothermia a month.

The danger of hypothermia increases as the men progress in their training. As they become more fit, the percentage of body fat, which normally serves as insulation, decreases sharply. A normally active person may have 17 to 22 percent body fat. But in the final phase of training, the would-be SEALs are often down to a body fat of only 4 to 7 percent.

One of those who has experienced hypothermia and lived to tell about it is Albert W. Winter, who went through training at Coronado in 1957. The trainees were assigned a relatively short swim, from their training center north along the coast to the rocks below the Hotel del Coronado. It should have been a simple outing for would-be SEALs, but the instructors had failed to take into account a strong southward current.

The men had been warned that they would be dropped from the program if they failed to make the swim, but one by one they gave up and had to be pulled from the water. Even though he was floating backward, one man fought off would-be rescuers until he was finally convinced that he would not be dropped.

Winter, who was a strong swimmer, was paired with an even stronger swimmer and he and his partner were among the few who made the full swim.

"We were making progress, and I think that kept me warm while I was swimming," Winter says. "But as soon as I hit the surf line, I almost didn't get through. I basically crawled up on the beach and lay down and started shivering. Had I had a weak heart I would have died, I'm sure. By all rights they should have lost me. I was really in bad shape. I was out of control. I couldn't get up, couldn't talk. They weren't smart enough to know they should have gotten me to the hospital. They covered me up, took me in a jeep to a warm shower. It was a long time before I could talk. I was just shaking."

By the late 1980s, the navy had become much more aware of the danger of hypothermia and knowledgeable about how to treat it.

The first step is to take the person's temperature, using a rectal thermometer. This gives a reading of the core temperature inside the person's body. In most cases of hypothermia, it is 90 or 91 degrees, compared with the normal 98.6 degrees. If it has dropped as low as 87.5 degrees, there is serious risk of heart failure.

Instead of being put into a hot shower, a man with the symptoms of hypothermia should be placed in a whirlpool bath with warm water. His arms and legs remain outside the tub and then are gradually warmed. If the cold extremities are warmed first, that causes a rush of cool blood to the core of the body and can make the person's condition worse. As soon as possible, the person should be taken to the nearest hospital emergency room.

The training base at San Clemente is equipped with a dry sauna— one of the few amenities—rather than a whirlpool bath, for use in warming swimmers. The instructors are all trained in dealing with hypothermia. But even that was not enough to save the life of Hospital Corpsman Third Class John Joseph Tomlinson after a five-and-a-half–mile swim at San Clemente on 14 March 1988.

The water temperature was between 57 and 59 degrees, and the seas were calm. In the last half of the swim, a current of about one knot was running against the twenty-three swimmers. Tomlinson and his swim buddy had been in the water for nearly four hours and were almost to the beach when he appeared tired and cold and then lost consciousness. When he was pulled from the water, his face was blue, his eyes were dilated, and froth was coming from his nose and mouth. The rescuers could discern no pulse or breathing.

He appeared to be dead. But victims of hypothermia have been known to revive from such a condition after being warmed. The instructors administered cardiopulmonary resuscitation and hurried Tomlinson to the sauna. A weak heartbeat was detected for about two minutes, and he took a couple of breaths on his own about an hour after he had been carried from the water. He was later flown to an emergency hospital, where he was pronounced dead of hypothermia.

The rules for the five-and-a-half–mile swim were later modified to require swimmers to wear wet-suit bottoms if the water temperature is below sixty degrees. The theory is that this will prevent a substantial heat loss through the legs, but it also adds to the burden the swimmer must propel through the water.

The final seven-week phase of the training at Coronado focuses on swimming underwater. The students are taught how to use two types of SCUBA gear: the air tanks familiar to recreational divers and the pure oxygen systems of the type developed by Lambertsen fifty years ago. On some assignments, the SEALs also use mixed-gas systems, in which the diver breathes both oxygen and another gas, such as nitrogen or helium.

Much of the training is conducted in a fifty-foot-tall diving tower filled with 110,000 gallons of water, which is normally maintained at a very warm ninety-four degrees Fahrenheit. In it, the trainees learn to function underwater in full view of the instructors. (Before the tank was built, the students actually went out into the ocean for their training dives.) At the bottom, the tank is equipped with the kind of lockout chamber found on a submarine. Originally designed to permit crew members to escape from a disabled sub, the chamber is now used routinely by SEALs to depart from a submarine and return.

To learn how to rise safely to the surface from a submarine, the trainees swim down to a bell-like shelter, which is suspended at twenty-five feet. While standing in the shelter, they breathe air that is compressed by the water pressure. When the instructor taps on the bell, the trainee takes a breath, grabs a rope, and starts up, hand over hand, one foot per second. But since the air in his lungs is under pressure, he has to blow air out as he ascends. He is taught to hold his head back and blow.

If he is not blowing enough, the instructor taps him on the chest. If too much, he gets a tap on the cheek. If he runs out of air near the surface, an instructor assists him the last few feet. If he runs out of air below ten feet, the instructors pull him, kicking and fighting, back down to the bell and "reload" him. Once back in the bell, they stand him up and make sure he is okay before sending him toward the surface again.

Once the diver successfully completes the ascent, using the rope, from both twenty-five and fifty feet, he is ready to make a free-floating ascent. He swims down to the bell at fifty feet and inflates his life jacket. On a signal from the instructor, he ducks out, begins his blow, and rockets upward. One instructor watches to make sure he doesn't bang into the side of the tank. Another, waiting halfway up, grabs his jacket to slow him and, if he is not blowing, gives him a knee in the stomach. The whole procedure takes less than five seconds.

After each ascent, the diver goes through a test to make sure air has not entered his bloodstream, causing an embolism. As soon as he reaches the side of the tank, he shouts, "I feel fine." One of the signs of an embolism is the inability to pronounce two words beginning with the letter *f*. After a quick check by a corpsman, he moves to a red line and stands at rigid parade rest for five minutes. Another sign of an embolism is the inability to stand still without twitching. The same process is repeated at a yellow line, a green line, and a black line.

When the students finish their training in the tank, they go out into the ocean for long underwater swims to perfect their skills at navigation in such combat operations as swimming into a harbor to attach mines to enemy ships.

When the successful trainees complete their six months at Coronado, they spend another three weeks at the Army Airborne School at Fort Benning, Georgia, where they learn the fundamentals of parachuting using a static line. Then they spend another six months in training with a SEAL team before being certified as full-fledged SEALs and permitted to pin on the SEAL badge—nicknamed the "Budweiser" because of its similarity to the beer manufacturer's trademark.

The Budweiser is a big, gaudy badge, a source of great pride to the SEALs and the result of a bureaucratic accident. Until about 1970, the SEALs had no distinctive insignia. Then several SEALs at the Pentagon began work to design a badge and get it approved for use by both UDT and SEAL team members. Al Winter, who was assigned to Washington at the time, recalls how they developed several sleek designs, similar to the wings worn by aviators. But the design needed the approval of a navy board, and the fliers turned thumbs down on the sketch. It looked too much like their wings.

The proposed badge had all the elements of the SEAL mission: an anchor representing the sea, wings representing the air, and a pistol representing the land. Winter suggested a blowup of the original design.

"I said, 'Why not make it look gross as hell? I know we can get this one approved. It's going to look bad. Then we'll do a design change. We'll just slim it down and make it the way we want it.' Everyone thought that was a hell of a good idea, but it backfired. When we went to the fleet and said, 'We've got a chance to get a really nice-looking emblem,' the guys said, 'No, we like what we've got.'"

Naval authorities have puzzled for years over the question of what kind of person becomes a SEAL, why some make it through training and even more don't. The concern works two ways. Any program with a dropout rate of 50 percent or more is obviously wasteful. It would be much better if tests could be devised that identified those most likely to succeed and weeded out the others. On the other hand, there is always the worry that those who have the potential to become superior SEALs might be eliminated by the selection process or fail, for unknown reasons, to make it through training.

Winter recalls one incident when trainees were being badly battered in attempts to land on the rocks near the hotel: "I know in my class, people were screened out who should not have been screened out. We were doing stuff at the rocks, surf up, at night. It was a really dangerous situation. We had guys hurt. One of the better officers just up and said, 'That's it! This is really dumb.' He was a strong leader. He took about six people with him."

Scientists have done a good job of defining the physical characteristics of the typical SEAL. Perhaps surprisingly, he is neither a huge Arnold Schwarzenegger nor a Rambo, overmuscled both below and above the neck. He is what physiologists call a mesomorph, with a chunky, muscled body, averaging 176 pounds and five feet, ten inches, tall. Dr. Thomas J. Doubt, a physiologist at the Hyperbaric Medicine Program Center at the Naval Medical Research Institute in Bethesda, Maryland, likes to think of the typical SEAL as an Olympic-class athlete, more closely resembling a star at water polo than either a marathon runner or a sprinter.

What is puzzling to the navy and its scientists is that the physical profile of the man who makes it through training and becomes a SEAL is almost identical to that of the man who doesn't make the grade. The difference is from the neck up.

In 1986, scientists studied 336 trainees in three consecutive classes at Coronado, trying to find out whether there was some difference that could have been detected beforehand between the 62 who completed the course and the 274 who didn't. At the beginning of training, the trainees were all subjected to a battery of tests. Those who completed the course were tested again in the final week before graduation.

The physical differences—age, height, weight, and percent body fat—between those who completed the course and those who didn't proved to be insignificant. What stood out was that the graduates tested higher on self-confidence, self-esteem, teamwork skills, and leadership potential.

But there were also interesting changes that took place during training. As might be expected, the graduates were more tired than when they started. They were also angrier, which might reflect their reaction to the rugged training course. More surprising is that the test scores of the graduates indicated that they were less likable, they responded with less validity, they were less service-oriented, and they were less reliable than indicated by their scores at the beginning of the course.

To succeed as a SEAL obviously requires a high level of intelligence, the ability to adapt readily to changing conditions, the ability to master one's fear, extreme self-control and self-discipline, and a great deal of self-confidence. But the scientists have not been able to devise tests that will identify the men with the mental and emotional characteristics to become successful SEALs. One reason is the difficulty of sorting out these subtle differences. But another is the SEALs themselves, who resist efforts by scientists to fit them into neat little slots.

When the first two SEAL teams were formed, they had barely had time to organize themselves when they were thrown into action.

On the East Coast, that first real test came during a nine-day period between 27 April and 6 May 1962 when a six-man team was sent on a highly secret mission to reconnoiter the Havana shoreline for a possible amphibious assault against Fidel Castro's Cuba. This was a year after the debacle at the Bay of Pigs and five months before the Cuban missile crisis.

Boehm, by then executive officer of Team Two, under Lieutenant Callahan, was put in charge of the operation. When the SEALs were being formed, he had argued unsuccessfully that the Underwater Demolition Teams should be converted into SEAL teams, a change that did not take place until two decades later. To emphasize his point, Boehm chose two more SEALs, in addition to himself, and three UDT men.

They flew to Key West and began practicing for the operation. George Walsh, one of the UDT swimmers, recalls nighttime drills off the coast near Key West. The men locked out of a submarine through the escape trunk and then waited in the water for the sub to retrieve them. The swimmers linked themselves together with a line. Those at each end of the line held little noisemakers that could be heard by the sub's sonar. Using this as a guide, the sub ran slowly between the two sources of sound and snared the line with its periscope. From the periscope, the swimmers followed a wire running at a forty-five-degree angle down to the escape trunk.

Every time they practiced this maneuver, Walsh watched the phosphorescence stirred up by the six swimmers and feared it would attract a hungry shark. "With all those legs going back and forth, we felt like live bait," Walsh says.

On the night of the beach survey, the six men had barely locked out of the sub and begun swimming toward the beach when they saw trouble coming in the form of several Komar patrol boats. One depth charge would have done them in, but the boats swept right past, apparently looking for the sub.

The swimmers lined up along the beach in pairs about twenty-five to fifty yards apart, one man in each pair in close, the other a little farther out. They were so close that they could see people in their apartments along the shore and make out footprints on the beach.

Boehm was up almost on the shore while his buddy, James C. Tipton, was a few yards out. Suddenly Boehm made out the form of a man on horseback riding along the beach toward him. He signalled to the others to lie low and then dashed into a clump of bushes just above the beach.

"Damned if he doesn't stop right there at that clump," Boehm recalls. "He lighted a cigarette. I'm figuring I have to grab the horse's reins with one hand, do him in with the other. I knew Tipton would be out of the water and with me. I was perched to take him out. My job was to get in there and get the information without anyone knowing we were there. But this guy kept looking out. He never made any moves."

Finally, the horseman continued his ride up the beach.

The swimmers completed their survey along four thousand yards of beach—more than two miles—and they were exhausted as they swam out toward the rendezvous with the sub. By that time, all the underwater-breathing devices had begun to fail. Walsh's breathing bag was full of water, and he discarded it.

For about half an hour they waited, treading water and swimming wearily in circles. One of the swimmers, Harry R. ("Lump-Lump") Williams, finally voiced the fears they all felt.

"Lump says, 'Maybe they ain't going to come pick us up. What do we do then, Roy?'" Boehm recalls. "I say, 'Swim to sea and drown.'"

My famous order. Lump says, 'What a chicken-shit order that is. I knew being a friend of yours would get me killed.'"

Almost desperate now, the men swam a little farther out to sea. And then they saw the periscope. They had been waiting above a coral head that prevented the sub from getting close enough to pick them up. As the sub snagged the line binding the men together, they had been in the water for almost eight hours, and they were near total exhaustion. But their ordeal was not yet over.

One man, Walsh, had discarded his "lung." The others still wore theirs, but they were not working properly. To enter the sub, they would have to swim down about thirty-five feet, crawl into the lockout escape trunk, and wait until the water had been expelled before they could get into the sub, a procedure that takes about four minutes.

Boehm and two of the men followed the wire from the periscope down to the trunk. Even when the trunk is open to the sea, a bubble of air is trapped inside. The three men took turns ducking inside long enough to fill their lungs. Boehm grabbed the intercom device that permitted him to talk to the skipper of the sub.

Boehm told him: "Well, Captain, we're back. We have the information. Now the ball's in your court. You can drown us or you can see if you can get these guys in."

On the surface, hanging onto the periscope, Walsh looked toward shore and saw several Komars headed in their direction. He took out his knife and tapped a warning signal on the mast. Suddenly, the sub rose slightly and a hatch in the conning tower opened. The swimmers tumbled inside.

Walsh could hear Boehm's voice, from the outside, booming through the intercom system: "If you don't surface this goddamn boat, somebody's going to get killed."

Moments later, satisfied that his men on the surface had been taken into the sub, Boehm and the other two swimmers locked in through the escape trunk.

Their survey had found the gradient of the beach too steep for an amphibious landing. And of course, no such landing in Cuba was attempted.

Five months later, both the new SEAL teams were called upon as the United States prepared to respond to the news that the Soviet Union was in the process of installing, in Cuba, nuclear missiles capable of reaching targets in the United States. Del Giudice and his Team One flew to Little Creek and prepared to parachute into Cuba. One plan called for the SEALs to jump along with a mass drop of army paratroopers. Del Giudice convinced his superiors that wasn't a good idea: the small SEAL contingent would be in more danger from the soldiers than from the Cubans.

The frogmen were called upon to make another surreptitious reconnaissance in Cuba. Lt. William T. ("Red") Cannon headed a unit of men from SEAL Team Two and UDT Twenty-two on the mission. He and seven other men—four two-man swimmer pairs—made the actual swim.

They locked out of a submarine off the harbor at San Mariel and then swam on the surface to save the oxygen in their artificial lungs. As they entered the harbor, they expected to find heavy chains across the entrance, but were surprised to find there weren't any.

Swimming underwater, they worked their way along the dock area, counting the Komar patrol boats. Their assignment was to determine whether it would be feasible, in the event of open hostilities, for the frogmen to swim in and knock out the patrol boats. They swam back out to the submarine, which was sitting on the bottom in about eighty feet of water, locked back in without difficulty, and reported that it would be an easy task to destroy the patrol boats.

Back in Little Creek, Cannon was briefed on the plan that would be followed in the event the Soviets refused to remove the missiles from Cuba. He and his swimmers were to set limpet mines with timers on the Cuban boats. They would also mine a big transport ship so the Cubans could not move it out to block the entrance to the harbor. And then they would work their way overland to link up with a unit from Team Two that was scheduled to parachute into an area near San Mariel.

Before any of these plans could be put into action, the crisis ended when the Soviets began removing the missiles.

The members of SEAL Team One returned to the West Coast and resumed their preparations for operations in the western Pacific and Southeast Asia. The land-bound nation of Laos was under growing threat by communist guerrillas. And the United States feared that, if Laos fell, that would expose its long border with South Vietnam to infiltration.

Del Giudice was already familiar with the area. In the summer of 1960, he led ten members of UDT-Twelve in the epic voyage of the

Mekong boat flotilla. Together with eight other sailors, Del Giudice and his men sailed up the Mekong River through South Vietnam and Cambodia in five fifty-two–foot LCMs (landing craft, mechanized). Nested on their decks were five smaller LCVPs (landing craft, vehicle and personnel) to strengthen the Laotian forces. Americans were a rarity in that part of the world in those early days, and the countryside was almost untouched by fighting. It was the lull between the French battles with the Viet Minh and the much bigger American and South Vietnamese war with the Viet Cong and the North Vietnamese Army.

Del Giudice particularly remembers how pleasant the cities of Saigon and Phnom Penh, the Cambodian capital, were.

"Saigon was a beautiful place," he says. "The Street of Flowers was just that, with beautiful smells. It was well organized, very pleasant. Phnom Penh was that way too. Very laid back."

The flotilla remained in Phnom Penh for almost two weeks and then continued, unarmed, up the Mekong toward the Laotian border. Residents of sleepy little villages along the way stared in awe as this strange flotilla worked its way up the river. Much of the route was uncharted, and several times boats became hung up on underwater obstacles. Most of one day was spent fighting the way upstream through the treacherous Sambor Rapids. The voyage had been timed to take advantage of high water. But that meant that, at times, the boats were slowed to less than one knot by the eight-knot downstream current. Finally, on the Fourth of July, the Americans turned the boats over to the Laotians at Voun Khom and were hurried to the airport for the flight back to Saigon.

Within two months of the creation of the SEALs, at the beginning of 1962, Del Giudice had gone back to Vietnam with a SEAL lieutenant and a marine colonel "to get the lay of the land and see what the SEALs might do." By the end of February, SEAL Team One was preparing to deploy part of its new force to Vietnam. In his own mind, Del Giudice had a clear idea of the direct-action type of operations at which the SEALs might excel.

But in many ways, the experience in Vietnam was to be a continuation of the long struggle by the navy's frogmen to define their mission and understand who they are.

CHAPTER SEVEN
A PLEASANT LITTLE WAR

Cathal L. ("Irish") Flynn later became an admiral. But in February 1964, when he arrived in Da Nang, he was a lieutenant (junior grade). As so often happens to SEALs, Flynn found himself a very lowly naval officer running a very secret and very important military operation.

Dave Del Giudice, the commander of SEAL Team One, had set up shop in the city itself in a building nicknamed the White Elephant, and he was busy building up the infrastructure to support the limited but growing American involvement in Vietnam. Flynn was in charge of a detachment of sixteen SEALs and four marines on the ocean side of the river that forms the large Da Nang Harbor.

Early 1964 in Vietnam was almost like B.C. in the Gregorian calendar. It was before the marines arrived, before helicopter gunships, before B-52 Arclight raids, before Rolling Thunder, Linebacker 1 and Linebacker 2, before search and destroy operations, before Agent Orange and defoliation, before Tet. The SEALs thus found themselves involved at the very beginning of the Vietnam War, as they were to be involved to the very end.

The first SEAL detachment of two officers and ten enlisted men arrived in Da Nang early in 1963 and became part of a small group of military men assigned to work under the Central Intelligence Agency. The goal at that point was to infiltrate agents into the north to stir up resistance against the government in Hanoi. Some of the agents were parachuted in or smuggled across the border. The job of the SEALs was to set up a system to land agents from the sea.

This whole effort was very small and extremely secret. Even today, many aspects of operations carried out nearly thirty years ago remain highly classified.

The hope in Washington was that raids from the sea could make life so unpleasant for the leaders in Hanoi that they would back off from their growing effort to take over the south. The Bay of Pigs fiasco had demonstrated that if an operation grew beyond a certain size, it should cease being a covert CIA activity and become a full-scale military operation. This is what happened early in 1964. The CIA backed out, the military took over the SEALs at Da Nang, and the whole nature of U.S. involvement in Vietnam changed.

Planning for the step-up in pressure on the north had consumed most of 1963. The result was a blueprint for a three-phase, year-long campaign of increasing intensity. It was given the code name of Operation Plan 34A, or, as it came to be known, OP 34A. The United States' involvement was to be carefully concealed, and the entire operation was to be very secret.

Although consideration had been given as early as the fall of 1962 to the use of American SEALs in these operations, that was eventually ruled out. Instead, the SEALs were assigned to train guerrilla fighters to carry out the harassing raids against targets along the North Vietnamese coast. The SEALs themselves were strictly prohibited from accompanying their charges north of the demilitarized line separating the two parts of Vietnam at the seventeenth parallel.

The Vietnamese commandos were hidden away in a chain of secret little camps along a ten-mile stretch of beach between two commanding promontories, Monkey Mountain on the north, and Marble Mountain on the south. At various times there were five to seven groups of forty or fifty men, each group in its own enclave. One group was trained as swimmers; the others were strictly shooters. Their boats were docked in a delightful little cove at the base of Monkey Mountain known as China Beach, where the SEALs had installed a base, with finger piers and a floating dry dock. In the early days, most of the commandos were ethnic Vietnamese. Later, there were Chinese, Thais, Nungs, Cambodians, and members of other minority groups in Vietnamese society.

Many of them had been discriminated against by the North Vietnamese, adding to their eagerness to fight. During the CIA days there were even a few German and Norwegian mercenaries serving as boat crews.

Irish Flynn was still a very junior officer, but his background had given him some perspective. Born in Ireland, he had received part of his education in a French military school. He was embarrassed to be put in the position of teaching these tough warriors how to fight.

"At the time," he says, "I was struck by our arrogance. I had never been shot at in my life, never shot at anyone. We had a few Korean War vets who had done some real shooting. But we were advising some guys who had spent ten years in the army with the French and had been in all kinds of fights. I thought it was an act of very great arrogance."

When Flynn arrived, the commandos were already in training for raids against the north in which a few men would be dropped near the coast to swim in and plant mines on North Vietnamese vessels.

One of the most urgent targets was a naval base at Quang Khe, about 120 miles north of Da Nang. Not only was Quang Khe a staging base for small boats smuggling high-priority arms and infiltrators into the south, it was also a base for the formidable eighty-three-foot Chinese-built Swatow motor gunboats, which posed a danger to guerrilla operations along the coast and even to American naval patrols offshore.

A first attempt to send in swimmers to attack the boats failed in mid-February 1964. Another attempt was scheduled for early March.

"They really had a tough job to do," Flynn says. "They had to go across a sand bar, go up a river a certain distance, dogleg left, swim accurately in on these patrol boats, and put two limpets on each boat. It looked like a really tall order."

The bulky SCUBA gear worn by underwater swimmers creates a good deal of drag, and this means that they move very, very slowly, less than a quarter of the speed of a person walking. Even a slight current is enough to slow them further or to push them off course.

The swimmers had demonstrated that they could swim impressive distances, but the Americans planned a rehearsal to make sure the mission was feasible. North of Da Nang, they found a river similar to that at Quang Khe and anchored a boat to represent the target of the actual mission. Then the four Vietnamese frogmen were dropped offshore to make the practice swim.

One American trainer remained on the boat. Two more Americans waited at the target boat to make sure the swimmers got there. Everything went perfectly. The men at the target boat signalled to the man offshore that the swimmers had carried out the mission, doing everything except planting live explosives. Then the swimmers returned to the boat and declared the mock attack a success.

The SEALs had already learned that any delay in carrying out a mission increased the odds that the North Vietnamese would be forewarned. So as soon as the swimmers were rested, they were sent off toward Quang Khe.

But after the mission was under way, the two SEALs at the target boat reported an unsettling discovery. They had found footprints along the bank of the river where the swimmers had walked, rather than swimming. Too late, Flynn learned that the rehearsal had been a sham. Whether the men could carry out their difficult mission was in serious doubt. But it was too late to call it off.

The skipper of the small boat that carried the swimmers north saw them off and then waited much longer than he should have for their return. Finally, he gave up and headed back south in broad daylight.

Flynn says he doesn't know what happened to the men. They simply failed to return. But North Vietnamese radio claimed the capture of four frogmen at about that time. One was said to have been killed resisting capture. Of the other three, one was sentenced to life in prison, one to eighteen years, and the third to seven years.

"The only way I could excuse myself was to blame youth and inexperience," Flynn says.

Despite the early failures, OP 34A scored a series of successes in the spring and summer of 1964. A junk was captured; a storage facility was destroyed; a bridge was knocked down; a lighthouse was shelled. The operations were becoming a constant irritant to the North Vietnamese. Whether they were causing enough disruption to be militarily significant was another question.

Flynn thought back to the French military men he had known, how extraordinarily tough they were. And yet they had lost as many officers in Vietnam each year as St. Cyr, the French equivalent of West Point, was turning out.

"I was only a lieutenant, but I wondered, what the hell are we doing here? This is not going to bring the guys who fought the war with the

French, who eventually won the battle of Dien Bien Phu, the battle of the Central Highlands, to their knees. This is not going to break their back, these pinprick raids we're doing."

William Colby, who was in charge of the operations for the CIA in the early days and who later became director of the agency, was one of the first to become disillusioned with the whole effort.

"Our experience demonstrated, quite frankly, that there was not much hope of generating any substantial resistance in North Vietnam. And having made a college try at it and having come to zero results in positive terms—minor effect, you know, tiny little pinpricks—I came to the conclusion—and I was in charge of them—that the operations just should be called off. They really were not contributing what they had hoped to, and they were suffering losses, and there was no point in it," Colby later recalled.

For many of the SEALs, life at Da Nang from 1963 up to, and even after, the arrival of the marines in 1965 was almost idyllic. Since they were forbidden to accompany the commandos to the north, they were in little danger. The uniform of the day was a pair of shorts and tennis shoes, and hair styles were a matter of personal choice. They had the beach area almost to themselves. And since they didn't bother the local Viet Cong, the VC didn't bother them. Rules against fraternization with the population were not enforced against the SEALs. Instead, they were encouraged to socialize with their Vietnamese counterparts.

At night, they gathered at little beach bars to talk and drink as they watched the moonlight sparkling off the breakers rolling in from the South China Sea. They didn't even bother to bring their weapons. Maynard Weyers, who, in the fall of 1964, relieved Irish Flynn in charge of the detachment advising the commandos, recalls running by himself for miles along the beach between Monkey and Marble Mountains without a weapon. He never felt threatened.

Later, when the marines arrived, a marine general took over a little hideaway near China Beach, causing one SEAL to comment, "Generals and SEALs know how to get through a war."

But the United States was moving inexorably toward deep involvement in the Vietnam conflict. And, although nobody knew it at the time, the little operations—the pinpricks—were to play a major role in the change from covert U.S. support of the South Vietnamese to large-scale involvement of American forces.

The increased tempo of commando raids against the north was made possible by the arrival in Da Nang, on 22 February 1964, of the first two of a fleet of Norwegian torpedo boats of the Nasty class. Although the name seemed to fit their job, the boats were actually named for a Norwegian sea bird. Before they arrived, operations had been limited by the fact that the boats available, ranging from junks to two 1950-vintage boats hurriedly removed from mothballs, were neither big enough nor fast enough and didn't have sufficient range to carry out the more ambitious raids.

Michael L. Mulford, who served as executive officer of one of the first two Nasties, was impressed when they arrived at the amphibious base at Little Creek, early in 1963. They were eighty feet long and had plastic hulls and a shallow draft of only three feet, seven inches. They were powered by two British-built Napier Deltic diesel engines, each capable of 3,120 horsepower. The boats were brand-new, just out of the Norwegian shipyard. They were even stocked with silverware, china, and small glasses fitting into the bar in the tiny wardroom, which was made of mahogany.

When the Americans took the Nasties out for a test run, they were greatly impressed by the engines and the automatic clutching mechanism. The engines had a deep, throaty roar that would make any hot-rodder cry with jealousy, and they could push the boat along at more than forty knots. And then when the helmsman grabbed the throttles and rammed them into reverse, the craft shuddered to a halt within two boat lengths and began backing up. Of course anyone standing on deck when that happened would be thrown flat on his face.

The boats had room for a crew and ten SEALs and enough room for provisions for a forty-eight-hour mission. The armament carried by the Nasties was constantly changing. Originally, they were equipped with two 20mm and two 40mm guns. The 40mm guns were removed to make room for more fuel, but then the craft seemed too lightly armed, so 81mm mortars were added. At various times, the boats were equipped with 20mm and 40mm guns, mortars, 57mm recoilless rifles, 3.5-inch rocket launchers, and flamethrowers.

Despite the fact that the Nasties were destined to take part in one of the most secret affairs in recent U.S. history, they received a remarkably public send-off. In May 1963, one of the Nasties sailed north to the Washington Navy Yard and took the secretary and under secretary of the navy and a collection of navy brass for a thirty-minute dash up and down the Potomac River. President Kennedy, who had skippered a PT boat in World War II, was invited along, but he was busy greeting an astronaut. The press was welcomed to photograph the new boat, and a press release described its purpose. The new boats, it said, were "designed to perform amphibious support and coastal operations" and were for use "by the navy's Sea-Air-Land (SEAL) Teams in unconventional and paramilitary operations." Only after the two boats had been shown off on the West Coast and in Hawaii, on their way to Vietnam, did the chief of naval operations order a stop to the publicity splurge.

The Americans who took the Nasties to Da Nang had little to do with the commandos who rode the craft north on their combat missions. Mulford recalled:

We never knew very much about the commandos. They were kept on the other side of the peninsula from us, on the beach side. They would come in by trucks, climb aboard the boats, and off they'd go. And we'd see them when they came back again. My greatest memory of the commandos is one time they—we had been out on a training mission, we came back, the guy jumped off the boat. He had one of these rocket launchers on his back. Three rockets on a backpack. He jumped off the boat and pranged the back of the rocket launcher on the stanchion, firing the rocket out over the camp. It went over Monkey Mountain and—oh, yeah, it took the hair off the back of his head. He thought it was hilariously funny. We wondered just how effective they were when they got to where they were going with that kind of attitude.

One of the first ones I remember was when they went up to shoot up a lighthouse to get nighttime gunnery practice. And that was without, as I remember it, landing anybody. They just went up into this small harbor and shot the lighthouse up, shot up the area around it, and got out of there again. Another time they were extremely jubilant about one operation. And that was when they had taken the commando crowd out, dropped them off. They crept into a North Vietnamese army camp, laid out their rocket launchers, got everything set, and then just fired the rocket launchers into the middle of the camp. When everybody came running out of the tents and hooches, they just shot them up with machine guns and got out of there. They came back just ecstatic over that one.

We wondered at the time just how much was getting accomplished. You'd have to leave at four o'clock in the afternoon, steam all night, shoot up a lighthouse, and come back. You can do the same thing with one airplane in an hour. It seemed like a rather romantic, but not particularly effective, way of getting a job done. To me, anyway. Never made much sense to us.

Despite the doubts of American officers in Da Nang about the effectiveness of the secret raids against the north, they were certainly proving an annoying irritant. Under pressure from Washington to step up the tempo of the harassment, American commanders in Saigon approved a plan calling for an increase of operations in August of 283 percent over the July level. At the same time, Hanoi beefed up its sentry force along the coast and began running more aggressive patrols with its own torpedo boats. Those actions set the stage for one of the critical turning points in American history. And the SEALs, or their South Vietnamese counterparts, were right in the middle of it, although most Americans were not to know that until years later. What happened is this:

Just after midnight on the morning of 31 July, four Nasties carrying South Vietnamese commandos approached targets on two islands off the central coast of North Vietnam. The men were prepared to land and plant explosives ashore, but the commander received intelligence that the enemy had been alerted to the raid. He decided to hit the targets with gunfire rather than land his commandos.

They shelled both islands, destroying a gun emplacement and a number of buildings on Hon Me and a communications station on Hon Nieu.

In addition to their mortars and automatic cannons, the four boats were newly equipped with 57mm recoilless rifles, and that could have had a significant influence on what occurred next. The recoilless rifle fires its shell in a flat trajectory, with a high muzzle velocity. For a person on the receiving end, it is difficult to tell the difference between being shelled by a small patrol boat with a recoilless rifle and being shelled by the five-inch gun of a destroyer.

As the Nasties sped south early on the morning of 31 July, they passed about five miles away from the USS *Maddox,* a U.S. destroyer involved in what was code named the Desoto Patrol off the North Vietnamese coast.

Three days later, as the *Maddox* approached Hon Me island, three torpedo boats attacked the American ship about twenty-five miles off the coast, launching four torpedoes. The torpedoes missed their target, and American planes destroyed one of the boats and severely damaged another.

At about midnight the next night, three Nasties, again firing 57mm recoilless rifles, shelled two separate North Vietnamese installations.

Despite worries expressed by the skipper of the *Maddox,* he was joined by another destroyer, the USS *Turner Joy,* and they were ordered to resume patrols off the North Vietnamese coast. About eleven o'clock on the night of 4 August, the two ships reported they were under torpedo attack. Although serious doubts were later raised about whether there had actually been an attack on the American ships that night, an official naval history based on both American and North Vietnamese records provides convincing evidence that such an attack did occur.

Back in Washington, the two engagements were portrayed as unprovoked attacks by the North Vietnamese against American ships operating in international waters. Although the North Vietnamese complained to the International Control Commission, which monitored the agreement that had created separate governments in North and South Vietnam, about the shelling of the two offshore islands, top officials in Washington denied there was any connection between those operations and the destroyer patrols.

On 5 August, planes from two American carriers delivered a devastating retaliatory attack on North Vietnamese installations. And on 7 August, Congress passed the Gulf of Tonkin Resolution. The vote was unanimous in the House and eighty-eight to two in the Senate. The Resolution authorized President Johnson to "take all necessary steps, including the use of armed force, to assist any member or protocol state of the Southeast Asia Collective Defense Treaty requesting assistance in defense of its freedom." It was the equivalent of a declaration of war, and it served as the legal basis for the massive American involvement in Southeast Asia for the next eight years.

Back in Da Nang, the SEALs, who were among the tiny group of Americans that knew about the U.S.-backed OP 34A raids on the north, listened in puzzlement to the less-than-candid reports coming out of Washington.

"I thought, oh shit, this thing has gotten out of hand," Flynn recalls. "The American people needed to be told about 34A to make a competent judgment of whether this was another sinking of the *Maine*. The North Vietnamese knew. The Russians knew. The Chinese knew. The South Vietnamese knew. Who were we fooling?"

Still, the SEALs at Da Nang remained so imbued with the need for secrecy about the operations in which they were involved that they didn't talk, even among themselves, about the inconsistencies between what they knew and what was being said publicly. Some of those involved still refuse to talk about those events of nearly three decades ago.

One of the questions that remains is whether any Americans were involved in operations against the north. A number of those who were there, among them Flynn, Weyers, and Mulford, say neither they nor any of their people went north. That was not for want of asking.

Weyers, who relieved Flynn, says: "I always said we would get better results if we went along. But we never got permission. I think sometimes they would go up there, get skittish, and come back without ever having done anything. If we had been able to send someone along, it would have made a lot of difference."

Ted Grabowsky, who served at Da Nang as a lieutenant from the spring until Christmas of 1966, about two years after the Gulf of Tonkin confrontation, almost went north inadvertently.

He would frequently accompany the commandos on training missions where they would swim ashore along the South Vietnamese coast. It finally occurred to someone that, when a Nasty boat roared out of the China Beach dock with an American aboard, his sun-bleached hair shining like a beacon, the boat was probably on a training mission. So a plan was worked out where Americans would accompany the Vietnamese on an actual mission and then be transferred to another boat when they were out of sight of land.

"This was a very important op, way the hell up north. I got orders to be on the boat, very visible. As we got underway, it began to rain," Grabowsky recalls. He told the petty officer accompanying him to go below and get some sleep. The three-boat formation, heavily laden with fuel and ammunition, started out slowly but gradually picked up speed. There was no English-speaking interpreter aboard. But the skipper managed to ask, "You go?" When Grabowsky said he was, the Vietnamese grinned and replied, "Number one!"

The transfer of the two Americans was supposed to be made at a point designated Alpha. Grabowsky tried to learn from the skipper and navigator where Point Alpha was. Both seemed puzzled.

The night was calm, with smooth seas and no moon. The three blacked-out boats raced north through the night. As they burned off fuel, Grabowsky could feel the surge of additional speed.

"I realized I'm going with these guys. I got the skipper to send a message to the officer in charge [in another boat] to say I was aboard. We got a message back: 'That's wonderful. We'll have a beer when we get back.'"

As Grabowsky watched, the commandos began putting on flak jackets and helmets, breaking out the ammunition, and checking their weapons. Grabowsky was wearing a pair of dark green tennis shoes, socks, shorts, and a light jacket. He had an M-16 rifle with one clip in the weapon and another in his pocket. He descended into the cabin to tell his companion they were going to war.

"He told me, 'I'm not going.'" When the officer insisted that they didn't have much choice, he replied, "I'm not mentally prepared."

Concerned not only about danger, but also about the international incident that would be caused if two Americans were captured by the North Vietnamese, Grabowsky made one more try to influence the officer in charge. He suggested they turn around and drop the two Americans at a U.S. Coast Guard vessel patrolling along the seventeenth parallel, the line dividing the two parts of the country. Even though this would throw off his timetable, the officer agreed. The three boats turned sharply and roared back down south.

Aboard the Coast Guard vessel, the silence of the night was suddenly shattered by the eighteen-thousand–horsepower roar of the six engines of the Nasties as they circled the American boat at top speed in the darkness. Two of the boats pulled up on one side and abruptly stopped. Then the big black bow of the third boat loomed over the other side of the Coast Guard vessel, powerful floodlights snapped on, and two half-naked Americans leapt aboard.

As suddenly as they had appeared, the Nasties backed off into the darkness and sped north to make up the lost time. After establishing their identity, the two Americans got off a coded message to confirm the mission was going ahead without them.

"The guys did carry out the mission. They did just fine. For us, it would have been just a long boat ride," says Grabowsky, who later rose to the rank of captain. And what was the mission? "A whole bunch of stuff—still classified."

Despite the prohibition on direct American involvement in the raids against the north, a few enlisted men did go along, although they did not go ashore. Later in the war, SEALs themselves carried out secret operations in North Vietnam.

In those early days, the SEAL involvement in Vietnam consisted almost entirely of men from the West Coast team, working out of Da Nang. One of the few exceptions to this arrangement was the assignment of one man from Team Two, on the East Coast, as an adviser to the Vietnamese equivalent of the SEALs—the *Lien Doc Nguoi Nhia* or LDNN, "soldiers who fight under the sea"—in the southern part of the country.

Lt. Roy Boehm, who had been the first acting commander of Team Two, was sent over as an adviser in 1964. Boehm couldn't get permission to operate as he wanted to, but on "training missions" he would happen to bump into the enemy and engage in a firefight. On weekends, he would visit villages in the area east of Saigon and treat those who were ill. In the process he met a man named Minh, a common name in Vietnam, who turned out to be the commander of the local Viet Cong battalion. The two became friends.

"They'd hit us and I'd see a flag come up on their side," Boehm recalls. "I'd call the action off and get up on the parapet. He'd walk out. I'm sure they had a sniper on me. I sure had a sniper on him. He'd say, 'Meet you at the tax building.'"

Minh drove a cab in Saigon when he wasn't engaged in combat. Boehm would climb into his cab and they headed for Cholon, the Chinese section of Saigon where few Americans ventured. They managed to converse in a mixture of French, English, and Vietnamese.

"We'd talk. We'd eat. I respected him more than some of the people I was working with," Boehm says. "Hell, I hated my supply officer more than I did my VC enemy. I learned a lot about their thinking and learned to respect them, to admire them. If you have an enemy you can admire and respect more than your [South Vietnamese] counterpart, you've got problems."

Boehm, a patriot and a professional fighting man, continued to carry out his orders and even developed an ingenious sensor system that caused

the Viet Cong in the delta all sorts of trouble. But on subsequent visits to Vietnam, he became more and more disillusioned.

"They really ruined a beautiful war," he says. "I felt that we had
corrupted and contaminated South Vietnam completely. The streets were
filthy. The black market was rampant. Military men were prostitut-
ing their most solemn and binding obligations. I was completely dis-
gusted. We kept escalating and escalating. And the more we escalated,
the worse it got."

SEALs continued to serve in Da Nang and other places in I Corps,
the northernmost of the four areas into which the Americans divided
their command structure, throughout the war. They continued to in-
struct and advise the Vietnamese frogmen. They carried out their own
secret operations under the American military's Studies and Observation Group (SOG), and they worked on special assignments for the
CIA. But as the American buildup began in 1965, the SEALs shifted
their attention increasingly to the southern part of the country, from
Saigon down into the delta.

While assigned at Da Nang in the early days, the SEALs were under
strict orders not to become involved in combat. In the south, they assumed
a direct combat role at a crossroads of the war. As in Da Nang, the
first SEAL platoons to arrive were members of the West Coast team,
SEAL Team One. Except for a few individuals in advisory roles, members
of the East Coast team, Team Two, were not to enter the Vietnam War
until later.

Saigon lies about forty miles from the South China Sea. Between
the capital and the sea is a delta area, then known as the Rung Sat
Special Zone. It is a huge mangrove swamp, crisscrossed by mean-
dering streams, a wonderful sort of mysterious place much like the bayou
area of Louisiana, and a favorite hiding place of pirates. For the Americans,
control of the zone was critical because ships carrying war supplies
to Saigon had to be able to move safely up and down the river. For
the Viet Cong, it was a critical transit route between the huge Mekong
River Delta south of Saigon and the area to the north. Both sides had
a similar goal: to be able to move safely through the area while disrupting the other side's use of the zone.

In their brief existence the SEALs had planned and trained for
the kind of hit-and-run raids from the sea that their Vietnamese counterparts were conducting against North Vietnam. They knew how to

slip ashore at night, blow up a radar station, and get away again. But they knew little or nothing about skulking around in a swamp in the darkness.

When Maynard Weyers arrived in the Rung Sat Special Zone in 1966 to take over a detachment from SEAL Team One, he found a thoroughly demoralized unit, unable to adjust to working in a swamp. The unit had stopped operating.

"Once you stop, these guys are going to get in a world of shit," Weyers says. "These guys want attention, one way or the other. If they're not operating and busy, there are going to be fights, all sorts of stuff."

The executive officer of the naval command in Vietnam told Weyers, "If I could, I'd get you guys kicked out of this country." Weyers's predecessor, Lt. James Barnes, told him not to unpack. Barnes was disillusioned, but he had made a lasting contribution to the SEAL structure in Vietnam. He began what came to be known as the barn-dance cards, in which every SEAL unit wrote a brief report after each mission. The cards served as a guide to others going on missions in the same area and were even studied back in Coronado. The information they passed on ranged from reports on enemy strength and tactics to such practical advice as "remove leeches with mosquito repellant."

Barnes told Weyers he had written to Captain Bucklew, by then commander of the Pacific Fleet's Naval Operations Support Group, saying, "This is not for us." He suggested the SEALs pull out of Vietnam.

As Weyers recalls, the response from Bucklew was blunt: "No way! This is the only war in town. If the SEALs want to stick around, they damn well better be involved."

Over the next few months, the SEALs set about finding how they could be useful in this strange kind of war. Night after night, they crept out into the darkness to set up ambushes. Patrols frequently lasted forty-eight hours and sometimes as long as seventy-two hours without sleep. Often the SEALs would take up their ambush positions and stand silently in one place all night, using Dexedrine to stay awake. A length of string stretched from one man to another. If one man began to snore, a gentle tug on the line would bring him back to wakefulness. The training in dealing with sleep deprivation during Hell Week began to make a lot of sense.

Many times, especially in the early days when their intelligence information was inaccurate, out of date, or nonexistent, the SEALs failed to make contact with the Viet Cong. But there were other creatures in the swamps to keep them company. The water level rose and fell with the tides in the South China Sea. When the tide was out, crabs could be heard scuttling through the mud. Sometimes a large snake slithered through an ambush position. Often, when the water was slack, an alligator, aware of some strange presence in its bailiwick, nosed up for a closer look. "Those damn things would flop their tails. Man, they'd flip that tail and just scare the shit out of you," Weyers recalls.

Very early in their time in the Rung Sat, the SEALs learned that they could operate in very small units, sometimes as few as two men, seldom more than five or six, if they planned ahead for support from helicopter gunships or artillery. That way, if they stumbled on a VC company or battalion, they could call in overwhelming firepower to destroy the enemy or at least to provide protection while they were extracted. In this way, they were able to take the night back from the Viet Cong, forcing them to move more cautiously, making them less effective.

In mid-August 1966, Weyers and a small group of SEALs were moving through the Rung Sat in a boat when American helicopter pilots reported spotting several Viet Cong craft nearby. It was daytime, a time when SEALs feel almost as uncomfortable as Dracula. But Weyers decided to send a squad to investigate the sighting.

Radarman Second Class Billy W. Machen was the point man. The scene is etched in Weyers's memory:

"Machen said to me, 'Jeez, I'm not real crazy about this daytime stuff.' I said, 'Well, the helicopters are going to be covering the whole time.' He said, 'Okay,' and they went in, patrolling toward where the boats were. Before they got there, the helicopters—there were two of them—said they were running out of fuel. So they left. And about that time the shit hit the fan. These guys got ambushed. Machen got killed. They were in dire straits in there, and it became an issue whether we can bring the body back. The helicopters finally came back and gave enough cover to get the hell out of there."

One of the men carried Machen's body out, fulfilling the promise SEALs make to each other that a dead or wounded SEAL will never be left behind.

Ten months earlier, on 28 October 1965, Comdr. Robert J. Fay had been killed during a mortar attack in Da Nang. But Machen was the first SEAL to die in a firefight, and his death had a profound impact on his comrades.

"When Machen got killed, I wondered, should we be doing this?" Weyers says. "Once somebody gets killed, then it becomes real. Before, it was a game. I had real questions in my own mind, should we be doing this? It was a bummer, anyway. I shouldn't have made the decision to send him in."

In the weeks following Machen's death, a number of SEALs decided this wasn't for them.

"Once we lost the first guy, guys bailed out of there. It is all well and good to play the role until the shooting starts. There were a lot of plank owners [original members of SEAL Team One] that bailed out. I've always had a bad feeling about that," Weyers says.

The reaction of those who left the team exposed one of the unavoidable shortcomings of the training the men had received. Combat is infinitely more dangerous and more frightening than anything else a person has ever experienced.

"There's no way you can tell how a guy will be under fire unless you shoot at him," Weyers says. "That's a real problem. A guy can parachute and free-fall and dive and mess with demolitions. But there is only one way to tell how a guy is under fire, and that is to shoot at him. And you can't do that."

For the SEALs, the death of Billy Machen on 16 August 1966 marked the end of the pleasant little war.

UDT members approach the beach at Saipan on 15 June 1944. (*National Archives.*)

Trainees place explosives on a rocky shore on Maui in the Hawaiian Islands. (*National Archives.*)

UDT member being inserted into the water by an early post–World War II experimental helicopter. (*National Archives.*)

UDTs in bulky dry suits ride a British Chariot manned torpedo. (*National Archives.*)

William Bain and Joseph DiMartino astride an Italian manned torpedo. (*Courtesy of Roy Boehm.*)

The Aqua Ho, powered by gas from a scuba bottle. (*Courtesy of Roy Boehm.*)

Early underwater propulsion devices. *From left:* two models of the Mark VI, the Sea Bat, the TRASS, two models of the Sea Horse, and the Mark I SPU. (*U.S. Navy photo.*)

Cockpit of the Sea Bat. (*U.S. Navy photo.*)

An early model dry suit. (*Courtesy of Roy Boehm.*)

Another type of American dry suit and an Italian suit. (*Courtesy of Roy Boehm.*)

Members of SEAL Team Two at Little Creek, Virginia, as they prepared to jump into Cuba during the missile crisis in 1962. (*Courtesy of Roy Boehm.*)

Vietnamese frogmen after an operation near the Cambodian border in 1968. (*Courtesy of Roy Boehm.*)

RD2 B. W. Machen, the first member of SEAL Team One to be killed in a firefight in Vietnam, *third from left, front row.* (*Courtesy of Maynard Weyers.*)

RD2 Machen, *left,* and fellow platoon members with captured Viet Cong equipment. (*Courtesy of Maynard Weyers.*)

SEALs going ashore in an area heavily infested by Viet Cong on the Bassac River in September 1967. (*U.S. Navy photo by PH1 D. S. Dodd.*)

SEALs leap ashore from an assault river patrol boat just before the enemy's Tet offensive. (*U.S. Navy photo by JO1 Tom Walton.*)

Photo from inside the plane of PH3 James Earl Fox being lifted during a test of the Sky Hawk recovery system. (*U.S. Navy photo.*)

PH3 Fox just before being pulled into the cabin of the plane. Moments later, the line snapped, and he fell to his death. (*U.S. Navy photo.*)

Two men being lifted by the Sky Hook system at Coronado after tests were resumed in October 1965. (*Courtesy of Maynard Weyers.*)

Two men being lifted from the ground during testing of the Sky Hook. (*Courtesy of Maynard Weyers.*)

Frogmen prepare to return and dock on the deck of the USS *Tunny*. (*Courtesy of Maynard Weyers.*)

The Dry Deck Shelter, shown attached to a submarine, serves as a hangar for an SDV. (*U.S. Navy photo.*)

Members of UDT Twelve placing a length of Mark VIII hose in position near Subic Bay Naval Station in the early 1960s. (*Courtesy of Maynard Weyers.*)

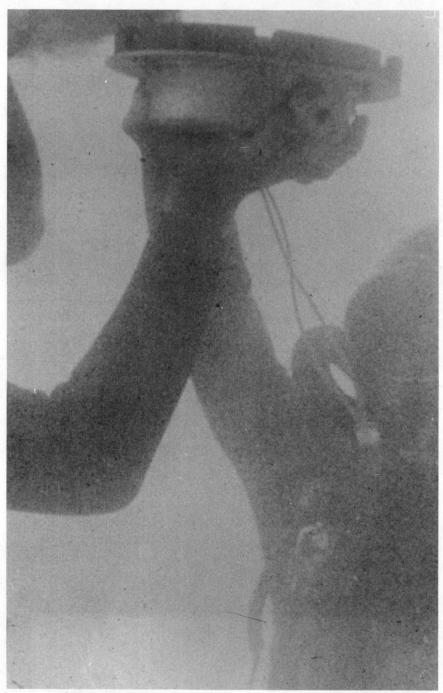

Frogmen attaching a small limpet mine to a ship's hull. (*U.S. Navy Photo.*)

In the "cast," a trainee rolls out of a rubber boat attached to the side of a speeding motorboat. (*U.S. Navy photo by PH1 Patrick C. Wilkerson.*)

During the recovery, the swimmer reaches for a flexible loop held over the side of the rapidly approaching boat. (*Courtesy of Roy Boehm.*)

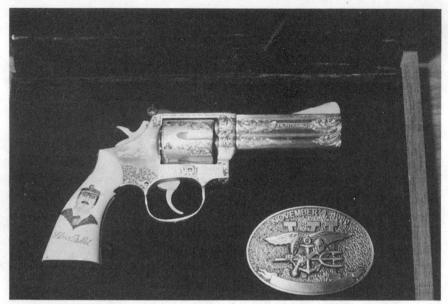

Pistol presented to Comdr. Richard Marcinko and SEAL Team Six belt buckle. False travel vouchers were used to pay for these items. (*Naval Investigative Service photo.*)

The four-man Mark VII became the navy's first operational Swimmer (later, SEAL) Delivery Vehicle in the 1960s. (*U.S. Navy photo.*)

CHAPTER EIGHT
THE MEN WITH GREEN FACES

When SEAL Team Two was preparing to send its first units to Vietnam in 1967, an uncle who had served in the rangers called James D. ("Patches") Watson aside and gave him a piece of advice: "When you go into combat, the first time you have to kill somebody, don't hesitate. Shoot!"

That moment came for Watson, a senior petty officer and plank owner of Team Two, on 13 May 1967.

Too often in those early days, the SEALs went out on ambushes, hoping enemy troops would come down a trail or float past in a sampan. Too often they were sent out with intelligence that was out of date or just plain wrong.

But on this assignment, the intelligence was specific, and it was good: A leader in the campaign to block ship traffic between the sea and Saigon would arrive at a hut hidden in the forest that night. Watson and a small group of SEALs were assigned to capture him.

Silently, Watson and two other SEALs crept through the mud and took up positions near the enemy hooch. Finally the man they were after approached, surrounded by his bodyguards. The SEALs' plan was to wait until the men had entered the hut and put down their weapons. Then they would burst through the walls of the grass shack and confront the men before they could react.

But before going inside, the target of the operation, exhibiting the caution that keeps some guerrilla fighters alive against all odds, took a look around the compound. Holding his AK-47 assault rifle at the ready, the man walked directly toward Watson—and then saw him.

Watson rose up from the mud. Clearly visible in his hands was a featherweight twelve-gauge shotgun with an eight-round magazine and a pistol grip. Gunsmiths at the Frankfort Arsenal had made the gun to his order. It was not automatic and required the user to pump each shell into the chamber. But it was so simple and reliable that a man could simply rinse it in a stream and be confident it would fire when he pulled the trigger. For close-in fighting, Watson much preferred it to a more complicated automatic weapon.

Perhaps he assumed the Vietnamese would be awed by his little shotgun; perhaps he still hoped to take the man prisoner; or perhaps it was reluctance to take a human life. Whatever the motive, despite the warning from the old marine and his own training, Watson hesitated. The Vietnamese, who had been at war a lot longer than the young Americans, didn't. A single shot from his AK-47 automatic rifle shattered the stillness. But the bullet missed. Watson fired, hitting the man in the chest and killing him.

As the bodyguards rushed out, Watson emptied his shotgun and then picked up the other man's AK-47 and chased the enemy soldiers off into the darkness.

When the shooting stopped, Watson turned to see one of his teamates rolling in the mud with laughter at this scene straight out of a Hollywood shoot-'em-up.

"I came over and pushed the AK-47 at him," Watson recalls. "I didn't think it was funny."

When the SEALs had time to think back on the incident, they realized why the American, despite his hesitation, lived and the other man died. The Soviet-designed AK-47 rifle is deservedly one of the most popular automatic assault rifles in the world. But it has a serious design flaw, and that flaw cost the Vietnamese his life.

A little lever on the side of the rifle is used to change it from single shot to semiautomatic or automatic fire. But instead of going in that order, through semiautomatic to automatic, the AK-47 goes to automatic and then to semiautomatic. In automatic, if the rifleman pulls the trigger, the weapon continues to fire. But in semiautomatic, he must pull the trigger for each shot.

In his excitement, the Vietnamese pushed the lever all the way down, through automatic, to semiautomatic. Before he realized he had to pull the trigger a second time after his first shot missed, he was dead. If he had gone into full automatic, he would have cut Watson in half.

Documents found at the scene revealed that the man killed that night had been a formidable foe, one whose skills the SEALs could well respect. He had twice been named soldier of the year and had been awarded the North Vietnamese equivalent of the Medal of Honor. He had been responsible, the year before, for the sinking of the *Jamaica Bay*, the world's largest dredge.

Another SEAL who hesitated when he first came face-to-face with an enemy soldier was Bill Bruhmuller, like Watson a senior petty officer and a plank owner of Team Two. Shortly after he arrived in Vietnam, Bruhmuller was crouching on the bank of a river in an ambush position. Although he didn't realize it at the time, his unit had stumbled onto a major Viet Cong crossing point. Before crossing, the VC sent their own version of the SEALs—scout swimmers—along the edges of the river to make sure the coast was clear.

"I can still very clearly see this one scout swimmer right dead in front of me. He could see me, see my outline. He was as surprised as I was. I had my M-16 on my lap," Bruhmuller says. From the muzzle of his rifle to the man's head was less than two feet.

"I hesitated," Bruhmuller says. "I wasn't sure what to do. Do I jump in and grab this guy? It all happened in a split second. I think I hesitated that split second, then I fired and killed him.

"I think when it happens the first time, there is a tendency to hesitate. We like not to think we will hesitate, but probably it is the reluctance to shoot somebody. Once you've done that, you don't hesitate anymore. Reality sets in. You realize these guys are trying to kill you. He who acts first is the survivor," Bruhmuller says.

Often, in that first face-to-face encounter with the enemy, there was no time for hesitation.

Rodney Pastore, who later became command master chief of Naval Special Warfare Group Two, had that experience on a "morning-glory" operation. Although the SEALs learned to feel most comfortable in the dark, one tactic they also favored involved arriving at the target at first light—hence the term *morning glory*. In this operation, Pastore was in a unit that descended on a suspected Viet Cong base camp in three helicopters. As the helicopters pounded the three hooches with rockets, the SEALs hit the ground running.

Pastore was carrying an M-60 machine gun. Although most infantry units consider the M-60 a crew-served weapon, requiring two or three men to carry the gun, tripod and ammunition, the SEALs made it a one-man weapon. One man could thus pack tremendous firepower; but even stripped down, the version used in Vietnam weighed about twenty pounds and was a cumbersome armful in a firefight.

As Pastore came around one corner of a building, he confronted a Vietnamese carrying an AK-47 rifle. With his relatively lightweight rifle, the VC probably had the advantage as both men fired. But Pastore's muzzle was pointed at the other man. The Vietnamese's was pointed slightly off to the side. Before he could bring it around, he was dead.

"He didn't have a chance. He didn't get it around fast enough," Pastore says. "That's how it works. It's not like the old cowboy days with the quick draw. The person who hesitates just doesn't get to tell the story."

As Pastore continued on around the building another VC began to shoot at him, but a SEAL quickly cut him down. Pastore stuck his head in the hooch and saw one man lying dead. Beside him lay two women. Just then a phosphorous shell hit the building, and the white-hot molten metal began to drip through the grass roof. Pastore ran to the helicopter.

As it lifted off, he thought back to the two girls he had seen in the building, by then enveloped in flames. "I remember looking down and noticing those girls didn't have any holes in them," he says. "I think those girls probably just fainted."

Unlike most modern military men—aviators who drop bombs on an unseen enemy, or sailors in an Aegis cruiser who launch missiles against a dot on the radar screen—SEALs are often so close that they can see, touch, and smell those they kill. For most of them, that first death of an enemy is easy to remember. But subsequent deaths tend to blur together.

"I personally think it is very easy to kill someone," says Ronald K. ("Ron") Bell, now a retired captain. "What's scary is that it's too easy. I didn't have any problem. And that's what scares me. You just pull this button and somebody dies in front of you."

Most SEALs quickly became inured to the sights and sounds of the death they inflicted. During training, they had come to terms with their consciences and looked upon what they did, under lawful orders, as morally justified.

The cruelty they often saw exhibited by the other side also seemed to justify their own actions. Lt. Red Cannon, who had been involved in the reconnaissance of the Cuban patrol boats in 1962, served in Vietnam in 1968 and 1969. On one patrol with a combined SEAL-Vietnamese force, they came upon a village that had just been looted by a Viet Cong unit. The people told them which way the VC had gone. Cannon and his men followed them for a while and then turned off to carry out their primary mission.

On the way back, they found the village in an uproar. Cannon tells what they found:

> The VC had come back and punished [the villagers] for telling where they went. They killed the two nuns at the girls' school, decapitated them, and hung them upside down with their heads in their crotches. They did the same with the little girls. There was a whole row of them, must have been ten or twelve, just lying on the floor, with their heads between their legs.
>
> That was what affected me most. They were vicious people. I had the feeling the war was just, because of the cruelty the VC inflicted on the people.

After a while, most of the SEALs became somewhat callous and a few may even have taken pleasure in killing. One officer recalls how, when they felt the need for a party, "we'd go out and kill a tax collector." An article in the *New York Times* reported a sign on the wall at a SEAL base in the Mekong Delta: "People who kill for money are professionals. People who kill for fun are sadists. People who kill for money and fun are SEALs."

Because they struck unexpectedly, and usually in the dark, the SEALs soon began to seem to many Viet Cong more numerous and perhaps even more ferocious than they really were. With their faces painted to blend into the darkness and the jungle, they became known as "the men with green faces."

In Vietnam, there was always the problem of telling the enemy from the friendly, the farmer violating curfew to get to or from his fields from the VC moving in for an attack. The SEALs, operating far from their bases in very small numbers, tended to err on the side of their own safety. Al Winter describes one such situation:

"You're sitting on a river bank in an ambush situation. You have some bad guys coming down. It's dark. You hail 'em over, and all they have to do is pitch a grenade in the dark and kill a couple of your guys.

We didn't take that chance. If they were curfew violators, and they were in a place where they shouldn't be, we would take them under fire and clean up afterwards. That bothered me. Sometimes you got the bad guys, sometimes you didn't."

While SEALs learned to accept the deaths of others casually, they have no tolerance for death in their own ranks. Most military commanders, preparing for an operation, calculate what it will cost in terms of dead and wounded. Plans are made to replace those knocked out of action. The SEALs are different. They tend to think that if a SEAL is killed or wounded, somebody did something wrong.

Larry W. Bailey, a retired captain who served in Vietnam and later commanded the training center at Coronado, says, "My experience is: every time somebody dies, somebody has screwed up. We don't charge enemy trenches. People get killed because that's their job. Ten percent of your troops going over the berm, across the barbed wire, are going to get killed, actuarially, demonstrably. We don't play that kind of game. Take this with a grain of salt, but every SEAL that got killed, that I know of, got killed unnecessarily, because somebody screwed up. That doesn't say anything bad about SEALs. It says we are so damn good we are the only ones who can get ourselves killed, in a perverse sort of way."

In fact, SEAL Team Two went through the entire Vietnam conflict with the loss of only nine men killed. Team One, which operated there longer, lost thirty-four men. But a number of those were lost in accidents or because of errors rather than enemy action.

One such tragic incident occurred on 20 August 1968. Warrant Officer Eugene S. Tinnin—one of the men involved in the reconnaissance of Havana harbor in 1962—headed a nine-man squad assigned to check out a suspected VC base area in Vinh Long province. A patrol boat dropped the men near their target, and they carefully worked their way in until they were in sight of a pagoda which they suspected was used by the VC. Tinnin left four of his men in an ambush position near the pagoda. Then he and the other four men set out to patrol in a circular pattern around the area. The two teams kept in touch with brief, whispered messages over their radios.

Then the men in the ambush heard sounds of movement in the darkness in front of them. The sounds came closer. When it seemed they were about to come under attack, they fired into the darkness. A rapid burst of fire came back. And then there were anguished cries in English.

Tinnin, lost in the darkness, had led his patrol back into the kill zone of his own ambush. He was killed in the brief exchange of fire, and five other men, four SEALs and one Vietnamese accompanying them, were wounded.

Bailey was personally involved in a similar incident. He was commanding a squad sent to ambush the Viet Cong at a river crossing. Bailey led his men into the ambush position, so close that they could hear the VC revving up the engines on their boats. And then he found that two of his men, an American and a Vietnamese, had gotten lost in the dark.

"I went back, to my great peril, I thought. We were in a hostile area and we could literally hear the boats knocking against each other. There I am, not knowing if the VC are going to get me or I'm going to run into my two lost troops and they're going to blow me away. I found them and brought them back to where I had mustered everybody else and told them exactly where to go," Bailey says.

Either the American did not hear Bailey's whispered instructions or he misunderstood. The two men remained where they were as Bailey crept back to his other men.

About two hours later one of the SEALs, assigned to face toward the rear of the ambush position, saw two silhouettes, outlined by the light of the setting moon. Bailey turned to face the rear: "I saw two heads looking around. They started moving from my center to my right. I really thought they were my guys, who, for some reason, had gotten up and started wandering around. That was really violating patrol discipline."

Bailey pointed at the leading figure. The man next to him said, "It's Hien," the Vietnamese member of the team. The two figures dropped to the ground. Bailey figured it was curious the man would drop when he heard his own name.

"I had made no move," Bailey says. "My weapon was on the ground between me and this other guy. They started moving again. I pointed to them, and he said, 'It's Hien.' This guy never learned to whisper. They dropped to the ground again.

"I got my weapon in under my belly. They started moving to the right flank of my ambush. They were moving right up on a guy who didn't know what was happening."

Bailey knew Hien always wore a baseball cap and carried a carbine. He looked for both telltale signs and couldn't recognize them. And he couldn't believe that the two men would have left their position and begun wandering around in the dark.

"I remember making a conscious decision: 'Hien, if it's you, you're about to die.' He was walking up on my ambush position. I just blew him away."

It was Hien. As soon as Bailey fired, the American, who was just behind the Vietnamese, began to holler. He was not hit, but he later found that one bullet had gone through his hat and another left a hole in his pants leg just below the tip of his penis.

Bailey hurried to the man he had shot. "If he died a painful death, he died a quick one," he says. "I gave him mouth-to-mouth. But when I blew in his mouth you could hear the bubbles coming out his belly."

A different kind of accident claimed the lives of four members of Team One on 18 May 1968. Two of the men took it upon themselves to take apart a captured Chinese 82mm mortar. Another SEAL was just approaching to tell them not to fool with the shell when it exploded. Three men died that day and one more died of his wounds a week later.

Five more members of Team One were killed on 23 June 1970. The men had just returned to Seafloat, a SEAL base on a cluster of barges anchored in a river near the tip of the Ca Mau Peninsula, the southernmost point of land in Vietnam. Eager for leave in the nearby city of Can Tho, they piled onto an army helicopter that had just returned from a combat mission.

As the chopper was at about twenty-five hundred feet, approaching Can Tho, its rotors came off, and it plunged to earth so violently that blades of grass were later found embedded in the metal of the weapon carried by one of the SEALs. All aboard the craft, including the five SEALs, were killed.

In the Rung Sat Special Zone and the delta, the SEALs formed a special bond with the crews of the boats that took them on their missions and got them back out again. One SEAL recalls with real affection, "They were very special guys, ordinary old-fashioned sailors, Mark one, mod zero, out of the fleet. They are hard to come by these days. Tattooed, dirty fingernails, foul language. They could make these boats work and get them into the places we went."

Actually, the SEALs almost always felt safer when they slipped into the water or stepped off into the mud. While cruising on the rivers, they worried constantly about a rocket attack from the shore.

They used a variety of boats. One was the thirty-foot PBR (patrol boat, river) that could make twenty-eight knots with its jet propulsion system. But dirty water, of which there was plenty, could clog the motor and bring the boat to a stop. Both the PBR and the larger Swift boat, or Fast Patrol Craft (PCF), carried .50-cal. machine guns and other weapons.

The light SEAL-support craft (LSSC), a twenty-six-foot vessel, was used frequently by the SEALs because it was just the right size for a squad. It, too, suffered from dirty water clogging its pumps. Two other high-speed boats used for squad-sized operations were the Boston Whaler and the SEAL team assault boat (STAB).

For bigger operations, the SEALs relied on the thirty-six-foot medium SEAL support craft (MSSC), which could carry a fully-equipped platoon, or the even bigger Mike boat—landing craft, mechanized (LCM)—which was modified for use in a variety of roles.

The tie between the SEALs and the boat operators was matched by their close link to the young pilots of the UH-1 Sea Wolf helicopter gunships and the fixed-wing OV-10 Black Ponies. While the SEALs could also call for help from other American or South Vietnamese air units, they always felt more confident if they knew their own friends were overhead. On a number of occasions, Sea Wolf pilots landed, lightened their helos by removing guns and ammunition, and then returned, unarmed, through enemy fire to pull out trapped SEALs.

The SEAL involvement in Vietnam went through a series of fairly distinct phases. First was the involvement in Da Nang, where they provided backup for Vietnamese carrying out harassing raids against the north. Then there was the assignment to keep open the shipping lanes and disrupt Viet Cong movement in the Rung Sat Special Zone. Then came intensive operations in the delta and in other parts of Vietnam. In each phase, the SEALs went through a period of learning, finding out how their special skills could be adapted to the particular situation.

One of their most intriguing experiments was with the use of scout dogs. Bill Bruhmuller of Team Two took the lead in this effort. They rigged a special harness so a man could parachute with the dog strapped to his chest and then let the dog down on a long leash before they reached the ground. Most of the dogs adapted readily to this new experience. But one, after the first jump, wouldn't even go close to an airplane.

In Vietnam, SEALs took their dogs on nighttime patrols. As they lay quietly in ambush positions, they would keep an eye on the dog. As the dog sniffed the air, his head would swing back and forth like a spectator at a tennis match. If he sensed someone approaching, his ears would go up. Then he would freeze with his nose pointing straight ahead, an indication that someone was close. The dog was able to sense anyone approaching the ambush well before the men could.

The one shortcoming of the dogs was that their legs were not long enough to propel them through the deep mud in which the SEALs frequently found themselves, so their usefulness proved to be limited.

Often, as the SEALs searched for their proper role, there was conflict with superiors, including those in the navy, who didn't understand what the SEALs were doing and didn't approve of it, either. Thomas L. ("Tom") Hawkins, who retired as a commander, tells with a touch of lingering bitterness of the army general, a division commander, who told him, "I know you SEALs. You SEALs are assassins. I don't want you here."

Ted Grabowsky later reflected on the way the SEALs were perceived by others in the navy: "We had no status, no standing in the regular navy. Some part of the navy saw us as some sort of quasi-criminal element, not a respected profession, that should only be used in desperate circumstances. And when you were through using it, you would stop forever. Like it was some sort of immoral activity."

Vice Adm. Robert S. Salzer worked with the SEALs for many years, first as commander of riverine warfare in 1967 and 1968 and again as commander of U.S. Naval Forces, Vietnam, in 1971 and 1972. He had mixed feelings about them:

They were in small detachments, and we kept them on a very firm leash. SEALs are a two-edged sword. It was something like having attack-trained German shepherds: you had to keep them on a very tight leash. They did good work, but what they really wanted to do was to get out and mix it up and have a shooting match. They had some real feats of derring-do. When General [Creighton W.] Abrams [American commander in Vietnam] was having a down period, I would always try and find some particularly hair-curling things the SEALs had done, because he loved tales of personal bravery, and those guys had that.

What they really were supposed to do is to lie very low. In that environment what I wanted them to do was to set traps, but not to give away their presence, to try to detect what the enemy was doing. They hate to sit still and do nothing. What they really want to do is find out what the enemy is doing by kidnapping some guy and getting it out of him.

One case in particular I remember. They had heard about a Viet Cong meeting, had gotten some intelligence on it down in the deep delta in the Ca Mau area, and they wanted to try and capture the politicos in there. You have to let the animal have his head once in a while. So they planned the thing. They came in by boat, quietly, and for once the intelligence was right. The guy who led them in pointed out the hut where the meeting was. I guess there were four SEALs, and they had an Australian SEAL type with them.

There were about twelve Viet Cong in this place. The guy kicked in the door, and all hell broke loose. Everybody drew their knives, and the rest of the Americans just came piling in. Afterwards, there were eight dead Viet Cong and one captured, another couple guys had run away, and one SEAL had sprained his wrist by swinging at a guy with his brass knuckles on. That tickled old Abe. It made his whole morning after an exasperating session.

One thing that frustrated Salzer was what he saw as the unwillingness of the SEALs to protect shipping in the route from the sea to Saigon by checking the ships for mines. "Searching muddy waters around the bottoms of ships for mines didn't really send them at all," he recalled.

Despite his apparent ambivalence about the role of the SEALs, it was during the period when he was commander of the riverine force that the SEALs began to come into their own. Many SEALs mark 1968 as the turning point, and they relate it to two events: the enemy's Tet offensive, at the time of the lunar new year, in January–February; and the arrival of Vice Adm. Elmo R. Zumwalt, Jr., as commander of naval forces in Vietnam, in September of that year.

For the Tet offensive, the Viet Cong put into action all of their forces in South Vietnam. For years, many VC had remained hidden, carefully avoiding combat against the heavily armed American forces. But during Tet, armed Viet Cong suddenly appeared in Saigon and other major cities. Their confident belief was that the people would rise up and join them in defeating the Americans and the South Vietnamese government.

Although intelligence reports had been hinting at some sort of enemy offensive, the likeliest target seemed to be in the far north, near the border between North and South Vietnam. The scale and ferocity of the offensive in the far south, in the delta, caught everyone—including the SEALs, many of whom were stationed there—by surprise.

Lt. John S. Wilbur, Jr., a member of Team Two, was stationed in a hamlet near Can Tho, in the lower delta. In the days before the offensive, he had spent most of his time working with senior intelligence officials planning a double operation.

"Everyone, including the entire regional CIA cadre, the highest ranking military command units . . . had absolutely no indication of whatever sort and from whatever source, (1) that there was going to be a massive military eruption of combat, or (2) that the Viet Cong infrastructure had the means or capability in place to even initiate that kind of multiple phase attack which, in actuality, immobilized the entire South Vietnamese government structure in the delta," Wilbur says.

At the time of Tet, Charlie Watson was a SEAL warrant officer stationed at My Tho. Watson had been a member of the UDT when the SEALs were being formed and was one of those prepared to parachute into Cuba at the time of the missile crisis. Because of the holiday, an uneasy cease-fire was in effect, and many South Vietnamese troops left their units to visit their families. Watson was ordered to take out a squad of six men and set up an observation ambush near the South China Sea. They were ordered, "Watch but don't kill."

During the night they heard laughter, and one of his men urged him, "Let's wax those guys." But Watson told him they couldn't do that. The SEALs saw no one moving during the night and, except for the laughter, made no contact. But they noticed that it was, as Watson says, "a very busy night . . . lot of bombing." When morning came, Watson got on the radio to call in a patrol boat to pick them up. But no one answered.

"I saw a PBR [patrol boat, river] racing along the opposite shore. I stood in the water and lit a flare, hoping he'd see me. Then I got to thinking, 'He didn't see me, but who the hell else did?' Then another PBR came right to us and told us My Tho was under attack. He says, 'the whole world has gone crazy.'"

When they reached the city, there was so much firing going on that they were told not to come ashore. Even years later, the words come tumbling out as Watson recalls the tension of those few days:

"We decided the hell with it. We grabbed a jeep and went roaring through town. Anyone stuck their head out, they got shot at. It was just like the rat patrol. We had to get back to the hotel. That's where we stayed, in the hotel. Ain't a bad way to fight a war, by the way. For five days we were not prisoners, but we were surrounded. My Tho was in bad shape."

From a hospital next door, a number of foreign nationals, among them Filipino nurses and Dutch doctors, crowded into the hotel. It fell to the SEALs to provide protection for them.

"I said, 'Goddamn, how are we going to protect all these people? There are only twelve of us.' We set up a pretty good fire, aimed at certain points, and hoped no one came. We saw those bastards climbing around the hospital. We would take potshots at them, kill them," Watson says.

The SEALs and the civilians they were trying to protect were on the fringes of a major battle for control of the city. From the hotel, they could see green rockets signalling a VC charge. Then they could see and hear the South Vietnamese marines and rangers meet the charge with point-blank artillery fire. "It was a terrible thing," Watson says. The sickening smell of tear gas hung over the whole city.

"On the fourth or fifth day, near the end, it was just getting dark, they were in the next street, and I was scared to death," Watson says. "And then here comes a jeep with the CIA guys. They wanted protection. I thought, Goddamn, we're gone. When them bastards come looking for help, it's a sad goddamn day."

But the South Vietnamese, their defenses bolstered by about thirty armored personnel carriers which had just happened to stop in the city, beat back the attack, and the shooting gradually tapered off.

By the time Zumwalt arrived to take over command of naval forces in Vietnam seven months after Tet, it was obvious to American commanders that the Tet offensive had been a terrible military disaster for the enemy. They had exposed their previously hidden forces, and they had been destroyed. The expected uprising by the South Vietnamese population had failed to materialize. But the surprise offensive had come as a devastating political shock back in the United States. President Johnson announced he would not seek reelection, and Richard Nixon, who said he had a plan to end the war, was nominated by the Republican party.

Zumwalt, an officer known for his openness to unorthodox ideas and willingness to try new approaches to old problems, quickly agreed to a proposal from Salzer, then commander of the riverine force: Put more effort into disrupting the use by the enemy of the delta's vast network of rivers, especially the smaller tributaries.

For years, the argument had waxed over whether most enemy supplies came in across the Cambodian border or whether they came down the coast on ships. As early as January 1964, Bucklew had been sent by his navy superiors on a survey trip to Vietnam to try to answer that question. His conclusion: While some supplies were coming down the coast, most were arriving from the other side, carried down by land from North Vietnam and then across the Cambodian border. The army liked to believe just the opposite, and Bucklew sent his report directly back to Pearl Harbor to prevent it being adulterated by more senior army officers.

Despite his clear conclusion, there were strong forces in both the army and the navy that favored a major effort to disrupt the infiltration of men and supplies by sea. Many senior officers in the navy remained far more comfortable with a blue-water strategy and continued to resist greater involvement in the messy riverine warfare, involving dinky little patrol boats, muddy water—and SEALs. Perhaps the navy had done about all it could by stopping infiltration by sea and along the major rivers. Still, as Tet demonstrated, the enemy continued to receive a substantial flow of supplies.

By the time Zumwalt arrived, there was growing evidence that these supplies were not only coming overland, down the so-called Ho Chi Minh Trail through North Vietnam, Laos, and Cambodia, but also by sea through Cambodian ports on the Gulf of Thailand. While there was a good deal of debate over the volume of supplies coming in by sea, it was obvious that moving supplies from the Cambodian ports and then down the river network, especially along the many small tributary streams, into the delta made for a much shorter supply route than the overland one from the north.

Zumwalt's new plan, called SEA LORDS, for South-East Asia Lake, Ocean, River and Delta Strategy, called for keeping the enemy off guard. "You can get away with almost anything once or even twice, but you must change strategies frequently in order to keep the enemy from exploiting you," Zumwalt told his staff.

Zumwalt was a great believer in the SEALs and wanted more of them. Kaine, by then a captain and commander of the Special Warfare Group, Pacific, which included UDTs, SEALs, Beach Jumpers, and training commands, got frequent calls from Zumwalt: "I need fifteen more, twenty more, one hundred more SEALs."

Anxious to increase the rate of training, Zumwalt called Kauffman, who had become an admiral and commander of U.S. naval forces in the Philippines, and asked for his advice. His recommendations didn't make sense to Kaine.

"Of course Kauffman hadn't anything to do with SEALs," Kaine says. "He didn't know a SEAL from a bowwow." Zumwalt got the two men together, and they quickly agreed that the way to speed up training was to restrict it to what the men needed to know to operate in Vietnam.

The SEALs were perfectly suited to Zumwalt's innovative, fast-moving strategy. But they faced one serious problem: the lack of accurate, timely intelligence. In the early part of their involvement in the war, they had been forced to rely on intelligence gathered by others. Often it was almost embarrassingly bad. The SEALs adopted a two-prong strategy of their own: They would gather their own intelligence and then act on it, sometimes almost immediately.

Platoon commanders were called to Saigon and handed bundles of piasters. The money was to be strictly accounted for, but the officers were told to use it to buy information on their own.

Down at the tip of the Ca Mau Peninsula, members of Team Two worked closely with a Chinese Catholic priest named Father Wa, who provided them with top-notch intelligence. Time after time, the SEALs amazed their superiors by coming back with high-ranking Viet Cong captives. Sometimes their intelligence was so good that they would wait at the side of a canal, knowing that a sampan carrying VC leaders would come along at a certain time. "The people we were looking for came down the canal at the time they were supposed to. They were this close. Just reach out. Just grab 'em. It was that easy a few times," Bud Thrift recalls.

Thrift commanded one unit in that area at a time when antiwar protests were mounting back home. He found himself with almost complete freedom to run his own little war. "I told my guys, 'Nobody gives a shit what we do down here as long as we do something. What we've got to do is win our little part of the war and don't give a shit about what the congressmen are doing back in the States and just get back out of here alive. We're just going to win our part and get out of here.'"

On at least one occasion, however, Thrift found that someone was paying attention to what they were doing.

"We went on an op, and the guy we were after didn't show up," he says. "I thought I'd do the smart thing. The guy's wife and kid were there. I took them back and left a note. It said, 'The men with the green faces have your wife. Turn yourself in.' The guy's brother was a major in the Vietnamese army, and we let the wife stay with him. But the guy we wanted had a girlfriend and had been trying to get rid of his old lady anyway. There was a lot of message traffic about taking hostages for trade. I didn't come out smelling too good."

Often when the SEALs began to penetrate the Viet Cong infrastructure, they found ties to the enemy cause very fragile indeed. William Cowan, a marine officer who often worked with SEALs in the Rung Sat Special Zone, says, "It was not unusual to have prisoners end up working for you. The first day, you capture a guy. The second day he is carrying the radio. The third day he is walking point without a weapon. After that he becomes our point man. That's how quickly those guys would turn. They didn't have in-depth loyalty. A lot of guys were just relieved they were not killed or eaten.

"Once they began working for the other side, the former enemy soldiers often provided remarkably accurate intelligence," Cowan says.

"One time we had a good hit on a base camp. The way we determined who we had gotten and who we hadn't gotten was by the serial numbers on their weapons. That's how we knew who wasn't there. We had very, very good intel."

Once, Cowan says, his unit captured a North Vietnamese warrant officer who agreed to guide them to his base camp. Even though it was his first flight in a helicopter, the man was able to direct the Americans right to the camp.

"It was amazing he was able to go up in the air for the first time and lead us. He walked us right up these rivers and said, 'that's where the base camp is.' When we rolled in the gunships, he went crazy. He was jumping up and down. I thought he was going to fall out of the helicopter, he was so excited."

One of the most amazing intelligence coups of the war illustrates how many of the Vietnamese were simply trying to get themselves and their families through the war safely.

Bill Bruhmuller was serving with Team Two in early 1971 when a Vietnamese he had developed as an intelligence source asked him out for a beer. How would he like it, the man asked, if he could put Bruhmuller in touch with a high-level enemy official who was willing to sell information for money? Bruhmuller asked a few questions and then demanded proof the man really had worthwhile information. A few days later, Bruhmuller's contact showed up with some documents.

"I purposely contacted the Defense Intelligence Agency rather than the army because I knew what would happen. They'd compromise him or not take it as seriously as I thought. The initial documents checked out, and they told me, 'You've got somebody very important,'" Bruhmuller says.

A meeting was set up. But there was one condition: Bruhmuller must come alone and unarmed.

The proposed meeting site was way out in bad country. Bruhmuller arranged for another Vietnamese contact to dress as a policeman and take him to the meeting in a closed police van. As the van approached the spot, the driver slowed but did not stop, so no one listening would realize anyone had gotten out. Bruhmuller wore civilian clothes: jeans, a green shirt, and a bandanna on his head. For protection in the jungle, he carried a knife and a .38-caliber or 9mm pistol.

From the road, he walked about a thousand yards off into the woods. "I never saw the man wearing a watch, but he was always there," Bruhmuller says. "I don't recall ever having to wait for him."

The two men introduced themselves. Bill Bruhmuller told the man, "You call me 'John'; I'll call you 'Mister.'" Bruhmuller never did learn the man's real name. He figured if he didn't know, he could never tell anyone.

Quickly the two men strode back to the road and hopped into the van as it rolled past. From there, they went directly to the airfield for the flight to Saigon. The DIA had assigned an interrogator who was fluent in Vietnamese.

"He was a black fellow, and he had just the personality, the language, to put this gent totally at ease. There was never any hesitation to answer questions."

Bruhmuller went off alone into enemy territory six times. Only once did he feel he was in imminent danger.

"On the way out once, Mister pushed me down into a hole. Within a couple of seconds, a VC patrol went by us. I saw eleven guys. I don't know why they didn't hear my heart going. If he ever was going to turn me in, this was it. The man saved my life."

Each trip took about twenty-four hours, and Bruhmuller stayed with Mister the whole time. "I stayed primarily as a confidence builder for Mister. We became almost friends. We trusted each other. I didn't want him messed over. I was there to protect him as well as to get information."

Bruhmuller didn't understand Vietnamese well enough to keep up with the interrogation, and he didn't really want to know the details of the information the man was providing. But he gradually learned Mister's story. Back during the war between the French and the Viet Minh, Mister was captured and sent to Hanoi for schooling. Later, he was sent back to set up his own organization in the delta.

"He wasn't doing this job because he hated Americans. He was doing it because he feared for his life. He was caught between two countries. He had no choice," Bruhmuller says.

After the crushing defeat suffered by the Viet Cong during the Tet offensive, life became bitterly hard for the survivors. They were ordered to grow their own food and fend for themselves. It was at this point that Mister, with a wife ill with tuberculosis and a sick child, decided to sell intelligence for money.

As each interrogation session ended, the results were flashed to Washington. There, analysts came to a startling conclusion: Mister was not only a top VC official, he was the number one man, in charge of all VC operations in the delta. Curiously, because of the contorted enemy command structure, the man himself didn't realize his own importance. But the information he provided laid bare the VC strategy, giving forewarning of attacks. A citation later issued to Bruhmuller said his intelligence coup "was responsible for saving thousands of American and South Vietnamese lives."

As the timeliness and quality of their intelligence improved, the SEALs found they were able to penetrate deep into Viet Cong sanctuaries where more conventional forces didn't know enough, or didn't dare, to go. Charlie Watson tells of one such foray into a VC enclave. The VC felt so secure that they had erected a huge archway at each end of the village, with a large VC flag nailed to each arch. Everyone was afraid to approach the village, but the SEALs sneaked through the brush and broke in through the back of one hooch.

"It was unreal," Watson says. "It was a jewelry store."

The SEALs erupted into the main street and found a row of stores lining the boulevard.

"We went down the street and burned the place," he says. "There was a feed store with fuel. We'd take the fuel, throw it in a store, shoot with a gun or throw in a flare, and burn the whole thing. There was a Vietnamese with us, one of the recon people. He's gesturing at this building. I can't understand. I gestured and said, 'Burn the goddamn place.' When we got to the boat, Ming, our interpreter, had watches all up his arm. Ming told me the recon guy, whatever his name is, said you really screwed up. He said it was a bank. There was an ungodly amount of money in it. And it was all burned. Hell, we could have had Ho Chi Minh parties every day for the rest of our tour."

Often, the SEALs found, it was not only the quality of the intelligence they gathered but also the speed with which they responded to it that counted.

In March 1969, two VC defectors showed up in the coastal city of Nha Trang with startling information. They said they had come from a tiny island in Nha Trang Bay. There, they said, the VC had a secret base, from which they sent out sapper teams to attack U.S. and South Vietnamese targets, and an intelligence unit that controlled a network of spies within the city. The defectors warned that they would soon be missed. If a surprise attack on the site was to have any chance of success in capturing key officials and getting the names of members of the spy network, it would have to be done almost immediately. The two men assured them they would find only a few lightly armed men.

Lt. (JG) Joseph R. ("Bob") Kerrey, a member of SEAL Team One, set out in the predawn darkness of 14 March to attack the site. With him were six other SEALs, the two VC defectors, and a South Vietnamese frogman. The men were dropped near the island from a small boat and managed to get ashore undetected. The first challenge was to scale a sheer 350-foot cliff in the darkness, without ropes. This put them above and behind the enemy camp, the direction from which an attack would seem least likely. Stealthily, they worked their way down the other side of the rock face until they spotted a group of enemy soldiers.

Kerrey assigned half his team to keep an eye on the soldiers. He and the other members of the team took off their boots and set out to check the rest of the camp. Suddenly, Kerrey and his men were spotted and came under heavy fire. The enemy soldiers were much more heavily armed than they had been led to believe. Kerrey didn't even see the grenade that flew through the darkness and went off at his feet. The lower portion of his right leg was torn apart, and he was thrown violently backward onto jagged rocks.

Despite his wounds, Kerrey called in fire from the other SEAL unit, surprising the VC in a withering cross fire. Seven VC soldiers died in the next few moments. Under Kerrey's direction, the SEALs took control of the camp and called in helicopters to carry him out along with the enemy prisoners.

For his heroism, Kerrey became the first SEAL to win the Congressional Medal of Honor. The citation signed by President Nixon says, "The havoc wrought to the enemy by this very successful mission cannot be overestimated. The enemy who were captured provided critical intelligence to the allied effort."

Kerrey's right leg was so badly mangled that doctors were forced to amputate below the knee. After a painful period of rehabilitation, he was fitted with a prosthesis that permitted him to resume a full range of normal activities—and some not so normal.

Chuck LeMoyne recalls seeing Kerrey shortly after he was wounded and finding him determined that the loss of his leg would not be a devastating impediment.

"I had a free-fall parachute and a couple of other pieces of equipment," LeMoyne says. "My new enterprise was surfing. I sold Bob the parachute so I could buy a surfboard. My wife thought we were both crazy. She thought Bob was crazy for wanting to jump out of an airplane with a missing leg. And that I was worse than crazy for selling him the parachute."

Kerrey went on to become governor of Nebraska, then to represent the state as a Democratic senator in Washington, and to seek the presidency.

As the quality of their intelligence and the speed with which they reacted to it improved, the SEALs found they spent less time sitting in long, boring, fruitless ambushes and more in operations where they killed or, better yet, captured enemy leaders. But with this came a growing sense of frustration. Everyone knew Cambodia was being used as a sanctuary by the enemy, and yet the SEALs were, for the most part, forbidden to cross the line.

Al Winter, who served in Vietnam with Team One in the latter part of 1968 and early 1969, says he had gray hair when he returned to Coronado.

"I was quite disillusioned with what we were doing over there, setting up ambushes and killing people," Winter says. "It wasn't exactly my idea of a fun thing to do. Let's say the war was not the war I thought it was. A lot of people felt that way."

Winter confronted Comdr. D. L. ("Dave") Schaible, who had led SEALs during their early involvement in the southern part of Vietnam and who was then commander of Team One. "I said, 'I don't mind going back, but let us go across the borders, let us do something that's going to help the war and not just entertain us.'

"I said to Schaible, 'Let us cross the border.' We were doing it illegally. That was happening. I didn't like that, either. We were doing good things, but it was against the rules for fighting that war. We were breaking the rules. I had guys in my platoon who said we ought to do more of it because now we were getting into the good things. And we could do it because we were well trained and we could move at night."

Winter says he did cross the border on occasion. But he describes himself as cautious, always careful to brief senior officers before an operation. Others, he said, were at the opposite extreme, carrying out operations and then talking about it afterward.

"I felt I was putting my ass, my guys, on the line. And if we got caught, we were doing something that wasn't sanctioned," Winter says. Winter felt that Schaible, who has since died, tended to agree with him. After opening himself up to his skipper, Winter might have found himself quarantined with the antiwar disease. He did not return for a second tour in Vietnam. Instead, Schaible told him he needed a gray-haired guy to represent him in Washington and sent him off to the Pentagon.

Because SEAL operations in Cambodia were both secret and illegal, it is still unclear today how often they occurred. Most often, such operations seem to have been illicit, although winked at by higher authorities. But sometimes they were carried out with official approval.

Jim Watson tells of one such operation that was carefully planned and authorized by higher authorities. He crossed into Cambodia, captured two men, and brought them back for questioning. He later received a commendation for the operation. What the commendation fails to mention is that the action took place in Cambodia and that the two men captured were Chinese intelligence officers. When the State Department heard about this foray into a country with which the United States was not at war and the capture of two citizens of a third country, there were demands that the SEAL responsible be court-martialled. Watson was spirited away from his base of operations, and an admiral told him, "Watson, we're going to have to hide you!" He was hidden until the storm blew over—and then quietly commended for the operation.

The ambiguity about crossing into Cambodia continued until April 1970, when U.S. forces crossed the border in a massive sweep designed to disrupt the North Vietnamese command and supply bases, at least long enough to permit the withdrawal of American forces and the turnover of responsibility for the conduct of the war to the South Vietnamese.

While the question of operating in Cambodia remained a sensitive subject until the assault in 1970, officially sanctioned penetrations into Laos and parts of North Vietnam were carried out regularly by SEALs operating out of Da Nang under the control of the Studies and Observations Group, the military unit which was responsible for the secret aspects of the war.

On a typical mission, the SEALs would fly to the large base at Nakhon Phanom, on the Thai border with Laos, where the United States had set up a major electronic monitoring system to process information provided by sensors scattered along the border between North and South Vietnam and along the Ho Chi Minh Trail through Laos.

From Nakhon Phanom, four or five SEALs would fly by helicopter to a "cool" place where the sensors indicated no enemy activity. Often, this was forty or fifty kilometers from the trail. The men worked their way through the jungle until they were three hundred or four hundred feet from the trail and quietly set up camp. They were equipped with powerful binoculars, to which a 35mm camera was attached. Special film permitted them to take pictures at night. They were careful to stay far enough back in the foliage that there would be no glint of sunlight on the lenses.

For several days, they would lie there quietly, counting and photographing traffic on the trail. Sometimes, the North Vietnamese would camp nearby. The SEALs held their breath for fear someone scouting for firewood would stumble on their position.

After several days, the SEALs carefully policed up their campsite so there would be no sign they had been there. Then they moved off to await the arrival of a helicopter to pluck them from the jungle. The helicopter crew dropped a probe shaped like a large dart down through the jungle canopy. Two metal arms folded down to form a seat. One after the other, the men straddled the probe and were reeled in by the chopper. The last man always ended up a little bruised and battered because, as he was being winched up, the pilot broke from the hover and headed for home.

Throughout the war, most of the SEALs operated in their own detachments. But a number of them were also assigned, often alone, to work with special South Vietnamese units. SEALs of Team One took credit for pioneering this kind of operation on an informal basis. The combination was a valuable one. The Vietnamese knew the language, the people, and the land. The SEALs were able to contribute the technology of modern warfare: helicopters, good communications, and a sophisticated logistics system.

John Wilbur first heard of these operations when a chief petty officer from Team One dropped by his headquarters. Up to that point, he had felt a good deal of frustration, "just wandering around in a foreign country at night with guns."

"We would often stumble around, try to collide with a contact target, have a firefight, try to kill a bunch of people, and then get out well before dawn. We were without any Seeing Eye dog at all. We didn't know what the sounds were. We didn't know which parts of the hamlets were trouble and which were not trouble. We didn't know which barking dog was going to alert who," Wilbur says. "The idea of working with knowledgeable, relatively well-trained counterguerrilla-type personnel was of tremendous benefit to us."

Late in 1967, a special SEAL unit—Detachment Bravo, or Det Bravo—was formed to work with what came to be known as the South Vietnamese Provincial Reconnaissance Units (PRU). Det Bravo reported to a cover organization that was actually an arm of the Central Intelligence Agency. Because of his enthusiasm for combining the talents of the SEALs and the PRU, John Wilbur was put in charge of Det Bravo. In effect he commanded a platoon, but his men were spread all over the delta, with one man assigned as an adviser to each PRU outfit in each of the sixteen provinces.

For a young lieutenant jaygee, it was a very exciting assignment.

It was not until later that Wilbur realized he was at the center of an intense power struggle between the two SEAL teams.

"This led to some sustained and eventually rather extreme internecine tensions and jealousies between SEAL One and SEAL Two," Wilbur recalls. "SEAL One thought they were the progenitor of this advisory proposal, and they coveted this as a SEAL One exclusively controlled assignment. All this was totally unknown to me, much to my later chagrin and some misfortune. This reveals how special, small, elite units got very involved in their self-imagery and internal competition."

Later, when Wilbur earned a law degree and became a prosecutor, he recognized the same kind of "fratricidal hostilities" between various law-enforcement groups.

As the commander of the PRU advisers, Wilbur had the opportunity to travel throughout the delta and to go on operations with the various units. They ranged in size and quality from a ragtag group of 30 to "really impressive, disciplined and capable companies of maybe 60 to 120 men." Wilbur found the best of them "as good a fighting unit as any that existed in Vietnam during the war."

On one of the operations in which he accompanied a PRU outfit, Wilbur had an extraordinary experience. He and five other men, four PRUs and an interpreter, set out in two sampans to attack what their intelligence told them would be a meeting of key Viet Cong leaders. It was a dark night, and much of the delta area was flooded. A few dikes could be made out as dim shadows above the dark waters. Occasionally they saw a hamlet looming up like a tiny island.

About a quarter of a mile from the target, they halted and went over their plans. The men in one sampan would attack the target while the others moved around to the other side as a blocking force. And then, out of the darkness came another sampan carrying two farmers. To make sure the farmers would not alert the VC, they were ordered to come along. Wilbur climbed over into their sampan and the three craft moved silently toward the target.

There was just enough light for Wilbur to make out a small shape huddled in the bottom of the sampan. It was a very frightened little boy, no more than three years old. According to the revised plan, the other two sampans would carry out the original attack scheme while Wilbur, with the farmers and the child, would follow them in.

Somehow, in the darkness, Wilbur and his little group arrived at the target first. They were in a marshy area at the edge of a muddy little island about the size of half a football field containing two small hooches.

"I had no idea what would happen," Wilbur says. "I didn't dare make any sound to abort the attack. I got out, clutched the little boy, and went up the embankment. The other sampan, the attack group, made a rush. There was screaming. Shots were fired. I crouched, trying to be out of the fire. Two armed men rushed out of the hut right at myself and this little tiny child. I had a Swedish K [a lightweight 9mm grease gun from the CIA arsenal] at the time. I got off a fumbling burst. Then I stood up, backed up and fell, clutching the child, into the marsh."

The water was about four feet deep.

"My total concern was on making sure the child was all right. I had a terrible fear he was going to drown. I flailed, got hold of him, and crawled up on the embankment. I checked the child. He didn't cry; he didn't do anything. I looked down into his face, and he simply stared up at me. He was like a little Buddha."

Wilbur could see the body of one of the two men he had shot at. He was sure he had wounded the other man, but he had gotten away. Wilbur put down the child and ventured about two hundred yards out into the marsh looking for the other man. Suddenly, he realized the "idiocy and stupidity of wandering around in a marsh after somebody with a gun without knowing where he was," and turned back.

The raiders had missed, by a day, the regional VC tax collector, but they did find a pile of documents. The child, frightened but unharmed, was reunited with the two farmers. The attack had alerted the local VC reaction force, and the raiders had to scramble to get away.

"We really had to paddle our ass off for the balance of the morning," Wilbur recalls. But he found the whole experience, where one American had been able to penetrate into an area where he would otherwise have been hopelessly lost, "fascinating, exhilarating, and intoxicating."

Wilbur was wounded during the Tet offensive, and Lt. (later Rear Adm.) Chuck LeMoyne, a member of SEAL Team One, was assigned to monitor the PRU program in the delta from January to September 1968. In the critical months after the Tet offensive, the PRUs had the job of mounting a systematic attack on the VC infrastructure. It was their task to identify, locate, and capture leaders of the VC. At that time, the PRU operated in fourteen of the sixteen provinces in the delta, and SEALs were advisers in twelve of those fourteen.

When LeMoyne arrived in Can Tho to take on his duties, he found a policy that tended to encourage killing the VC rather than capturing them. But this was counterproductive. Far better to capture people and, if possible, get them to work for you.

"When you're running a combat operation," LeMoyne says, "it's easy to talk about capturing someone, but it is a lot easier to talk about than to do. We learned as we went along. When I first got there, we were paying a bounty on weapons. We found we were getting a lot of weapons but not nearly as many prisoners as we would like. The reason was, it's a hell of a lot easier to get a weapon from someone you have shot than from someone who is alive and kicking. The economic-man principle was alive and well in Vietnam. The PRU would say, 'There's a weapon. I'm going to get a bounty for the weapon. Bang, you're dead. Now I have a weapon.' We didn't really care about the weapon—certainly we did, but it was the individual we wanted, and we wanted them alive. Because captured members of the infrastructure could give you more information about other members of the infrastructure. Some of them would surrender and become *hoi chanhs* [working for the South Vietnamese]. We could put them back to work. We couldn't stop paying the bounty on the weapons, once we'd started, but we started paying a larger bounty for prisoners by order of importance. Capture rates went way up. It was remarkable. We were capturing, in the delta, a thousand to twelve hundred VCI [Viet Cong infrastructure (personnel)] monthly."

Those captured were taken to an interrogation center. Often the PRU knew the men they had captured because they had lived in the same village. But the Viet Cong tried to involve everyone in their activities. With that volume of captives going through the interrogation center, there was a constant problem of identifying those who were really important leaders and those who had cooperated with the VC for self-preservation. Often the SEAL adviser had to step in and act as a quality-control officer.

The advisers worked six-month tours of duty, and LeMoyne wondered if that was too short a time to learn the territory and run effective operations. But he found that after six months in an active province, the advisers were visibly tired. Fatigue showed itself in various ways.

I had an adviser in Ca Mau, a fine petty officer. He was a very quiet, almost laconic, individual, a man of few words. I went down to see him right after the Tet offensive. We sat up almost all night. He never stopped talking. That was uncharacteristic behavior. It didn't affect his operations. But that wasn't him. When he got home and relaxed, it was back to Silent Sam again.

I had another adviser who was a corpsman by rating. He ran

an awfully good operation, doing a marvelous job. He had one of the best intelligence organizations in the whole corps. But his hands shook badly. When they were loose, they shook noticeably. He never left them loose, laid them on things. He would put his pencil on the paper and write. But if he lifted the pencil, you would see his hands shake.

I relieved a couple of advisers, one because he didn't like being in the field by himself at night with the PRU. He tried, but he just wasn't comfortable at it and asked to be relieved. Another I fired. He was just a disruptive person, abrasive. He was in a good province with a good PRU and wasn't getting results.

As the PRU program proved its worth, it was absorbed into a much broader effort known as the Phoenix program, whose goal was to destroy the VC's ability and willingness to fight by identifying individuals through a census program, removing the VC leadership, and replacing them with a revolutionary development cadre loyal to the Saigon government.

Phoenix amounted to a deliberate plan of repression and control of the population. And it quickly gained a reputation for brutal assassination of VC leaders and their families. Studies after the war indicated it had been quite effective in sapping enemy strength.

Wilbur later felt he had been very fortunate to be in at the beginning, before "the great surrender to the Phoenix program."

"The PRU was an impressive and satisfactory success, but recognition of its success would spell its undoing. It would attract attention, become a pawn of bureaucratic jealousies and meddling. The uniqueness of my experience is, I was there at the beginning, before it got administratively restricted and before too many cooks and too many hands started struggling for the helm," he says.

Soon after Richard Nixon took office as president in January 1969, the United States set in motion the process known as Vietnamization, which would prepare the South Vietnamese to take over the war and permit the withdrawal of American troops. One after another, SEAL detachments and platoons were pulled out. The dwindling number of SEALs remaining in the country increasingly found themselves in the lonely, demanding role of advisers to the Vietnamese frogmen, the LDNN.

Two of the most remarkable feats of bravery performed by SEALs occurred late in the war, after most of the Americans were gone and the few remaining SEALs were operating with LDNN.

In April 1972, the North Vietnamese took advantage of the American withdrawal to launch a broad offensive with the goal of overrunning South Vietnam and toppling its government. The Easter offensive was met by fierce resistance from the South Vietnamese, and the attack was turned back. Even though most American ground troops were gone, the United States weighed in with heavy use of air power to pound North Vietnam and provide air support for the South Vietnamese troops.

In the midst of the battle, an American EB-66 electronic-warfare plane was shot down on 2 April 1972 while escorting B-52 heavy bombers on a mission. Although the plane suffered a direct hit from a surface-to-air missile, the plane's electronic warfare officer, fifty-three-year-old Lt. Col. Iceal Hambleton, got out. While still in his parachute, he radioed his position. But he was in deep trouble, far behind enemy lines. A desperate standoff then began. Other air force planes dropped a circle of mines around Hambleton to keep the North Vietnamese soldiers away. But he was still surrounded by enemy troops who knew his approximate location.

Even though they couldn't reach him themselves, the North Vietnamese decided to use the downed officer as bait in a trap for would-be rescuers. One Huey helicopter was shot down with the loss of all on board. Another was so badly damaged it had to crash-land on a nearby beach. A big HH-53 rescue helicopter succumbed to enemy fire, as did two small OV-10 reconnaissance planes.

The air force will go to great extremes to rescue a downed airman. But there was added urgency in this case when it was learned that Hambleton had worked in the Strategic Air Command and had a wealth of information in his head about U.S. missile forces and their targets. Officials were determined that he not be captured by the North Vietnamese and passed on to their Soviet allies.

Only after it became obvious that the traditional method of retrieving a downed flier simply would not work did the authorities call on Lt. Thomas Norris, one of the few SEALs remaining behind in Vietnam. On the night of 10 April, Norris and four other frogmen crept a mile and a half through the enemy-controlled area and rescued one of the spotter-plane pilots. The next day, he tried twice with a three-man team to get to Hambleton. They couldn't penetrate the ring around the officer. By this time, Hambleton had been on the ground nearly ten days.

Norris decided on a new tack, one that fit in with the way he had always liked to operate. Earlier in the war, when Norris was a member of Team Two in the south, he had preferred to go on missions with only one or two companions.

Capt. Michael Jukoski, who was Norris's platoon commander, recalls Norris at the time as quiet and unassuming but very aggressive. "I didn't like him to go out with just two people," Jukoski says. "It is a lot easier to move with less people, but he couldn't fight his way out."

As he prepared for the rescue attempt, Norris donned the clothes of a Vietnamese fisherman. He was joined by Nguyen Van Kiet, a Vietnamese frogman. They climbed into a small sampan and paddled up the Song Mieu Giang River on the night of 12 April. Hambleton had carefully nursed the batteries of his emergency radio. He was instructed to move down to a pickup point on the river.

The two frogmen found Hambleton and quickly helped him into the sampan, covering him with banana leaves. Then they set off down the river, moving close to the bank and stopping whenever they heard signs of an enemy patrol. Several times they called in an air strike to clear the way. Finally, after three hours, they had almost reached the forward operating base that was their goal when they came under fire by heavy automatic weapons. Air force planes, circling above to cover the rescue operation, quickly moved in to silence the enemy guns.

For his feat, Norris was awarded the Medal of Honor. The citation, signed by President Gerald R. Ford, says, "By his outstanding display of decisive leadership, undaunted courage, and selfless dedication in the face of extreme danger, Lieutenant Norris enhanced the finest traditions of the United States Naval Service."

Nguyen Van Kiet, who accompanied Norris on the rescue mission, became the only Vietnamese to receive the Navy Cross. The citation, signed by Navy Secretary J. William Middendorf II, says, "Due to Petty Officer Kiet's coolness under extremely dangerous conditions and his outstanding courage and professionalism, an American aviator was recovered after an eleven-day ordeal behind enemy lines. His self-discipline, personal courage, and dynamic fighting spirit were an inspiration to all, thereby reflecting great credit upon himself and the Naval Service."

Norris displayed a distinct kind of bravery, repeatedly returning into enemy territory with the same kind of cool calculation that Bruhmuller displayed in his repeated trips to escort Mister out for interrogation. There is quite another kind of bravery encountered more often on the battlefield, the kind that is seen when men, in the heat of battle, do things that seem almost superhuman. By a strange twist of fate, Norris was the object of a feat of this kind of bravery.

The Easter offensive had been beaten back, but in the fall of 1972, the North Vietnamese were still a major threat in the area of the demilitarized zone. To keep track of the NVA forces and identify targets for bombing attacks, small units of LDNN, with their American advisers, patrolled the six-kilometer-deep strip of South Vietnamese territory between the Cua Viet River and the DMZ.

By that time, the SEAL presence in Vietnam had dwindled to three officers and nine enlisted men. Douglas P. Huth, who later, as a captain, commanded the Naval Special Warfare Center at Coronado, was one of the officers. Typically, he says, two Americans would accompany four Vietnamese. They would sail north, out of sight of land, in a cement-hulled junk and make contact with a destroyer standing by to provide gunfire support.

"The ship vectored the junk in to a couple of thousand meters off the beach. Then we'd go over the side into a rubber boat and paddle ashore," Huth recalls. The boat returned to the junk while the SEALs patrolled four or five kilometers inland.

"We could see and hear the NVA," Huth says. "We got close enough to tell what kind of weapon a guy was carrying. But it wasn't our job to capture them. If you make an attempt to do something other than recon and surveillance, they know you're in the area. The object is not to let them know you are there. Offensive action is not doing the mission because it defeats the opportunity to go back in that area again."

The SEALs were warned that if they got in trouble, they could not expect air cover or helicopter support because of the formidable air defenses the NVA had installed in that area. The only help available was from the five-inch guns on the destroyer. And for that to be useful, the SEALs had to know exactly where they were.

On 31 October, Norris and Engineman Second Class Michael Thornton accompanied an inexperienced LDNN officer and two veteran LDNN enlisted men on such a patrol. Their plan was to land south of the Cua Viet River and patrol north to check out the Cua Viet River Base, which the NVA had captured earlier in the year. They landed about four o'clock in the morning and carefully patrolled northward, working their way around the numerous NVA encampments. To their surprise, they did not find the river where it should have been.

They were lost. Instead of inserting them south of the river, as planned, the skipper of the junk had left them off north of the river. Instead of moving north toward the river, they had been moving north away from it, almost across the DMZ into North Vietnam.

By the time they were convinced of the error, it was nearly dawn. Norris ordered the patrol to pull back to the shore where he would try to find a landmark and determine where they were. Without an accurate fix on their position, he could not call for fire support from the USS *Newport News,* lying offshore.

Just as the men had crept to within sight of the shore, they were spotted by an NVA patrol. Within minutes, they found themselves surrounded by more than forty enemy soldiers, who moved to within twenty-five yards of their position. Norris managed to figure out where they were and radioed for naval gunfire. But the NVA were so close that the American gunners could not hit them without also hitting the frogmen.

The battle raged for forty-five minutes. Thornton had shrapnel wounds in both legs and his back, and one of the Vietnamese had been hit in the hip.

Norris decided on a desperate gamble. He radioed the ship to give him five minutes and then target his own position. While he and one of the LDNN provided covering fire, Thornton and the two other Vietnamese sprinted 125 yards to the last dune line and prepared to pin down the NVA long enough for Norris and the remaining LDNN to move back before the ship's shells rained down.

As Norris raised up to fire an antiarmor shell, a bullet struck the left side of his head and knocked him to the ground. The Vietnamese frogman looked at the gaping wound and dashed back to the last dune line. He told Thornton that Norris had been killed. Still, a SEAL does not abandon a buddy, even if all he can do is recover the body. Thornton ran back to their last position and found Norris, still alive, but only barely so.

Thornton is a hulking man and Norris is slight. If their roles had been reversed, both probably would have died right there. But Thornton was able to carry the wounded officer back through the enemy fire. The Vietnamese looked to him for guidance. He told them they were going to swim. Somehow, they covered the 275 yards of open beach without being hit and plunged into the four-foot surf.

Once past the breakers, Thornton inflated Norris's life jacket and pushed him ahead of himself, while also helping one of the LDNN. The NVA soldiers pursued them a few feet into the water, firing their weapons. But they soon lost sight of the fleeing SEALs and cheered their victory.

Out at sea, the crews of the American ship and the junk from which the patrol had departed many hours before watched the final barrage rain down on the SEALs' last known position and waited for radio contact. Instead, there was silence. Long after everyone had given up hope, an enlisted SEAL on the junk insisted that they continue the search. Finally, shortly before noon, the five men were found and lifted from the sea.

They were transferred to the *Newport News* for emergency treatment, and then Norris was taken to a hospital in Da Nang. Huth, who saw him the following morning, some fourteen hours after he had been hit, says, "He didn't look very good." He is convinced that the salt water, by cleaning out the wound and stopping the bleeding, saved Norris's life. But perhaps because of the long delay in reaching medical treatment, doctors could not save his eye.

Later, Norris became an FBI agent, spending months working under cover to make cases against drug dealers and white supremacists.

Thornton, later a SEAL officer, became the third SEAL and the first enlisted man to receive the Medal of Honor. "By his extraordinary courage and perseverance, Petty Officer Thornton was directly responsible for saving the life of his superior officer and enabling the safe extraction of all patrol members, thereby upholding the highest traditions of the United States Naval Service," the citation, signed by President Nixon, says.

CHAPTER NINE
THE SUPER SEALs

In the early morning darkness of 6 June 1972, Lt. Melvin S. ("Spence") Dry stepped from a helicopter and plummeted into the Gulf of Tonkin near the North Vietnamese city of Thanh Hoa. The twenty-six-year-old officer fell at least thirty-five feet and hit the water so hard that his neck was broken. He became the last SEAL fatality of the Vietnamese war, almost six years after Billy Machen became the first SEAL to lose his life in that long conflict.

Dry was a key participant in Operation Thunderhead, a bold but badly bungled effort to assist the escape of as many as five Americans from a North Vietnamese prison camp near Hanoi. The operation, long cloaked in secrecy, marked the first use in combat by U.S. forces of tiny swimmer (later, SEAL) delivery vehicles (SDVs).

The operation was set in motion when the prisoners managed to send out word that they planned to break out of the prison, steal a small boat, and make their way down the Red River into the Gulf of Tonkin. This meant that, if everything went smoothly, they would emerge from the sprawling Red River Delta somewhere along a fifty-mile stretch of coastline, running from just above Thanh Hoa north to a point slightly below the big port of Haiphong, sometime between 29 May and 19 June.

Aboard the USS *Long Beach,* command center for the operation, plans were made for helicopter patrols that would cover the entire area two to four times a day, looking for a boat with a red or yellow cloth flying from its mast, the signal the prisoners had selected to enable the rescuers to pick them out of all the boat traffic in the delta and along the coast.

Just north of Thanh Hoa, however, the coastline swings in, almost due west, and then curves south, with several islands a short distance off the shore. This meant that the helicopter searching for the escapees could come under cross fire from the island and the mainland each time it ran this five-square-mile gauntlet.

This is where the SEALs came in.

They agreed to send two men in to hide on one of the little islands and, through their binoculars, watch the boats moving along the coast for the red or yellow signal. This would provide complete coverage of the area where the men were expected to emerge into the gulf without adding to the danger to the helicopter and its crew.

But sneaking the SEALs onto the island posed a problem. If they tried to come in so close to the Vietnamese mainland by helicopter, surface boat, or even parachute, they were likely to be detected. The decision was made to try something the U.S. Navy had never done before in a combat situation: bring them in close to shore in a submarine and then send them the rest of the way in an SDV.

The skipper of the USS *Grayback* met with planners of the operation in the Philippines and told them he could do the job.

The *Grayback* was an old diesel-powered submarine originally built in the 1950s to carry a Regulus missile. It had a large hangar for the missile on its deck. When the Regulus was phased out, the frogmen were quick to propose that they team up with the crew of the sub. The hangar area, they explained, was big enough to hold two SDVs or one SDV and a good deal of other equipment. And since the hangar area was dry, the frogmen could prepare for a mission in relative comfort.

The SDV is sometimes called a minisubmarine, but that is a misnomer. Unlike a submarine, which contains an airtight crew compartment, the SDV is not sealed against the sea. The men must wear underwater breathing apparatuses, and their only protection against the cold water is their wet suits.

Well before the creation of the SEALs, the UDT teams had for many years worked with submarine crews, learning how to use the escape tower to "lock out" of and "lock in" to the sub. But the *Grayback,* with its big, dry hangar, gave them an entirely new capability. Their only complaint was that the sub, designed to loiter for long periods until it was called on to launch a missile attack, was slow, only capable of creeping along at five knots.

In Operation Thunderhead, speed was not a problem, but stealth was all-important. The entire operation was so secret that the crews of the surface ships crowding the Gulf of Tonkin were not told about it. This meant the *Grayback* had to work its way past three aircraft carriers, plus cruisers and destroyers; maneuver in close to the Vietnamese coast; and then settle gently to the bottom without being detected.

A more modern nuclear-powered submarine might not have been able to slip through an entire American fleet undetected. But the *Grayback* was an older model. On the surface it was powered by diesel engines. But when submerged, running slowly on electricity from its batteries, it was almost inaudible, even to the most sensitive passive sonar.

The skipper promised not only that he would reach the designated point, but that he would remain there for the nearly three weeks that the operation might go on, surfacing only at night when necessary to recharge his batteries.

In the middle of the night of 3–4 June, Dry, who was a member of SEAL Team One, and three other men climbed from the submarine up into the hangar and prepared for their "takeoff." Two of the men, Lt. (jg) John C. Lutz and Fireman Tom Edwards, belonged to UDT Eleven, and they served as the crew—the pilot and navigator—of the SDV. Their task was to deliver Dry and another SEAL, Warrant Officer One P. L. Martin, to the island and then return to the submarine. After two or three days they would repeat the process, picking up the two SEALs and replacing them with two more.

When everything was in readiness, the hangar door was opened, and Lutz slowly "flew" the nineteen-foot-long SDV off into the dark waters. The craft was an early model of the Mark 7 SDV, the first to go into service with the navy. It was little more than a prototype, intended for training rather than for a combat mission. With its four-man crew it had little positive buoyancy to spare for carrying weapons and other gear. Its navigation equipment amounted to little more than a clock and a compass.

As the SDV slowly made its way toward its target, the crew members became aware that they were fighting a much stronger current than they had expected, and that their batteries were running out of power. They weren't going to make it. Before reaching the island, they were forced to surface and lie there, dead in the water. When Lutz and Edwards failed to return, the submarine sent a prearranged message: "Briarpatch tango." This meant the SDV team was in trouble.

Shortly after dawn a helicopter was dispatched to search for the four men. Just east of the little island they were spotted in the water, alongside the black shape of the SDV. As the helo hovered overhead, the men were hoisted to safety. The helicopter crewmen were surprised to see how much equipment they were carrying: radios, survival gear, ammunition, M-16 rifles, and even communications equipment from the SDV.

As the last of the survivors was hoisted into the cabin, one of the helicopter's crewmen swung the craft's automatic machine gun into position and raked the SDV with bullets, sending it to the bottom. The frogmen were flown to the cruiser *Long Beach*.

On the following day, 5 June, the submarine radioed a message asking to have its "package"—the four men—delivered about midnight that night. The plan was for the sub to send a swimmer to the surface with an infrared lantern to signal his position. As the helicopter moved slowly overhead the frogmen would step out into the darkness, in a procedure called a helo cast. The man from the submarine would lead them back to the sub. One part of the message from the submarine was a mystery to officers on the cruiser. It said, "Will be conducting abbreviated ops." Even though this didn't make any sense, it was decided not to force the sub to compromise its position by pressing for an explanation.

The frogmen asked to be dropped from thirty feet, with the helicopter moving forward at five knots. This would be like jumping from the top of a three-story building onto water, which can be as hard as concrete from that height. In practice, it had been found that the forward momentum of the chopper would help the man maintain the proper body position so he would slice into the water rather than pancake. The thirty feet at five knots was a compromise from standard operating procedure, which called for matching the helicopter's speed to its altitude: ten knots at ten feet, twenty knots at twenty feet, thirty knots at thirty feet, and so on. This compromise reflected the SEALs' instinctive feeling that jumping out of a fast-moving helicopter was not a smart thing to do.

James L. ("Gator") Parks, a plank owner of SEAL Team One and one of the navy's most experienced SDV operators, says, "I'm not jumping out of any helicopter at thirty knots and thirty feet. I have done it, and

I'm not ever going to do it again, I guarantee. That was SOP [standard operating procedure]. We were not smart enough to get the SOP changed."

As the helicopter crewmen and the four frogmen emerged onto the deck of the *Long Beach* and prepared to board the helicopter, it became obvious that the fine points of helo casting were just so much theory. The night was dark and overcast, without even the hint of a horizon. The pilot said he'd try for thirty feet and five knots, but they had better plan on forty feet and ten knots.

Once airborne, the crewmen scanned the area ahead with an infrared detector, looking for a signal from the submarine. At one point, they saw a line of dim lights and flew toward them. Only as they swept in over the breaker line did they realize the light they saw came from candles, shining dimly from the windows of homes along the shore.

The pilot banked sharply back out to sea. But then, flying on instruments, he dipped so low that ocean water splashed onto the floor of the helicopter.

The infrared detector never did pick up the signal from the submarine. But the men in the helicopter saw several small, flashing strobe lights near where the submarine was supposed to be.

The pilot zeroed in on one of the strobes. Dry, still burdened with equipment, handed his rifle to Lt. Comdr. Edwin L. Towers, the officer in charge of the rescue attempt, and stepped into the darkness. The chopper was hovering, without the forward momentum that would have helped the men maintain the proper position to slice into the sea. Lutz, Martin, and Edwards followed quickly, in that order. As each man stepped out, the helicopter became lighter. By the time Edwards jumped, he may have been some one hundred feet from the water, equivalent to jumping from the top of a ten-story building.

As Edwards disappeared out the door, a startling message came from the sub: "Do not deliver my package! I say again, Do not deliver my package!"

The helo crew flashed back a message that the package had been delivered about thirty seconds before. The sub responded that it had detected a North Vietnamese patrol boat approaching and had to move.

The helicopter wheeled away toward a nearby amphibious ship, leaving the four frogmen alone in the darkness of the Gulf of Tonkin until a search could begin at dawn.

Lutz was stunned by hitting the water, and some of his equipment was torn away by the impact, but he was not injured. He and Martin, also slightly dazed, soon located each other and then found Edwards, seriously injured and moaning. Martin inflated Edwards's life vest, and Martin and Lutz called for Dry. There was no answer.

Soon, however, the three men made contact with four other swimmers in the water and learned the meaning of the mysterious strobe lights they had seen from the helicopter.

Although those aboard the *Long Beach* who were masterminding the operation didn't realize it, the *Grayback* carried two SDVs. When the first craft failed to return, it was decided to send another SDV, with a two-man UDT crew and two SEALs to take up the surveillance mission on the island. This second SDV mission was the meaning of the enigmatic reference to "abbreviated ops." But the SDV was improperly ballasted. As soon as it left the hangar deck of the submarine, it sank to the bottom. The four men were fortunate to escape before the sub, rolling gently, crushed the SDV.

Although their tiny craft foundered right beside the sub, the currents were so strong that the men were not able to get back inside. They began to flash their strobes, hoping that the helicopter coming to drop the package, consisting of the four men from the original SDV, would realize their predicament and pick them up.

The four men who had escaped from the second SDV—Lt. (jg) McGrath, Lt. (jg) Conger, Seaman McConnel, and Petty Officer Birkey— joined up with the three survivors from the first SDV. They were apparently caught in a giant whirlpool, for during the night Dry's body floated into their midst.

When the helicopter returned to the area shortly after dawn, the crew members were startled to see eight, rather than just four, forms bobbing in the sea. As they got closer, they could see that one of the men was dead. Even though it strained the capacity of the helicopter, all seven men and Dry's body were lifted from the sea and taken to the *Long Beach*.

Just after dawn on the morning of 9 June, alert lookouts on a U.S. destroyer spotted the wake made by a submarine's snorkel. The crew had not been told of the presence of a friendly submarine, so they began firing with their five-inch gun. As soon as the destroyer radioed that the sub was under attack, the cease-fire order was flashed from the *Long Beach*. It was not until late that night, however, that the skipper of the *Grayback* felt comfortable coming to the surface and reporting that he had suffered no damage. He also said he would send a small rubber boat to pick up the six frogmen remaining after Edwards had been flown to a nearby aircraft carrier for treatment, along with Dry's body.

It was not until three o'clock on the morning of 12 June that the rubber Zodiac boat from the sub, its outboard motor disabled, was paddled up to the *Long Beach*. Quickly, the six frogmen joined the two men in the boat and paddled off into the darkness. Why they felt such a strong urge to get back to the submarine, even though both the SDVs had been lost, is not clear. Perhaps it was the simple fact that they thought of the submarine as home.

The planners of Operation Thunderhead later learned that the prisoners had called off their escape attempt but had had no way to pass word of their change in plans. The official navy accident report on the death of Dry says the helicopter was hovering at about thirty-five feet when he jumped. But a number of SEALs familiar with the operation believe the helicopter, maneuvering on instruments in inky blackness and having, a few moments before, dropped so low that water splashed onto the flight deck, was at a much higher altitude when Dry stepped out the door.

Operation Thunderhead was not one of the U.S. Navy's finest hours, and that may help explain why it long remained highly classified. But it was also the navy's first chance to test in a combat environment a type of technology in which it had lagged, but which other nations had pioneered, on several occasions with spectacular success.

The leaders in the use of small submersibles were for many years the Italians, but the British were probably the first in modern times to give serious consideration to the use of combat swimmers. In 1909, a Royal Navy officer proposed a scheme in which men—human torpedo riders—would sit astride torpedoes and guide them toward enemy shipping. At the beginning of World War I in 1914, the concept was proposed to Winston Churchill, then first lord of the admiralty and a man with a well-developed penchant for the unusual and the unorthodox. But the idea of having men ride torpedoes into an enemy port was too much even for Churchill. He turned thumbs down on the proposal. In Italy, a similar suggestion was greeted initially with similar skepticism. But perhaps because Italy was not blessed with a navy as powerful as that of Britain, the Italian brass gave the go-ahead. The plan called for surface swimmers to be dropped from a mother ship, swim into an enemy harbor, plant mines on ships, and then swim back out again.

The scheme was workable, and on 1 November 1918, just days before the end of the war, it proved itself in combat. An Italian swimmer towed a mine into Pola Harbor, on the coast of what is now Yugoslavia, across the Adriatic from Venice. There he planted the explosive on an Austro-Hungarian ship, the *Viribus Unitus,* and sank her.

In World War I, Italy was one of the Allies, along with the United States, France and Britain. But by the mid-1930s, the British navy was seen as a major threat to Benito Mussolini's plan to create a new Roman Empire. When Il Duce launched his attack on Ethiopia in the winter of 1934–35, the Ethiopians, with their spears and primitive rifles, put up little resistance. But the British Mediterranean fleet could, at any moment, cut the Italian supply lines to Africa.

Two submarine officers, Lts. Teseo Tesei and Elios Toschi, revived the idea of using combat swimmers. Their proposal was very similar to that rejected by Churchill two decades before. But their torpedo riders would wear breathing devices as they rode into enemy harbors with their eyes just above the level of the water. Once inside the harbor, they would dive, attach the warhead to a ship, and set the timer. In theory, they would then ride the propulsion unit of the torpedo back out to sea. Practically, they would be lucky to be able to surface and surrender without being shot. Tesei and Toschi contemplated a major surprise attack that would sink or disable the bulk of the British Mediterranean fleet.

The plan was abandoned, and the small group trained by Tesei and Toschi was disbanded, after the British and French made a secret deal that gave Mussolini a free hand in Ethiopia, effectively removing the Royal Navy as an obstacle to his ambitions. But as war became more imminent, the plan was revived again in 1939, and by early 1940, Tesei and Toschi were learning to ride a twenty-two-foot-long torpedo with a detachable warhead containing 660 pounds of explosive. It was capable of a speed of two and a half miles an hour, had a range of ten miles and could reach a depth of one hundred feet. It was an awkward beast to ride, and the Italian swimmers dubbed it *maiale* (the pig). The goal of the plan was the same as it had been half a decade before: to disable the British fleet that dominated the Mediterranean.

The months that followed Italy's entry into World War II on the German side on 10 June 1940 were frustrating ones for the Italian swimmers. Early tests forced them to concede that a lengthy period of intense training was needed. When they were finally ready to go to war, each of their first five attempts—at Gibraltar, Malta and Alexandria—failed. In the process, both Tesei and Toschi were captured. Finally, on the sixth attempt in September 1941, three British ships were sunk while at anchor at Gibraltar.

This was just a prelude to what the Italian frogmen accomplished on the night of 18–19 December 1941. An Italian submarine surfaced a little more than a mile off the Alexandria lighthouse and launched three *maiali*. Moving cautiously in the darkness, six men climbed aboard their aquatic steeds, two on each torpedo. As they approached the entrance to the harbor, luck was with them. The submarine nets were swung aside to let three British destroyers enter. The frogmen followed so closely behind that they were battered by the wake of the ships and became separated, but they were safely inside the first line of defense.

The team leader, Lt. Luigi Durand de la Penne, and his copilot, Emile Bianchi, cruised slowly through the harbor toward their target, the *Valiant*, a thirty-two-thousand–ton battleship. As they approached the ship, the men were forced to push their torpedo over a torpedo net. In the process, their craft sank about forty-five feet from the ship, and they became separated.

Groping in the mud at the bottom of the harbor, de la Penne found the torpedo, detached the warhead, and tugged it through the mud to a position beneath the keel of the ship. He quickly set the fuze and then surfaced, panting for breath. He found Bianchi clinging to a buoy, but both men were soon spotted and captured. When they refused to reveal the location of the explosive, they were locked in a cabin in the bowels of the ship—directly above the warhead.

When the blast came, de la Penne and Bianchi were badly shaken up but not seriously injured. And they found the door of the room that could have been their death cell hanging from its hinges. They hurried to an upper deck in time to witness two more powerful explosions in the crowded harbor. Their teammates had sunk another battleship, the *Queen Elizabeth*, and a tanker.

In those few moments, six men had sunk two battleships and a tanker, totalling some eighty thousand tons. They had completely changed the balance of naval power in the Mediterranean, leaving the British without a battleship in that area for the next year. Although the British tried to hide the disaster, the Axis navies soon learned what had happened but failed to capitalize on their advantage.

The Italian swimmers continued their operations until Italy signed an armistice agreement in August 1943. They never repeated the success of the Alexandria raid—partially because they had reduced the number of highly lucrative targets—but they are credited with sinking or damaging ships totalling 150,000 tons in three years.

Even though the two Italian officers responsible for developing this formidable weapon were captives, the British did not learn of their role and the navy brass did not fully grasp the fact that a handful of men, riding torpedolike craft that were barely seaworthy, were capable of wreaking havoc with their navy—until the disaster at Alexandria. Shortly after that attack, Churchill wrote in a letter, "One would have thought we should have been in the lead."

Although at the time of the attack at Alexandria the British were not in the lead, they were already strong contestants in the race. They were developing their own manned torpedoes, called Chariots, and training teams of torpedo riders, equipped with breathing devices based on Lambertsen's invention. In October 1942, they made their first combat swim against a most formidable target, the German battleship *Tirpitz,* then hidden in the inner harbor of Trondheim, far up the Trondheimfjord from the Sea of Norway.

The powerful *Tirpitz* was a threat to all Allied shipping in the Sea of Norway and perhaps out into the Atlantic as well. In January 1942, Churchill ordered his forces to sink the ship, warning that "the whole strategy of the war turns at this point on this ship."

The plan called for two Chariots to be loaded aboard a merchant ship, disguised as one of the small freighters carrying peat from the offshore islands to the Norwegian communities up the fjord. Using false papers this ship, the *Arthur,* would thread its way up the fjord until it was close to the anchorage of the *Tirpitz.* Then the two men assigned as crew of each of the Chariots would dress in their cumbersome diving gear and climb aboard their torpedo craft. Moving underwater, they would approach the battleship and place their explosive warheads under its keel.

To get through the German patrols, the crew of the *Arthur* lowered the two Chariots over the side and towed them beneath the water. And then, just as they were in sight of Trondheim and trying to pick out the outline of the battleship, they hit a large wave, and their propeller cut the tow lines. When a diver went down to see what had happened, he found both lines dangling loose in the water. Their mission thwarted, the men scuttled the *Arthur,* rowed ashore, and made their way overland to Sweden.

The first attempt to sink the *Tirpitz* ended in failure on 31 October 1942. But the British didn't give up.

Three months later, in January 1943, eight two-man Chariots were dispatched for an attack on the ships of the Italian navy berthed in the harbor of Palermo, Sicily. The raid was a spectacular success. The Chariot riders sank a cruiser, three submarine chasers, and two merchant ships.

While the Chariots had proved their worth, the British were also busy developing a much more sophisticated undersea craft, a true minisubmarine called the X-craft. The goal was still the same: sink the *Tirpitz.*

In September 1943, six submarines set off from the secret British naval base at Loch Cairnbawn, in the far north of Scotland. Each had an X-craft in tow. And strapped to each X-craft were two large containers, each containing two tons of explosives. For ten days the subs made their way northward across the rough North Atlantic. This time the *Tirpitz* and two other German warships were anchored in a fjord near the North Cape of Norway, far above the Arctic Circle. On several occasions, tow lines parted and had to be replaced. One of the minisubs was lost at sea on the crossing. Another began leaking and was forced to abandon its explosive charges. The skipper of the parent submarine decided to scuttle the ailing X-craft rather than try to tow it back to Scotland.

Thus, four X-craft survived the ten-day crossing, having traveled more than a thousand miles, most of the time submerged. With fresh crews, who had made the voyage in the relative comfort of the parent submarines, the four craft set off by themselves at about 6:45 on the evening of 20 September. In these far northern latitudes, they would have only a few hours of darkness, with dawn at about 2:00 A.M. Their major target was the *Tirpitz,* but two other powerful German ships, the *Scharnhorst* and the *Lutzow,* were also docked nearby. With luck, the sixteen men manning the four X-craft would have the chance to strike a crippling blow at the German navy.

Two of the craft wriggled through mine fields and antisubmarine nets and actually bumped against the gray hull of the *Tirpitz* as they jettisoned their explosive charges, set to go off in one hour. One of the minisubs, disabled by the collision with the battleship, surfaced, and her crew surrendered. Another X-craft almost got away, but was disabled by machine-gun fire and sank. Two of her crew survived and were captured.

When the explosives laid by the two X-craft went off, the *Tirpitz* had moved slightly. She was seriously damaged, but not sunk. One of the other X-craft entered the harbor but was unable to plant its mines. Another became disabled and was not able to participate in the attack.

The *Tirpitz* never again put to sea on an offensive sweep and was finally put out of action when it was hit by fourteen bombs in a mass attack by four-engined bombers on 3 April 1944.

By the end of the war the British had an array of underwater attackers, including the Chariots, the X-craft, and the swimmers themselves. Hitler became so furious with the depredations of the swimmers and other commandos that he issued a secret order that all captured commandos, including those in uniform, were to be "slaughtered to the last man." The X-craft crew members captured in the attack on the *Tirpitz* were fortunate. Officers aboard the German ship, impressed by their bravery, offered them hot coffee, schnapps, and hammocks. They spent the rest of the war in a prison camp.

In the Far East, the Japanese had developed a small fleet of quite sophisticated little submarines. They were seventy-eight feet long and six feet wide, carried a crew of two, and were powered by diesel engines capable of a top speed of nineteen knots. Five of the subs were carried across the Pacific, each lashed to the deck of a mother submarine, to take part in the attack on Pearl Harbor. But even though several of the little subs, each carrying two torpedoes, managed to get inside the harbor, they inflicted no damage during the attack.

The U.S. Navy took little or no interest in this form of warfare during World War II, even though officers were familiar with the British and Italian efforts and knew of the Japanese minisubs. But in the period of intense experimentation and innovation that followed the war, members of the UDT forces obtained two-man torpedoes from the Italians and X-craft from the British. They were especially interested in the X-craft because, being a true minisubmarine, it provided a good deal of protection for the crew members from the cold and darkness of the sea.

American frogmen became adept at "flying" the X-craft and looked forward to developing a fleet of minisubs of their own. They even managed to develop such a craft.

But navy politics intervened. The submarine force, a much larger and more powerful part of the service bureaucracy, was willing to permit the UDT and its parent, the amphibious force, to operate free-flooding submersibles in which the occupants were surrounded by water. But the submariners insisted that any true submarine belonged to them. The little sub that the UDT men had developed disappeared into the clutches of the submariners, and they never saw it again.

The frogmen faced a dilemma. If they chose to use true submersibles, they would be at the mercy of the submarine force. They would have limited control over the type of craft developed, and they could never be sure the little subs would be available when they needed them. If they chose free-flooding boats, they would have control over the design and operations, but they would face all the problems of operating under the sea with only limited protection from the cold.

The decision was that it was better to be cold and independent. The UDT force decided to focus on developing its own wet submersibles rather than rely on the submarine force to provide it with minisubs.

W. T. ("Tom") Odum, head of the ocean engineering department of the Naval Coastal Systems Center, in Panama City, Florida, has been involved with the development of these little swimmer-propulsion devices since the early 1950s. The first he remembers is a one-man vehicle in which propulsion was provided by the man pedaling a bicyclelike system that turned a small propeller.

Then, in the midfifties, came the Mark 2, built by Aerojet General according to a design from General Electric. From the outside, the Mark 2 looked like a little airplane, with the two-man crew sitting side by side. Inside, it looked very much like a 1956 Ford pickup. Odum says the designers reasoned that the crew members would find the little craft extremely claustrophobic but that they would be more comfortable in familiar surroundings, so they modeled it after the interior of a popular truck.

The Mark 2 was the navy's first effort at a sophisticated swimmer delivery vehicle. It was powered by silver zinc batteries, used a gyroscopic compass, and was equipped both with a hovering system and with thrusters that permitted it to maneuver left, right, up, and down.

Unfortunately, it was, as Odum says, "a hydrodynamic nightmare—it just didn't have any stability." The little craft never got beyond the experimental stage. It was so unstable that it could not even be towed through the water until it had been pulled up onto a large sheet of plywood.

About the same time, the navy also developed the Mark 1 SPU (swimmer propulsion unit) which was powered by silver zinc batteries and designed to drag the swimmer through the water a little faster than he could swim on his own. He controlled the speed with a pistol-grip throttle. The device worked, but the navy decided not to use a one-man vehicle, and the program was killed.

In the midsixties, with the war in Vietnam heating up, work began on the kind of free-flooding SDV now in use in the fleet. Beginning in 1964, the coastal systems center developed the Mark 6 SDV. It was a two-man vehicle, but the front and rear could be separated for the insertion behind the cockpit of a five-foot-long pod that held either electronic equipment or two more swimmers. The Mark 6 was extremely stable and easy to fly, and it was the first SDV with a usable Doppler navigation system.

Next came the Mark 7, a four-man boat modeled after a two-man Italian submersible. The Convair division of General Dynamics built about a dozen of the craft, and the Mark 7 became the first SDV to move beyond the experimental stage and into use by the fleet. The Mark 7 never won any beauty contests. It was an awkward-looking boat, with a square shape, a rounded nose, and a tapered tail. It wasn't very fast or very maneuverable, but it was stable and very dependable. "Just a work horse," Odum says. Two of the early model Mark 7s were used—and lost—in Operation Thunderhead.

The Mark 7 proved to the navy that SDVs could be very valuable because of the way in which they increased the range of the combat swimmer and yet permitted him to remain hidden under the water. But it was also obvious from the experience with the Mark 7 that something better was needed.

Work began on the Mark 8, and the navy quickly decided to build the craft itself at China Lake, a naval research facility in the southern California desert that normally focused on the development of missiles. There, far from the sea, the six-man Mark 8 was put together and then taken to a fresh-water reservoir for testing. The Mark 8 was bigger than the Mark 7, capable of carrying six men rather than four, and its equipment was much more sophisticated, including sonar and an inertial navigation system. The goal was a craft that could operate for six hours at a speed of six knots.

While work was under way on the Mark 8, the navy decided it also needed a separate two-man boat to do reconnaissance and carry weapons. This became the Mark 9.

In the Mark 8—the SEALs call it the bus—the six SEALs sit up-right, with the pilot and navigator in the two front seats and four combat swimmers behind them. In the Mark 9, the two swimmers lie on their bellies, side by side. With two propellers and a flat shape, the Mark 9 is highly maneuverable. Flying the Mark 9, the SEALs say, is fun, like driving a sports car or a fighter plane.

Operating an SDV is not an occupation for anyone with even the slightest tendency toward claustrophobia. Even many SEALs, brave men who don't flinch at jumping from a high-flying plane or engaging in a firefight, don't want anything to do with what seems to them like being locked in a little black coffin deep under the water. Men in an SDV have virtually no room to move about; they are surrounded by cold water, and they are in total darkness except for the dim glow from their instrument panel.

With the Mark 8 and the Mark 9, which came into service in the late 1970s, navy special warfare finally had a unique capability for operating clandestinely under the seas over relatively long distances.

By that time, too, many of the tactics for use of the SDVs had been worked out with the earlier Mark 7s. The SEALs learned how to maneuver into a harbor, slide back the canopy, and photograph the bottom of a ship, even at night. They adapted the Mark 37 torpedo and found that the two-man Mark 9 SDV could carry two of them. The SDV's aiming system was much more primitive than that of a full-scale submarine, but the frogmen found that, lying just below the surface, they could aim accurately enough to hit and disable a ship.

Much of their effort was devoted to mine warfare. With their sonar, they could help to locate mines. And with their ability to move about undetected, they could approach enemy ships and place limpet mines on their hulls. In this procedure, one man causes the SDV to hover while another, linked to the craft by a safety line, swims to the ship and attaches the mine.

One of the key innovators was then-Lt. Comdr. Tom Hawkins, who served as commander of UDT-22, an East Coast team that pioneered the use of SDVs, and later as the first commander of SDV Team 2, when the SEALs and UDT were combined in 1983. Hawkins says they got extremely good at what they did.

He tells about one demonstration attack on a flotilla of destroyers anchored in Chesapeake Bay.

"I went on board and the admiral offered me coffee," he recalls. "I said, 'Admiral, you have seven ships anchored here. At the slack tide, we'll bring an SDV out of that channel over there. These guys are going to come over here and systematically hit that ship, that ship, that ship. . . . They will put an inert limpet mine on each ship. Within several minutes, a flare will come to the surface.' This guy gives me the ho, hum.

"I told him, 'At eight o'clock you're going to see the first flare go off over there. I would like you to alert all your sonar operators, tell everyone manning the gunnels to be aware, try to catch us.' Ho, hum. The first flare went off at eight o'clock. All of a sudden he had seven destroyers lying on the bottom. He became concerned. We're going to go back and write an after-action report on this thing. We're getting graded, and he's getting graded."

Hawkins told the admiral they would be back the next night and told him the order in which the ships would be hit.

"We did the same thing to them again," he says. "They never knew we were there."

In another demonstration, swimmers were parachuted into the Intercoastal Waterway near Eglin Air Force Base in Florida, mated up with an SDV that had been positioned there, and maneuvered in toward the air base. They parachuted with what Hawkins will describe only as "a very classified weapon." Their job was to place it on a dock at Eglin. For many years, UDT and SEAL teams were trained in the handling and use of small nuclear weapons, and it is probably such a device that Hawkins was referring to. The SEALs are no longer trained to use nuclear weapons.

Hawkins waited on the pier for the swimmers to arrive. He was confident he would see them coming. He knew where they were coming from and when. They were using old-style breathing apparatuses that left a trail of bubbles, and Hawkins had a well-trained eye for such telltale signs. But they caught him by surprise when one of the swimmers surfaced and handed the device to a petty officer waiting with Hawkins.

"A lot of times we had trouble selling the SDVs," Hawkins says. "People said they were just toys. But they cease to be toys when you can do something like that. It was an incredible event. Even I was impressed."

SDVs can, of course, be detected, but that is very difficult. They are virtually silent, and their plastic shell makes a poor target for detection devices.

"We've measured the signature of an SDV," Hawkins says. "Of course it has a signature. But I used to tell my men they'll never get you the first time. If you go into a harbor and shoot off one of those torpedoes, how in the name of God are they going to know where it came from? If you do it two times, three times, four times, in the same harbor, they're going to get you."

For a number of years, the navy experienced serious problems with the reliability and maintainability of the Mark 8 and 9 SDVs. The skipper of one team complained that his force was only a paper threat because his craft were laid up for repairs most of the time. But that situation has changed. Lt. Comdr. Doug Lowe worked in SDVs a decade ago and then was ordered back as executive officer of SDV Team Two in the fall of 1990. He was not overjoyed at the assignment.

"In most of our dives, I don't think we had a 50 percent success rate. We were shitty. When people talked about me coming back to SDVs, that was real frustrating for me," Lowe says. But, when he joined the team at Little Creek, he was much impressed by the progress that had been made. Reliability, he found, was more like 90 percent than 50 percent.

The Achilles' heel of the SDV is the problem of mobility—getting it to the war. SDVs can be flown anywhere in the world, but then there is the problem of unloading that strange-looking device at a foreign airfield. Or they can be carried aboard a surface ship and dropped into the sea by a crane. But that has to be done well out of sight of a potentially hostile shore, and there is always the chance that it will be seen. The U.S. Navy has never found enough money to do what the Italians did during World War II: restructure a surface ship so SDVs can be operated through a door below the waterline.

On one occasion, the navy wanted to get a look at a Soviet ship. But the ship was anchored in a Cuban harbor, about eighteen miles upriver from the sea. With fresh batteries, an SDV could probably have made the thirty-six–mile round trip. But it didn't have the range to carry out the mission if it was launched from a surface ship well outside the territorial waters claimed by Cuba. The mission had to be called off.

SDVs can also be lofted by helicopter. One of the early experiments in transporting an SDV in this manner turned out disastrously.

Command Master Chief Herbert H. Haskin, of SDV Team Two, in Little Creek, was one of two SDV operators taking part in the test. He and another SEAL positioned themselves in a boat offshore. The plan was for the helicopter to pick up the SDV, carry it across the base, and deposit it in the water. The two SEALs would then climb aboard, submerge, and fly away.

As the CH-46 helicopter pulled the SDV free from the water of Little Creek Cove, it began to swing. The two SEALs offshore could see the helicopter and its ungainly load moving toward them. Suddenly, just as the helicopter passed over a picnic area at the nineteenth hole of the base golf course, the SDV broke loose, fell across a sidewalk, and broke open like a cantaloupe. Batteries spewed sparks. High-pressure air bottles ricocheted around the area. The two SEALs drove their boat onto the shore and ran to the scene.

"We were over there in five minutes or less," Haskin recalls. "At the picnic tables, the people were still frozen. These people had not moved. Their mouths were open, half-chewed food hanging out of their mouths."

No one was injured, but the SDV was a mess. They found parts as far as two hundred yards away. The lesson learned, Haskin reports wryly, is that "the boat is not dropable."

Through all the experiments with helicopters, airplanes, and surface ships, it was always fairly obvious that the best way to get an SDV to the war was by submarine. That way it could be brought in as surreptitiously and as close to shore as possible.

When the *Grayback* became available in the 1960s, it made an almost perfect match for the SDV. Although the ship still remained a part of the submarine force, it was assigned to work full-time with the frogmen, offering plenty of opportunity for training. But the *Grayback* provided only a limited capability. The original plan had been to adapt another older sub, the *Growler,* as an SDV carrier and assign it to the East Coast, while the *Grayback* remained in the Pacific. But money ran out before the second sub could be modified and put into service in the Atlantic.

Submarines, of course, have only a limited lifetime, and the navy was forced to think about a successor to the *Grayback.* There were no more subs with a big hangar deck that could be modified to transport SDVs. The solution was the development of what is called a dry-deck shelter (DDS). A big metal cylinder, it is designed to be bolted to the upper deck of a submarine and connected to the interior of the sub by a watertight hatch. The DDS is nine feet wide and divided into three sections: a hangar area capable of holding one SDV, a transfer chamber for moving in and out of the sub, and a decompression chamber.

Two submarines designed to carry the original Polaris submarine-launched intercontinental missiles were taken out of the strategic submarine force and converted to carry the dry-deck shelters. They are the USS *John Marshall,* home-ported at Norfolk, near Little Creek, and the USS *Sam Houston,* home-ported at Pearl Harbor. They are big boats—410 feet long and 7,880 tons submerged—capable of carrying a full platoon of SEALs plus a platoon of specially trained sailors who operate the DDS. When they carried missiles, they were known as boomers. Now, the sailors call them slow-attack boats or spook boats.

The only complaint the SEALs have is that the *Marshall* and the *Houston* are not always available. Often they unbolt the DDS and go off to operate as attack boats with the fleet. As a result, the SEALs don't get as much training time as they would like.

Unfortunately, both subs are at the end of their service life. The only choice to replace them seems to be conversion of several fast-attack "long boats" of the Sturgeon class to carry the shelters. But those subs are much smaller—292 feet long and only 4,640 tons displacement. Members of the SDV teams say those boats are not a good answer to their needs. The boats don't have enough room for the SEALs and all their equipment, they can't take the SEALs on a long deployment, and they are difficult to control at the slow speeds required for SDV operations. But modified fast-attack boats may be the best the SEALs will get.

Well before they began using SDVs in regular operations, the UDT and SEAL team members had often worked closely with the submarine force. They were trained to lock out of and lock back into a submerged submarine. On a number of occasions in Vietnam, UDT members carried out difficult beach reconnaissance missions and even fought battles ashore after locking out of subs. They also adapted the method Fulton had worked out for the recovery of surface swimmers—the method the navy promptly forgot. After finishing an operation, swimmers get into their rubber boats with a line between them. Then the sub snags the line with its periscope and carefully tows the boats far enough out to sea so the sub can surface and take the swimmers aboard.

All of their experience in swimming and submarine operations, however, did not prepare the frogmen for the physical demands of working with an SDV. When the navy began thinking about SDV operations of six hours' duration, no one knew whether men were capable of remaining underwater that long, let alone whether they could carry out their assigned tasks.

The first concern, although not the only one, was the loss of heat during long submersion in cold water. A free-swimming SEAL might spend a couple of hours underwater on a mission and during that time he is physically active, generating heat. A man in an SDV, on the other hand, may spend eight or more hours underwater, much of the time sitting or lying passively in his little craft, generating little heat. He is also likely to go deeper and stay longer than the free-swimming SEAL.

Capt. Edward Thalman of the Navy Diving Center at the Naval Medical Center in Bethesda, Maryland, explains that a wet suit of the type worn by sport divers is made of foam neoprene that insulates the swimmer by surrounding his body with little bubbles of gas. If he goes to sixty feet, the gas becomes compressed and he loses heat at about the same rate he would without a wet suit. But the suit makes his skin feel fairly comfortable, and he does not realize his core temperature is dropping, perhaps dangerously. A number of SEALs have done their part for science by diving after having swallowed transistorized thermometers and while wearing rectal thermometers so the doctors could monitor their internal temperature.

The loss of heat can result in death. But long before that point is reached, a swimmer in cold water may lose the ability to carry out his mission. Of particular concern is the loss of heat in the hands. The muscles that provide strength in the hand are in the forearm, with tendons connected to the fingers. But the fingers also have their own little muscles that stabilize the joints, with major muscles at the base of the thumb. If these muscles in the hand become too cold, manual dexterity is lost. It is virtually impossible to tie a knot, use a knife, or operate a zipper.

One partial solution to this problem is to fit the swimmer with something like the gloves worn by skiers, covered with a big, waterproof outer glove that is removed only when there is work to be done. Research is also under way on heated gloves. But heating the diver's entire body poses a much more difficult problem. That would require a large amount of energy, enough to drain an automobile battery every forty minutes.

And it might not help that much because, as a heated garment increased the diver's skin temperature, his body would slack off on its production of heat.

Members of SDV teams spend long hours under the water, as much as a thousand hours a year, the equivalent of six full weeks. And because of this long exposure to cold water, they suffer permanent physical changes. After a while, an SDV operator notices that he gets cold quicker than other people. His fingers quickly turn blue. In effect, his body says, "Oh, oh, here it comes again," and begins to shut down.

Water temperature limits the usefulness of the SDVs. They cannot be used in areas of the world where the water is extremely cold. But in training missions, they have operated in water so cold that, on return from an operation, the men inside had to wait until someone outside chipped away the ice before they could emerge.

As the doctors had a chance to study these men spending such long periods of time underwater, they also discovered other physical changes that had not been apparent in their studies of divers who remain submerged for much shorter periods of time.

On land, gravity pulls blood down into a person's legs. But swimming underwater, a person is in a state of near-weightlessness, much like an astronaut. Without the pull of gravity, more blood finds its way to the chest. In the upper chamber of the heart is a little sensor that detects the amount of blood in the body. The sensor mistakenly interprets the unusual flow of blood to the chest as an indication of an overall increase in blood volume. It releases a hormone that serves as a messenger to the kidneys, ordering them to start dumping fluid.

"Almost as soon as you get in the water, you start urinating," Thalman says. The cold also stimulates the urge to urinate, and the salt water causes dehydration. The result is a serious loss of body fluid and a drop in blood pressure.

In a period of eight hours in the water, a swimmer may lose 17 percent of his blood volume, as much as two quarts. When he tries to do some work, his heart has to work harder to get the blood to his muscles. Instead of 120 beats a minute, it may race at 160 beats to get the same job done.

The danger is that a diver might ride his SDV for several hours, swim up on a hostile shore, stand up, and faint because his blood pressure has dropped so low. Actually, he probably wouldn't pass out, but he would be unable to perform as much physical activity as he would normally be able to do.

A new underwater breathing device now under development will have a full face mask that will permit a diver to drink liquids while under the water. But this is not really a solution, Thalman says, because the added liquid will be quickly dumped by the kidneys. One possible solution is to have the swimmers replace the lost liquid shortly before they go ashore on a mission. Thought has also been given to the use of some form of medication to regulate urine production, but the doctors worry about possible side effects on a person going into a combat situation.

One of the most difficult problems for the experts in medicine and physiology is to overcome the SEALs' deeply ingrained belief that they can do anything. No matter what happens, they believe, they can tough it out. But when they embark on missions that may keep them underwater for many hours and then require them to carry out demanding assignments ashore, the physical limits may prove insurmountable. Dehydration can sap the strength of the toughest SEAL, and cold can even kill him.

Dr. Thomas J. Doubt, of the Hyperbaric Medicine Program Center at the Naval Medical Research Institute in Bethesda, says, "SEALs have a can-do attitude about things. Virtually nothing is perceived as too dangerous, too hard, too difficult. They say, 'You want that done? We'll do it.' I preach to them like you would to a professional football team. I tell them a 5 or 10 percent difference in performance makes a big difference for the elite athlete. And I say that, in three days, I can change anyone's performance noticeably by what I have them eat and do."

Doubt's basic approach is the same as that used by marathon runners: carbohydrate loading in the few days before the race, or combat mission. But SEALs, he says, work so hard preparing for an operation that they don't find time to prepare themselves by eating properly. And when they are confined to a submarine, they tend to overeat with foods that build fat rather than the carbohydrates that can be called upon for energy during a mission.

Haskin, the veteran SDV operator, agrees that performance would be improved if some admiral would order the SEALs to pay as much attention to nutrition as they do to preparing their equipment for an operation. But then he expresses the gut feeling of a SEAL:

"These people say, 'I could improve your performance.' A lot of times the people they are using are divers or non-SEALs. A SEAL is a SEAL. There's nothing like that in the world. If you're a SEAL, it amazes people how you can do things. I agree on what they say about food, and I think it should come out in black and white. But on the other hand, I'm one of the poorest examples. I'll go out on an eight-to twelve-hour op. I won't eat breakfast. I'll drink a Coke or soda, I'll eat a couple of candy bars, and I'll be out there for twelve hours. I'll come back, and I'll be hungry. If there is any decline in my abilities, it doesn't show. Either I'm above their standard, so even if I lose 15 percent I'm still above the standard. Or the figures are off. I relate that to the SEALs. I learned a long time ago, if I set my mind to it, I can do it."

He referred to a visit, the day before, to an explosive-test range on a chilly, overcast spring day. "You saw my hands out there. They were blue. But you saw me cutting fuze, tying knots. My hands were cold to the point I couldn't feel them. It is an attitude in the mind. I have had a lot of shrinks test me. There's a group of people who can do things they shouldn't be able to do. That's what makes us cost-effective."

Largely out of concern over the limitations imposed by cold water, leaders of the navy special warfare community have finally overcome their long reluctance to consider using dry boats. Work is now underway on development of the advanced SEAL delivery system or ASDS, a minisubmarine in which the SEALs would be freed from wearing all their protective gear and would be protected from the cold.

The members of the two SDV teams are probably justified in thinking of themselves as, in a sense, super-SEALs. They not only have their own little boats, but they wear the special Mark 15 mixed-gas under-water breathing apparatus, and they get more training than other SEALs. They also get more money—$300 a month dive pay, compared to $175 for other SEALs, and $110 a month "pro pay," the incentive money given to those who volunteer for jobs that are hard to staff. Other SEALs only receive half as much pro pay.

"I feel the SDV is the future of naval special warfare," Haskin says. "The ability to do things very few people can do is very satisfying to me. I can do what they can do. They can't do what I can do."

In the future, much of the emphasis in the use of SDVs will probably be on mine warfare. Today's SDVs are capable of carrying mines much larger than the limpets carried by a free-swimming diver.

"Mine warfare, that's the future," says Gator Parks, now an engineering technician at the navy's research center in Panama City, Florida. "I'm not opposed to putting things under a ship. Big, big things that will ruin their dock, too. I've always resented the fact that I might have to go under a ship with a little limpet mine that's not going to do anything but piss them off. If I go in there, I want them to know I've been there."

CHAPTER TEN
THE LIEUTENANT (JG) SAYS NO

The SEALs have always been a tiny part of the navy. And the officers in charge of their platoons have almost always been heavily outranked by almost everyone, from admirals on down. To protect their own men, who are very skilled but can also be very vulnerable, low-ranking SEALs have, on a number of occasions, been forced to stand up to senior officers, no matter how many stars on their shoulders, and explain what it is that SEALs do and don't do.

In the spring of 1975, Comdr. R. T. ("Tom") Coulter found himself in just that position. He was a lieutenant junior grade commanding a platoon of SEAL Team One at Subic Bay in the Philippines.

American prestige was at a low point. In the fall of 1974, with impeachment proceedings moving forward on Capitol Hill, President Nixon had resigned, to be succeeded by Gerald Ford. The new president's approval rating plummeted after he granted an unconditional pardon to his predecessor.

On 29 April 1975, the remnants of U.S. forces withdrew ignominiously from the rooftop of the embassy in Saigon. And then, two weeks later, on 12 May 1975, an American-owned ship, the 10,485-ton *Mayaguez*, was seized while sailing through the Sea of Thailand sixty miles off the Cambodian coast. The thirty-nine members of the crew were spirited away in a Cambodian gunboat.

Ford and his two key advisers, secretary of state Henry Kissinger and secretary of defense James Schlesinger, were outraged. The last thing they needed was this kind of affront to the nation's battered self-esteem. But they also saw the incident as an opportunity to demonstrate that the United States was not to be toyed with by pip-squeak Third-World countries.

By chance, the carrier USS *Coral Sea* was in the area, on the way to Australia. Rear Adm. R. T. Coogan, commander of Carrier Task Force 73, was ordered to retrieve the ship and the crew.

Pilots reported spotting the *Mayaguez* anchored near Tang Island, thirty-four miles off the coast. The supposition was that the ship's crew members were being held captive on the island.

A hurried meeting was convened at the U.S. Naval Base at Subic Bay, to begin planning for a rescue operation. There was intense pressure from Washington to do something, and to do it fast.

Coulter recalls that initial meeting: "Our original question was, 'Who says they are on the island in the first place?' Nobody answered that. We said our first course of action should be to go in and do strategic reconnaissance and see that they're on there."

But instead of sending a few SEALs in to size up the situation, the decision was made to send in the marines to retrieve both the ship and the captives. From the Philippines and Okinawa, eleven hundred marines were flown to a base in Thailand about an hour and a half's flying time from the island. The move was made without getting permission from the Thais, and they were furious.

On 14 May, two days after the ship had been seized, eleven big CH-53 helicopters took off from the Thai base at U-Tapao and headed for the scene. Three of the helos lowered their marines to the deck of an American destroyer escort. Their job was to board and search the *Mayaguez*. While the remaining choppers headed for the broad beach at the eastern end of Tang Island, the first group of marines sprayed the *Mayaguez* with tear gas and then climbed aboard. They found hot food on the table in the mess, but the ship had been abandoned by its captors. The ship was recovered relatively undamaged, without a shot fired.

The plan called for the remainder of the marines—about one hundred of them—to sweep across the island, a C-shaped, jungle-covered, six-square-mile scrap of land, searching for the crew members. They were assured that they would meet little, if any, opposition. As the choppers approached the island, it became brutally apparent that that particular bit of intelligence was badly off the mark. They came under intense machine-gun fire. One helicopter crashed on the beach. Another went down just offshore. A third belly flopped into the sea.

The surviving marines found themselves pinned down in a perilously thin defensive perimeter on the beach. Another hundred marines were flown in as reinforcements. But any hope of sweeping the island in search of the captives was abandoned. Instead, the marines had all they could do just to remain on the beach and stay alive.

Before the landing, a softening-up bombardment had been ruled out for fear of harm to the captives. But the rules were changed when the marines' precarious position became apparent. Not only did the marines call in naval gunfire to cover their withdrawal, but a lumbering C-130 cargo plane winged its way over the island and delivered the biggest piece of conventional ordnance in the U.S. inventory, a fifteen-thousand–pound bomb.

Back in Washington, it was reported that one marine had been confirmed killed and that casualties were light. Officers aboard the *Coral Sea* didn't have an accurate toll of the casualties, but they knew the operation had been a disaster. Not only had the marines been forced to withdraw, but they had left without recovering the captives and without retrieving the bodies of their dead comrades or the secret black boxes in the downed helicopters.

An urgent call went out for the SEALs.

Coulter, another officer, and twelve enlisted men loaded their boats and all their gear into two C-2 COD (carrier on-board delivery) planes at Subic and set off to hopscotch across the South China Sea. On the way, they landed on one carrier, refueled, flew on to a second carrier, refueled, and finally arrived on the *Coral Sea.* Coulter told his men they had completed their carrier qualifications that day.

Aboard the *Coral Sea,* Coulter was hurried to Coogan's cabin. He glanced around the room. There were about twenty-five officers there. He was the lowest ranking, by about four pay grades.

Coogan told him what he wanted done. He wanted the SEALs to sail to the island in a boat carrying a white flag and then to retrieve the bodies of the marines and the helicopter crew members, along with the black boxes and the coding devices from the helicopters.

The young SEAL officer was startled. "I told him we wouldn't go. Nope, we're not going on that one. We're not going in unarmed with a white flag after thirty marines just got their ass blown off," Coulter recalls.

Coogan, who already had more problems than he needed, was furious. Coulter was on very thin ice. To refuse to carry out an order is a court-martial offense. Naval officers just don't do that. But Coogan stopped short of issuing a specific order.

The admiral and his staff argued that leaflets would be dropped to assure the Cambodians of the peaceful intentions of the SEALs. Coulter had had a brief chance to talk to marines just back from the beach. They reported there were 125 to 150 paramilitary troops on the island, some of them U.S.-trained and -equipped. They were armed with American M-16 rifles and M-60 machine guns, as well as Soviet or Chinese AK-47 rifles and grenade launchers. Coulter was not confident they would rely on what they read in the leaflets. And he knew some of them couldn't read.

"He didn't order me to go. My option to him was, if he ordered us to do it, I had room on the front of the boat for him to come in with us. I said, 'We have room on the front of the boat for you, Admiral, if you want to wave the flag. But I personally don't think that's a very good idea.' He said, 'Well, no one asked you your opinion.' I said, 'Well, we're . . . not going. We're not going in unarmed. That's not what we do.' "

Coulter proposed instead that he and his SEALs swim in at night, do a strategic reconnaissance of the situation, and recover the bodies and the secret devices from the helicopters. Although the SEAL officer had already put his career in jeopardy, the fact that he proposed a workable alternative to the admiral saved him from further trouble.

While the officers aboard the *Coral Sea* pondered their next move on the island, other events had been moving swiftly. Air strikes had been made against a Cambodian airfield and an industrial target. They were designed to pressure the Cambodian government into releasing the ship's crew members. Actually, the thirty-nine crew members had already been placed aboard a Thai fishing vessel that had been seized previously, and they were soon picked up by an American destroyer.

Back in Washington, the rescue operation was hailed as a demonstration of American power. Defense secretary Schlesinger declared it "an eminently successful operation incorporating the judicious and effective use of American force for purposes that were necessary for the well-being of this society."

Only later was the casualty toll revealed: fifteen killed, three missing and fifty wounded. In addition, a helicopter crash in Thailand killed
twenty-three other men preparing to take part in the rescue effort.

Coulter was not the first SEAL officer to balk at leading his men
into a no-win situation. A precedent had been set a decade before, in
the formative days of the SEALs.

In April 1965, President Johnson sent a brigade of marines and part
of the 82d Airborne Division to the Dominican Republic, a Caribbean
island nation, to halt a civil war pitting leftist rebels against the government. Also involved were army Special Forces and a platoon of SEALs,
who dressed in casual clothes and attempted to blend into the population. Larry Bailey was one of the SEAL officers.

When I was in the Dominican Republic in 1965, we had a SEAL
platoon that was going to be sacrificed along with a Special Forces
A team or two to prove we were macho men, to prove we could
do something really hairy and glorious. There was a radio station in downtown Santo Domingo owned by the leftist rebel group.
The Special Forces group commander decided the radio station
should be taken out by special operations people.

We were going to cross the mouth of the Rio Ozama in rubber boats and seize a sea wall. Then other SEALs would ferry
Special Forces across the river. Then we would go up over that
sea wall and go down the street through a completely hostile area
for a half mile to a mile and then blow up this radio station.

That was really a John Wayne–type event. Had it gone off, it
would have been a testimony to our masculinity and all sorts of
stuff. The simple fact was, there were sixty ships offshore. Any
one could have fired one spotting round and one for effect and
blown that radio station to smithereens. They wanted it to be
nonattributable, for God's sake. My platoon commander [Lt. Jack
Macione] raised bloody hell. He said, 'We're going to get killed
over there, and there's no reason for it.' He was absolutely right.

Fortunately for everyone involved, a deal was made with the rebel
leftists under which they would be permitted to go to Cuba. The mission was cancelled before the SEALs got themselves killed—or a SEAL
officer got himself court-martialed.

When a SEAL officer finds himself in a position where he knows his men will be endangered by trying to carry out an ill-advised operation, a strong sense of SEAL tradition tells him that he has an unwritten contract with his men to make sure they do not get killed or hurt needlessly.

Steve Elson, a retired commander and one of the most outspoken SEALs, puts that philosophy this way: "Rules are fine. But unless it's absolutely imperative to the welfare of this country to follow those rules, you don't get anybody killed. When you get out in the field, you've got to let the guy take charge of his unit. These young people have been preached to: do what the boss says. When it comes to my men, my people, screw the boss. He's not out there. You've got to keep your guys alive. You don't want anybody getting killed."

CHAPTER ELEVEN
THE MARCH OF THE JEDI

When sixty-three Americans were taken hostage at the American embassy in Teheran on 3 November 1979, the United States possessed the most powerful military force in the history of the world. Its nuclear arsenal bristled with weapons of incredible power. Its carrier battle fleets dominated the world's seas. Its army and air force were a match for any other force they might face.

And yet the Pentagon had nothing in its awesome arsenal suited to the task of extracting the hostages safely from Iran. A raggedy band of young men who styled themselves as "students" were able to sneer their hostility at the United States and get away with it, month after month.

While the television anchormen counted off the days of the hostages' captivity, and the political damage suffered by Jimmy Carter's White House mounted, the Joint Chiefs of Staff, acting in great secrecy, set in motion a military operation designed to pluck the hostages from downtown Teheran and whisk them away to safety.

The problem faced by the chiefs was that they had no small, highly trained military force capable of such a feat. To be sure, the army had its antiterrorist Delta Force, but how were they to get in and out of Teheran? The rescue force had to be cobbled together out of bits and pieces from all the services. As the plan evolved, it called for marine helicopters to fly from a carrier in the Arabian Sea deep into Iran to

181

an isolated spot code named Desert One. There they would meet a fleet of C-130 cargo planes carrying the Delta Force soldiers plus their equipment and fuel for the helicopters. From Desert One, the plan was for the soldiers to go on to the outskirts of Teheran by helicopter, hide out during the daylight hours, then sneak into the city, storm the embassy, and escort the hostages to the waiting helicopters and thus on out of the country.

It was a bold, imaginative, and very risky plan. Top Pentagon officials thought they had a chance for success. President Carter agreed and gave the go-ahead in mid-April.

During the night of 24 April 1980, the whole venture came apart in an embarrassing disaster at Desert One. Several of the helicopters, lost in a dust storm, failed to arrive, and the decision was made to abort the mission. Then during refueling, the rotors of one of the helicopters slashed into a tanker plane, causing a fire that killed five men and injured eight others. The survivors clambered into their C-130 transport planes and fled Iran. Pictures of the wreckage were broadcast by the Iranians as vivid evidence of the humiliating failure of the rescue mission.

In the backlash from the disaster at Desert One, Carter lost his bid for a second term to Ronald Reagan. The fifty-two hostages still in captivity were not released until moments after the inauguration of Reagan on 20 January 1981, 444 days after the takeover of the embassy.

It was in this atmosphere of crisis and frustration that the Joint Chiefs determined to create a hostage-rescue force that would be trained and ready to respond instantly in any future emergency. Not only would it have the soldiers of Delta Force, but the air force and army would have specially equipped aircraft on call, ready to move rescue teams in and out of remote parts of the world. The navy would designate ships and submarines to carry the rescue teams. And the navy would create a force specially trained to carry out a rescue effort in a maritime environment.

To form this special navy hostage rescue team, the chief of naval operations singled out thirty-nine-year-old Comdr. Richard Marcinko, gave him direct orders to create the force as rapidly as possible, and armed him with a "pri one"—priority one—that permitted him to take the men and equipment he needed from other commands.

In those early days, the name, even the very existence, of this new unit, was highly classified. But this was the genesis of SEAL Team

Six. To many SEAL officers, Marcinko's new assignment was fraught with dangers. Hurrying to put together a team, he was sure to step on toes and make enemies. Everything Marcinko did would be watched carefully from the highest levels of the navy and the Joint Chiefs. And if SEAL Team Six were ever called upon for an actual hostage rescue, its performance would have to be perfect. There was no margin for error. The death or injury of even a few hostages was simply not acceptable.

To Marcinko, the chance to form and lead Team Six was a marvelous opportunity to show what he could do—and to advance his career. He had become an officer to lead instead of follow, and that is what he intended to do.

A product of a broken home, Marcinko dropped out of high school in New Brunswick, New Jersey, and joined the navy at seventeen. As an enlisted man, he became a second-class radioman, and acquaintances who knew him then recall that he used to boast that he would one day be chief of naval operations. His early career seemed to lead him in that direction. He was selected for officer candidate school and became an ensign. Attending night school and the Navy Postgraduate School, he earned a bachelor's degree in government, and then qualified for a master's degree in political science from Auburn University while attending the air force Air University.

By the time Marcinko was tapped to lead SEAL Team Six, he was one of the best-known officers in the SEAL community. He was the most charismatic, the most flamboyant, and one of the most respected SEAL officers. Men who served with him in Vietnam say they would follow him anywhere. A man who served under him in Team Six recalls how, on their first free-fall jump from a C-130, flying at ten thousand feet, Marcinko, wearing a bright red jump suit, led the way out of the cavernous opening at the back of the plane. Whatever he asked his men to do, he was willing to do—and do it first.

He had a way with people that permitted him to get away with behavior that, as one friend said, "would get me killed." He casually called strangers by racial epithets, and got a smile in return. Rear Adm. George Worthington, who succeeded Marcinko as naval attaché in Cambodia in the mid-1970s, recalls a reception for Gen. Lon Non, brother of Lon Nol, who had been president of the country.

"He [Marcinko] was well loved, if not revered, by the Cambodian officer corps and the troops, too. He had a sort of Lawrence of Arabiaesque leadership quality about him. . . ." Worthington says. "Marcinko had never laid an eye on Lon Non. But he walks up behind him and grabs him with a big bear hug. This guy is a general, the brother of Lon Nol. Marcinko did that to him, and the guy loved it."

But there was another side to Dick Marcinko. By midcareer he could also qualify as the most-hated, most-despised, most-envied SEAL officer. His own attorney, who later represented him in a serious brush with the law, acknowledges that he was regarded by some of the other SEALs as "a boastful braggart."

One high-ranking navy officer was startled, when Marcinko visited him at the Pentagon, to notice a pistol tucked in his sock. Another officer invited Marcinko to present a briefing at the Pentagon and then called the session off because he was so embarrassed by Marcinko's flamboyant profanity.

Marcinko served in Vietnam as a member of SEAL Team Two in 1966, 1967, and 1968, earning Silver and Bronze Star awards and picking up a new nickname. As a child he was known as "Dick." When he was an enlisted man, friends called him "Rick." And in Vietnam, he became known as "Demo Dick," later embellished into "Demo Dick the Assassin" by a magazine writer.

When Marcinko received his marching orders from the CNO, he found that SEAL Team Two, on its own, had foreseen the need for a special new SEAL antiterrorist unit and was already well along in creating such an outfit.

More than two years earlier, in February of 1978, Lt. Norman J. ("Norm") Carley, operations officer of Team Two, had formed what they called Mob Six. Since the team had five platoons, this implied the mobilization of a sixth platoon. Carley and about twenty of the senior enlisted men in the team devoted about half their time to planning for what turned out to be a new kind of SEAL team.

They had a chance to practice some of their theories that same year when a major NATO symposium, called Sealink 78, was held at Annapolis. Terrorism was on the rise. There had been threats, taken very seriously, against top NATO commanders. Carley was tapped to form a platoon from Mob Six and provide waterfront security at Annapolis during the conference.

Whether or not it was due to the presence of the SEALs, the symposium went off without a terrorist attack. Top navy officials were impressed with what they had seen of Mob Six.

In March 1980, Carley was transferred to the West Coast. It was a short tour of duty. Shortly after Desert One, he was called back to the East Coast to become Marcinko's executive officer in SEAL Team Six.

Many of the prospective members of the new team were not even aware of its existence when they were recruited. Lt. Theodore ("Ted") Macklin, one of the original members of the team, recalls how he was flown back from an assignment in the Arabian Sea and reported in to SEAL Team Two, of which he was a member, at Little Creek. Both the commander and the executive officer were overseas. In charge was the operations officer, Comdr. Bill Shepherd, who had put Macklin through his SEAL basic indoctrination and who later became an astronaut.

"I said, 'Bill, why am I here?'" Macklin recalls.

Shepherd pointed to the door leading out to a small physical-training area: "See that door? Go out that door, take a right, cross the parking lot, and don't look back."

"I said, 'What is it?'"

Shepherd told him, "Ted, if I had the opportunity, I'd do it."

"I trusted Bill. I said, 'Okay, Bill.'" Macklin went out the door, turned right, didn't look back, and found himself one of the first members of Team Six.

Marcinko personally visited SEAL units to interview men being considered for membership in the team. In many cases, he was able to pinpoint men he had operated with in Vietnam. A number of the officers were, like Marcinko himself, mustangs who had entered the navy as enlisted men and later earned their commissions.

That early recruiting relied largely on the old-boy network. The SEAL community was small enough that almost everyone knew everyone else, although there was a tendency to feel that you didn't really know another SEAL unless you had operated with him.

Later a more formal method of screening was set up. In 1983, Marcinko brought on board Comdr. Thomas Mountz, a clinical psychologist who has spent his entire career in operational commands.

"As the teams got larger, we were getting people in who were untested in the operational arena," Mountz explains. "We had to develop something to some degree artificial to tell if this person is capable of doing the job. These are people to whom the U.S. government is looking to do *the* hardest mission. It is scary to bring a person in for a mission and not know if he can do it. These guys are absolutely professionals in everything they do. They are the best in the world at any task they take on, be it parachuting, diving, shooting. They do a nasty, nasty job, a job most people don't want to do and are glad they don't have to."

Although not a SEAL himself, Mountz participated in many of their activities, including parachuting. He remained at Team Six for five years and became an unabashed admirer of the SEALs he knew there.

But others in the SEAL community worried about the type of personalities that might be attracted to the team. This is how one veteran SEAL officer who had an opportunity to observe Team Six over a period of years put his concerns:

You get a bunch of people, smart, strong, aggressive, and you require them to kill other people. You are requiring guys to do some really tough things. They are going to go in and find that terrorists are women, terrorists are children, anybody. You're up close. This is very personal. The psychologist looks at whether you can blow a hole in a man two feet away and watch his brains come out the other side of his head—and do it.

You give them this training. I'm talking about concentrating year after year on parachuting, making guns, sniper shooting, scaling mountains, swimming, diving. You give them all this training and require them to kill people, not from a hundred yards away, not from two hundred yards away, not from thirty thousand feet with a bomb, but from three feet away.

Can you imagine that group of people together? All of a sudden in that group of 150 or 200 men, who are so highly trained, all keyed up and required to do such hazardous things, you are going to find some amoral people. They're there because they're smart and aggressive and they have no morals. You have guys who have no morals, will do anything. That's how you get a reputation for being really bad.

But the great majority are really dedicated, straight, hard working people. The reason the amoral man doesn't get away with more is that a lot of people watch him. He is controlled. But you are going to find that kind of person when you have a group of people required to perform what these people are required to perform.

Many SEALs say Marcinko skimmed the cream of the SEAL community, taking the very best from each platoon. But one officer told friends he was startled when Marcinko visited his unit. Although reluctant to lose his top performers, he pulled the personnel files of the very best at each pay grade and had them on the desk when the commander of the new team arrived. Marcinko glanced quickly through the folders, brusquely brushed them aside, and demanded to be taken to the records room. There, the officer later recounted, he went through the files and "uniformly, he pulled out the scum."

Those chosen for service in Team Six certainly considered themselves the *creme de la creme*, the elite of the elite. Among other SEALs, they were regarded with a mixture of resentment and envy. And they quickly picked up a nickname—"the Jedi"—from the Jedi warriors of the motion picture, *Star Wars*.

An officer in another SEAL unit reflects the mixed feelings about the team: "They are nobody, Six. Those guys are a paramilitary fitness club. That place is just a mess."

But then, almost in the same breath, he adds, "SEALs [in the other teams] aren't number one anymore. Those guys go first. They get all the assets and all the training. The rest of you guys are sort of second-string jayvee. Those Six guys have a lot of experience. They do a lot of high-speed stuff. We drive up to Camp A. P. Hill to do a training mission. In their training, their beepers go off, they fly to Germany, and do a full-profile op. That's an op! Those guys come as close to the cutting edge as they can without shooting each other. They have so much money thrown at them, and they're really well trained."

And what would this officer like to do next? Join Team Six.

Even Marcinko's most outspoken detractors are forced to acknowledge his accomplishment in creating this new command with little guidance about what exactly he was expected to do. He had to recruit a hundred men or more, acquire everything from typewriters to exotic weapons, train his men in antiterrorism and hostage rescue—something nobody knew much about at the time—and even find a place to set up shop.

At first, the team made room at Little Creek, the East Coast SEAL headquarters. It was later moved to another naval installation in Virginia.

The new team was formally commissioned on 1 October 1980. On 31 December, Marcinko declared his command mission capable. To create, in three months, a new military unit prepared to carry out an unfamiliar assignment, even with the benefit of the preliminary work done by Mob Six, was a remarkable achievement.

Team Six was not just another SEAL team with a special mission. In many ways, it really was a new kind of SEAL team.

Instead of operating in platoon-sized or smaller units, the members of Team Six are trained to work in much larger units. They practice operating in assault groups—called color teams—of thirty to forty men and, if the hostage rescue situation calls for it, multiple color teams.

They are trained to board a ship at sea or an oil platform, by climbing aboard from the sea or parachuting from the sky. When the cruise ship *Achille Lauro* was hijacked in the Mediterranean Sea near Egypt on 7 October 1985, members of SEAL Team Six hurried to the scene. Their assignment was to board the ship and kill or capture the terrorists who had taken it over. Before they could go into action, the hostages were released. Later, when an Egyptian airliner carrying the terrorists was forced by American fighters to land at an Italian airfield, the SEALs almost got into a shooting scrape with the Italians.

One officer who had watched the earlier formation of the army's Delta Force was in a position to compare the two units. "Inside of a year," he says, "Marcinko had Team Six as good as Delta. I saw them competing. They could crack an airplane. They could do anything Delta could do, at least as well."

Capt. Ronald K. ("Ron") Bell, who had an opportunity to observe Team Six when he served as commodore of Naval Special Warfare Group Two, says, "Marcinko accomplished some very significant things in standing up the team. They are extremely capable. If I were a hostage and had to pick someone to rescue me, I'd pick Six. I would pick Six over Delta, the Germans, the Israelis, or anybody. SAS [British Special Air Service], anybody."

Tom Hawkins, now a retired commander, recalls envying the money available to Team Six. "It gets a significant portion of the special operations budget, and it should," he says. "I can say that, having been in charge of a team always looking for money. I would look at those guys and they never lacked for money. I used to get pissed off about it. But as I got into more senior positions, I saw that it was tax dollars well spent, in my view."

Team Six eventually grew into what the navy calls a major command, headed by a captain, rather than a commander. It also was given a new cover name to distance it from problems that occurred during the Marcinko era. SEALs still tend to refer to it as Six, or simply the Jedi.

The training for members of the team is extremely demanding, involving constant travel. Tom Mountz recalls being asked once how long he had lived in the Norfolk area. He replied, "Five years." His wife broke in to correct him: "No, I've lived here five years. You've lived here one year." He figured he had been on the road 80 percent of the time. Members of the team joke that they work only half a day: twelve hours.

It is not surprising that men who work so hard also play hard. And that, as it turned out, meant trouble.

Because they might have to infiltrate into an area in preparation for a rescue attempt, members of the team dressed casually and wore their hair and beards any way that suited them. They also used first names, regardless of rank. This made sense because no one wants to be addressed as "lieutenant" or "sir" in the midst of a take-down situation.

This combination of casual dress, fraternization among officers and enlisted men, and hard partying soon made the members of Team Six a familiar and recognizable sight on the streets of Virginia Beach, the resort town closest to Little Creek. According to one story, two men wearing beepers were in a bar and introduced themselves to two young ladies. "I'm Doctor Jones from Detroit and this is my friend, Mr. Smith," said one. "He's in insurance." The girls sized them up and responded in unison, "Oh, you're from Six!"

Their op-sec—operational security—left a good deal to be desired.

Members of the team liked to congregate at the Raven, a bar and restaurant on Atlantic Avenue, one of the two main streets paralleling the ocean in Virginia Beach. There they drank, fought, broke glass, and even, on occasion, ate glass. The trick is to grind the glass into dust between your teeth before swallowing it. Members of the team were arrested for everything from public intoxication and fighting to child molestation.

Everyone familiar with the team agrees that most of the trouble was caused by a very small percentage of its members. But they were not brought under control, and a major reason may be Marcinko's own reputation for partying and hard drinking. One officer who served under Marcinko in Team Six says, "The man liked to drink. To be with him, you had to drink—to be in the 'in' crowd. I drink when I want to drink. This went against the grain."

Often, Marcinko conducted interviews with men being considered for the team in a bar. Mountz, who doesn't drink, says Marcinko offered him a beer when he came for an interview at seven A.M. and, when he declined, told him he might not fit in.

"I do have a capacity to drink," Marcinko wrote in a letter to the author. "Especially gin (Bombay). Team members (East Coast) weaned on Rum/Coke at St. Thomas during annual winter training. I polished these skills in attaché training and converted to gin. Gin is powerful but my safest drink—consume more. It demoralizes the opponent drinking mixed drinks or slurring while I casually rant and rave. I do play 'head games.' I use booze as a *tool.*"

Carley, who understood that his job as executive officer of the team was to keep his boss out of trouble, says he never recalls an occasion when Marcinko's drinking interfered with his performance. Often, he says, Marcinko could break down the reserve of the younger sailors by sharing a beer or two with them. But he also says that Marcinko's drinking may have proved a bad example for some members of the team.

The off-duty behavior of team members became so notorious that it came to the attention of top admirals at the nearby Norfolk Naval Base. Officers at the SEALs' headquarters at Little Creek were ordered to clean things up, even if it involved firing Marcinko.

Comdr. Jack Schropp, who was on the staff at Little Creek, found himself in a position where he was responsible for checking out the rumors about the behavior of the Team Six men that came to him from junior officers and enlisted men. He called in an outside investigator, a captain from SURFLANT, the Atlantic fleet surface command.

"When I complained," Schropp says, "I was told to keep quiet because of national security. National security, hah! Marcinko was causing me more trouble than Abu Nidal."

Senior officers were also troubled by a series of accidents during the team's training. One man lost an eye when hit by a rubber bullet. Another was killed during a live-fire exercise when the man behind him stumbled and cranked off a round as they entered a "kill house." A third was severely crippled as a result of a parachute accident. Several other men died. Details of these accidents are shrouded in the secrecy that surrounds all Team Six activities, so it is not possible to determine whether they should have been avoided or whether they were an unavoidable by-product of the dangerous, realistic training done constantly by members of the team. Marcinko says simply, "People died. We worked hard and fast."

When Maynard Weyers, then a captain, took over as commander of Group Two in 1982, he found a black book, a big three-ring binder, filled with information about problems with Team Six. An admiral at SURFLANT told him, "That is one area you've got to clean up."

But the problem was complicated by the fact that Team Six did not really belong to the navy. While it looked to the navy for administrative support, it was under the operational control of the Joint Special Operations Command at Fort Bragg, North Carolina. Part of the command structure set up by the Joint Chiefs to deal with the hostage problem, JSOC was headquartered at an army fort, commanded by an army general, and generally army-oriented. Marcinko thus had two bosses, and his navy bosses felt he tended to play them off against each other.

Weyers won't even use the name of the operational command that Marcinko reported to, but he says, "Of course Dick, with his personality, if he couldn't get the thing he wanted from one guy, he's going to go the other way. That happened a lot."

Spending by SEAL Team Six probably paled in comparison with that of the army's bigger Delta Force, which managed to acquire the fuselage of a large airliner and erect a multistory building for use in hostage-rescue practice. But by the hand-to-mouth standards most SEALs were accustomed to, Team Six did very well for itself. Perhaps too well. As part of its equipment, the team acquired three large Mercedes Benz sedans. The team could drive its Mercedeses onto a special air force plane, fly to a distant country, and hit the ground ready to roll.

But the autos were too nice to sit idle. Team members took to using them as liberty cars on nighttime drinking forays. That went on until the night that one of the cars was involved in an accident.

The result was that Marcinko was subjected to a disciplinary proceeding known as a captain's mast and received a letter of reprimand and an unsatisfactory fitness report. Everyone knew that a commanding officer with such a blot on his record had reached the end of his naval career. Weyers sent an aide to have the fitness report screened by navy lawyers to make sure they hadn't missed anything, that there weren't any loopholes.

A short time later, in July 1983, Marcinko was replaced as commander of the team by Comdr. Robert Gormly, who had also won a Silver Star in Vietnam. Marcinko had had three years in the job but didn't want to leave such an exciting command. Other SEALs felt Marcinko resented being replaced and failed to give Gormly a good turnover. Marcinko describes himself and Gormly as "competitive peers" from Vietnam and adds, "No strain, other than two egomaniacs walking through life. All SEALs have a degree of egomania."

One disgruntled enlisted man who had been a close associate of Marcinko left soon after Gormly's arrival. He later recalled the situation:

"Morale was at an all time low as of that summer. . . . It was awkward down there. . . . Captain Gormly had checked on board. Everything had changed, becoming more of a military organization. . . . There was a lot of turmoil with the transition. And Captain Gormly instituted a lot of military regulations. And rules that were in effect, he just started enforcing them. And it changed the complexion of the unit as well as the capability of the unit."

Others there at the time say morale among most of the SEALs remained good, and they deny that the capability of the unit suffered. But there was no question that there was change and some turmoil.

Marcinko found himself in Washington waiting to begin classes at the National War College. But world events intervened to save him from being put out to academic pasture.

On 23 October 1983, 241 marines and sailors were killed when a truck loaded with TNT exploded at the entrance to their barracks in Beirut, Lebanon. Vice Adm. J. A. ("Ace") Lyons, Jr., was vice chief of naval operations for plans, policy, and operations at the time. Like everyone in the military community, he was shocked at the loss of life. He decided to do something to prevent a repetition of the tragedy.

"Our people had been schooled since World War II that you're going to take the first hit," Lyons says. "Well, the first hit with a terrorist, you ain't going to get a chance to come about."

He proposed the creation of a special team to test security at key naval installations. The goal was not only to find lapses in security but to raise the awareness of the entire navy to the threat of sneak attack by terrorists. He described the plan in a memo to the chief of naval operations:

> I have established the Red Terrorist Cell under the code of OP-06D. This cell will plan terrorist attacks against U.S. naval ships and installations worldwide. They will identify the vulnerabilities of the targets and plan the attacks within the known capabilities, ethnic characteristics of the terrorist factions and the political objectives of the sovereign states involved. In conjunction with the attack scenario, this group will also recommend actions which can be taken which will either inhibit or so complicate any planned terrorist actions that they will not occur.

Lyons looked around for someone to run this special team and he spotted Dick Marcinko, "sitting on his ditty bag," waiting to begin classes.

"It looked like we could take his unique talent and put it to work for the navy," Lyons says.

Lyons and Marcinko had known each other for a number of years and had hit it off together. Lyons had become the younger man's mentor, his "sea daddy." When Marcinko told off superior officers and got away with it, it was because he had a bigger admiral on his side.

"As I've always told people, if you're going to war and you have to have somebody at your side protecting your six, then Dick Marcinko is your man," Lyons says. "Dick Marcinko would go out and do unusual things for the betterment of his men, not for Dick Marcinko's sake, but to get equipment to help his men. Did he always go through channels? No. Did he get the job done? Yes. Did he have people who resented him? Of course. When you break rice bowls, that's what happens. You understand that, but you get on and get the job done."

As an early test of the concept, Lyons and the vice CNO asked the commander of the Charleston Navy Base whether he was satisfied with his security arrangements. He assured them there was no problem. Marcinko and an enlisted man were dispatched to South Carolina to check out the base security.

Dressed in scroungy clothes, unshaven, and with long hair, they drove through the gate at Charleston, breezed past the pass office, and spent the next several days wandering throughout the installation, even penetrating the supposedly most secure nuclear storage areas and going aboard nuclear-powered submarines. During the entire visit, they were never challenged.

To staff the new Red Cell organization, Marcinko leaned heavily on his contacts in the SEAL community, especially on SEAL Team Six. Gormly later insisted that Marcinko had not "raided" his command and that he had cooperated in providing men for the new organization, but the loss of members of Team Six certainly added to the turmoil.

It was obvious to Lyons and Marcinko that Red Cell, whose job was to expose problem areas, would be greeted with less than enthusiasm in many parts of the navy. To help smooth the path, they brought in Bill Hamilton, the same officer who had been charged with setting up the SEAL organization back in 1961. Shortly after that assignment, Hamilton had, as far as many of his navy friends were concerned, simply disappeared. In fact, he had signed on at the Central Intelligence Agency as head of its maritime department.

In late 1979, he had returned to the navy and had held several assignments in the ordnance and operational security areas. Hamilton, by then a captain, was familiar with many of the admirals then in major commands, and he was named head of OP-06D, with Marcinko as his deputy. Marcinko ran the operational side while Hamilton paved the way by explaining the program to his admiral friends and getting their cooperation.

The plan was, over a period of several years, to make mock terrorist attacks on about fifty bases—some 10 percent of the total—at a cost of about $125,000 apiece. The hope was that this would not only improve security at those bases but expose enough areas of weakness to protect the entire navy from terrorist attack.

Advance warning was given of each of these "terrorist" assaults, which would not be the case with a real attack. Those expected to be involved were briefed beforehand and given the opportunity not to take part. Even though this was all playacting, Marcinko himself could be pretty terrifying, and the exercises were frighteningly realistic.

Because of the sensitive nature of what they were doing, Capt. George Vercessi, a navy public affairs officer, was detailed to Red Cell, and he went along for the exercises.

"There were always a lot of rumors because he and his colleagues were coming to do the exercise," Vercessi recalls. "He would say things to shock or get your attention. He'd go into a briefing and say, 'We won't break any skin. We won't draw any blood. No broken teeth. Everything else is mine.' He would tell the women, 'We're not going to pull the skirt over your head and tie your hands behind your back.' He wanted to get attention. He enjoyed twisting tails. I used to tell him, 'Dick, be a little less emphatic. These things get magnified.'"

The exercises often terrorized unindoctrinated participants. Middle-grade petty officers, used to a sedentary office life, were forced to do jumping jacks and push-ups. One security officer was kidnapped from his home and held hostage in a motel room. He later complained in a lawsuit that he had suffered a cracked rib and that his head had been held in the toilet while it was flushed. Often, those taken hostage by the team told Vercessi they began to believe they were victims of real terrorists and that they had been told it was an exercise just to trick them.

The SEALs assigned to Red Cell continued to do all of the things they had done as SEALs: shoot, work with explosives, jump out of airplanes, swim. When they were asked why it was necessary for them to be armed, even though they were involved in training exercises, two

explanations were given. One was that they would soon return to a
SEAL team and that they had to retain all their skills.

Another explanation was that some of the members of the team, and
perhaps Marcinko himself, thought of Red Cell as a new Team Six.
And because it was ready to hand, it, instead of Team Six, might be
called on to deal with a real-world crisis. Lyons insists this was never
his intention or that of other top navy officials. But one of the enlisted
men who had served in Team Six and then in Red Cell gave this
explanation later in a court case: "The concept was to possibly form
another unit similar to SEAL Team Six, doing exciting things during
the last twelve months of my career. . . . All the while we were trying to form a formal OP-06D like SEAL Team Six, having equipment
for each man, having X number of men to respond to whatever happened around the world."

Hamilton says Marcinko never told him that was his goal, but it seemed
very clear to him.

"When Marcinko lost the SEAL Team Six command, he saw this
as another opportunity to build another SEAL Team Six, if you will,
another elite organization. Which was unrealistic on his part. That's
why he recruited all the prime, key guys out of SEAL Team Six to
come up, telling them they were off and running in a new organization that was supersecret and super this and that. He never talked to
me about it. I could feel that was what he was trying to do. That isn't
the way the navy traditionally does things. You don't have an organization sitting in the office of the CNO that's going to be deployed to
fight Arabs in the Persian Gulf. That's contrary to everything."

Apparently the closest that anyone in Red Cell got to a real-world
operation was when Adm. James Watkins, while he was CNO, tapped
Marcinko to accompany him as his bodyguard on a trip to the Persian Gulf area.

While Marcinko was involved with Red Cell, his name came up for
consideration for promotion to captain, and he was selected. This decision
was to have a profound effect on Marcinko's life and on SEAL Team
Six.

A number of officers read that Marcinko had been selected
for promotion and were astounded. One retired officer thought for a
long time and then decided to do something about it. He wrote a long
letter, six or seven pages, and sent it off to President Reagan at the
White House.

"I was concerned about the impact [of the promotion] on the other SEALs," he says. "If I hadn't written, there is no way I could live with myself. I was astounded no one else had done it. All I was after was that he not be promoted. He is not fit to command people."

By the time the letter to the president found its way from the White House down through the navy bureaucracy, the Naval Investigative Service already had an investigation underway. And while the letter dealt with alleged improprieties, not with criminal activity, the investigation focused on possible criminal offenses by members of SEAL Team Six.

The investigation had apparently been triggered by another SEAL who had contacted the office of the inspector general of the navy, directly detailing what he thought were criminal offenses. He says,

When I saw his name on the captains' list, I knew that his record went before the board with a punitive letter of reprimand in it. Active punitive reprimand. I'm sure he got it pulled. I had just seen the stuff they were doing, completely illegally, doing with their eyes wide open, having been warned by me that it was illegal. Marcinko would say 'up yours,' just keep on doing illegal and unethical things. I just made a conscious decision that, if I had anything to do with it, Dick Marcinko should not be a captain.

I wrote a letter to the inspector general of the navy, cited chapter and verse of where some documentation was, of what I was talking about.

Before sending his letter, the officer "dillydallied around for weeks."

"I tried to talk to my conscience. I knew I had deep grudges against Marcinko. I knew it would be unethical to nail him just because he was vulnerable. But I decided, if this is the kind of guy we're going to nominate as captain, that's the wrong cotton-pickin' signal to send to junior officers. He screwed up several junior officers, both those who tried to imitate him and those who tried to play straight and narrow."

Eventually, this officer set the letter aside and made a phone call instead. He was subsequently interviewed three times by an agent of the Naval Investigative Service and provided lengthy statements about his allegations.

Whether because of these statements, or because of information provided by others, by the spring of 1986 the probe of SEAL Team

Six had become a full-fledged investigation of the possible misuse of public funds. It even had its own code name: Iron Eagle.

Heading the investigation was Clifford R. Simmen, one of the investigative service's crack investigators. He had served in Vietnam as an army Ranger and had earned a Bronze Star. He had a good deal of empathy for the SEALs. Agents with specialized knowledge were drafted from the Hawaiian Islands, Camp LeJeune, Norfolk, even the Philippines.

At one point, they hired a truck, backed it up to the door at Team Six headquarters, and carted away the team records. About fifty boxes of them. It was an extraordinary scene: a government agency raiding, in effect, one of the navy's most secret and most vital military units. Gormly watched glumly. He cooperated fully with the agents, but he did not face an easy task in keeping his team operating at top efficiency. The investigators made copies of documents he needed, but they took the originals.

The whole SEAL community was astounded, especially when they considered that the head of the Naval Investigative Service was a SEAL: Cathal ("Irish") Flynn, newly frocked as a rear admiral. Two conspiracy theories evolved. One was that Flynn was using his high office to "get" Marcinko. The other was that, as a new admiral, Flynn wouldn't dare to throw a large percentage of his investigators into a vendetta against a fellow SEAL unless he had been told to do so by top navy officials or perhaps even the White House.

Neither theory holds up. Flynn was acquainted with Marcinko but didn't know him well. He admired what he had heard of Marcinko's combat record in Vietnam. He didn't have any motive to "get" him. And while the investigation may have seemed excessive to many SEALs, it involved, at its peak, only about 20 agents and clerks, fewer than two percent of the agency's force of 1,050 agents. Simmen says he reported regularly to Flynn on the progress of the probe but felt no pressure to push harder or to let up. "He never once tried to influence the investigation," Simmen says.

By May 1986, the agents had compiled a file of documents that suggested possible wrongdoing. But they had found no smoking gun. They decided to call Marcinko in for questioning.

Shortly after eight o'clock on the morning of 15 May 1986, Simmen, Marcinko, and another agent, Mark Fallon, crowded into a tiny interrogation room in the NIS's regional fraud office in Building 200 at the Washington Navy Yard. It was not an unfamiliar situation for Marcinko. He had been through escape and evasion training. He had been taught by the navy how to handle himself with interrogators who could torture or even kill him, not merely ask him questions.

The questioning went on all day and then, with a couple of hours off for dinner, continued until three o'clock the next morning. Marcinko began the session confrontationally but frequently brought humor into the conversation. He never, at any time, gave any visible sign that he was under pressure. But the agents sensed the pressure. They could smell it on him.

At the end of the session, Marcinko typed a twenty-two–page statement. It was loaded with classified information about events in his own career and the activities of SEAL Team Six.

The matter might have ended there. The agents were not sure a case could be made against Marcinko. And some of the allegations had been resolved in his favor.

Many in the SEAL community knew of the letter of reprimand contained in his personnel file. They suspected it had been improperly removed from the file before it went before the promotion board. Weyers, who was responsible for the punitive letter, remained puzzled years later.

"Even with a bad fitness report as a CO, he still got picked out for captain. If the report was taken out of the file, how did it get taken out? You have to have fitness reports covering every period. If you have a day missing, you have to have a letter saying why that day is missing. He still made captain. That is almost impossible to do, but he did it. I'm not sure how."

Marcinko says: "My record went to the 0-6 board [the board responsible for recommending promotion to grade of 0-6, or captain] complete. It was pulled during the board, and some words in the fitreps [fitness reports] were removed by the VCNO, my commanding officer, by proper legal administrative procedures. I only used the *book*."

Lyons recalls that Marcinko appealed to the Board for the Correction of Naval Records and also wrote a formal request to the CNO. Lyons had a lawyer on his staff go over the appeal in great detail and then endorsed it and sent it to the vice CNO, who agreed to pull out the unfavorable report.

"It was done totally above board. No corners were cut. It was done in accordance with set procedures," Lyons says.

During the period when he was under consideration for promotion, it was no secret to Marcinko that many SEAL officers did not think he should become a captain. An incident that occurred at that time demonstrates the lengths Marcinko was willing to go to to protect his chances for promotion, and also demonstrates the extent to which he deserves his reputation as a tough guy.

While at SEAL Team Six, Marcinko injured his leg. "At the time of the injury," he says, "I had one of my corpsmen look at it. I was busy overseas. Upon return, I felt I could manage rather than turn myself in at Portsmouth Hospital. Enough [people in the] USN were pissed off at me and I was afraid they'd use the injury as an excuse to relieve me for 'medical reasons.' I still had lots of work to do."

Finally, seventeen months later, he saw a doctor at Bethesda Naval Hospital, who diagnosed the problem as a broken leg. He told him the navy did not, at the time, have a specialist in sports medicine. He recommended contacting the doctor who tends the Washington Redskins professional football team, but warned that the navy would not pay for the procedure. Marcinko, who always seemed to be short of cash, borrowed the money for the operation from an enlisted man and checked into the hospital.

"I did not want to explain how or why I had been walking around (jumping/diving/shooting) for seventeen months without medical attention," Marcinko says.

While the investigators naturally focused their attention on Marcinko, the founder and former commander of SEAL Team Six and the subject of the original charges, they also spent hundreds of hours analyzing the records they had seized. And as they did so, they became more and more interested in John Mason, a hospital corpsman and weapons expert who had been one of the original Mob Six and a plank owner of SEAL Team Six. A good-looking blond-haired man who was one of the best shooters in the navy, Mason had become a close friend of Marcinko's, despite the disparity in rank.

The team relied on him when it put on secret demonstrations of its skills for top navy and government officials. Once, demonstrating the powerful .50-cal. sniper rifle used by the SEALs, he fired at a metal disk that made a satisfying clang when hit. Unexpectedly the disk broke free of the line from which it was suspended and went whistling through the air over the heads of the dignitaries. Mason, cool under pressure, calmly treated the accident as part of the program and continued smoothly with his lecture.

But there was also a disturbing dark side to Mason's character. On one occasion, when he was sent to represent the navy in a national shooting championship, he scored lower than he had expected. Instead of merely accepting the fact that he had had a bad day, he obtained a blank score card, filled in a better score, forged the judge's name, and replaced the original card. He was caught when the judge happened to notice the scores on Mason's card were not the ones she had recorded.

The investigators began to see what they thought was a similar pattern in the records of SEAL Team Six. They met several times with Mason and he denied any wrongdoing. Then in June 1986, about a month after the marathon session with Marcinko, Simmen and Agent Ralph J. Blincoe went to Mason's home, sat him down and started laying out travel claims they had sorted out of the team's files.

"He was using false receipts he had had printed at print shops on his travel claims to substantiate reimbursements," Simmen says. "That's when we realized this was not a witch-hunt, realized we were getting to the meat of the allegations."

They confronted him with a stack of receipts from Mariner's Rest, supposedly a yacht anchored at Water Street in Washington, D.C. The documents indicated a number of members of the team, including, on at least one occasion, Marcinko, had been reimbursed for lodging after submitting receipts from Mariner's Rest. But the agents had checked carefully. There was no such address or yacht. The receipts had simply been ordered from a printing house. The agents concluded that the team members stayed with friends or at cheaper hotels and were then reimbursed for their lodging at the higher rate.

Most embarrassing for Mason were the documents showing that he had submitted false receipts for travel and schooling totalling several thousand dollars and then used the funds to buy a going-away gift for Marcinko when he left SEAL Team Six. First, he bought a Smith & Wesson Model 56 .357mm pistol, with ivory handles made from the heart of the elephant's tusk. Then he had Marcinko's image scrimshawed into the ivory. Finally, he ordered a custom-made walnut case for the weapon. Simmen, who saw the gun when the government seized it, termed it "beautiful."

Mason also purchased two hundred bronze belt buckles, and two sterling silver buckles for Marcinko and one other team leader. The one hundred serialized buckles for the original plank owners each had Marcinko's signature engraved on the back. Each buckle carried the

SEAL insignia and the Roman numeral *VI* embossed on the front. The investigators were fascinated by the thought of members of one of the navy's most secret units identifying themselves with fancy belt buckles. They were also intrigued by the fact that a collection had been taken up for the buckles and the gift for Marcinko. They never did find out where that money went.

As Mason was confronted with one document after another, he gradually provided details of the scheme in which he had been involved. Even as he confirmed the agents' suspicions, he seemed to be trying to protect Marcinko. By the end of the session, Mason had signed a detailed confession. "John Mason was the key to the kingdom," Simmen says.

Mason was indicted on thirty-seven counts alleging he had obtained some $15,000 by use of false travel claims. He pleaded guilty to four counts and agreed to cooperate with the government investigation and repay more than $11,000. He received a five-year suspended sentence.

The false travel claims and other hanky-panky involving SEAL Team Six paled in comparison to another scheme the investigators stumbled across involving Mason and Marcinko. As outlined in court papers, the two SEALs made a deal with a Phoenix, Arizona, grenade maker to provide the seed money to set themselves up in business after they left the navy.

This is the way the scheme was described: Marcinko, Mason, and a former SEAL created a company known as RAMCO. Then Marcinko and Mason arranged for the navy to buy forty-three hundred grenades from Accuracy Systems of Phoenix for use by SEAL Team Six for $310,500. Then Charles Byers, the owner of Accuracy Systems, allegedly kicked back more than $100,000 to RAMCO.

Byers is a brilliant inventor, whose catalog offered for sale a dazzling variety of low-lethality antiterrorist munitions. They are designed for use in a hostage situation, where the purpose is to shock and disorient the terrorists, but not to cause permanent injury to the hostages. Among the items in the catalog are these:

• Thunder-Flash Stun Grenade. "A non-fragmenting submunition container that explodes with a deafening blast and dazzling flash to temporarily blind and stun terrorists."
• Sting Ball Stun Grenade. "Blasts out a large number of marble-sized soft rubber sting balls which are designed to further disorient the terrorists and disperse rioting mobs."

• Combo Sting Ball Grenade. "In addition to the rubber sting balls, the M-452C Sting Grenade is filled with CS tear gas."

• Star Flash Stun Grenade. "This highly effective munition not only provides the blast and flash of a regular stun grenade, but also explodes in a terrifying shower of white hot sparklets to insure thorough disorientation of the target suspects."

• Multi-Flash Grenade. "The difference between this grenade and the above listed stun grenades is that the Multi-Flash Grenade ejects seven smaller sub munitions that are fuzed to explode over a period of one to two seconds. Each individual blast is less than a stun grenade but it provides a significantly enhanced period of disorientation."

• Multi-Star Flash Grenade. The seven sub munitions of the M-470 are loaded with a special explosive "for the occasional situation that requires a much more powerful stun grenade. It contains over four times the explosive power of the standard stun grenade. Aircraft hangars or other large rooms are typical applications."

• Magnum Star Flash Grenade. "The M-471 is truly awesome, producing the increased blast of the M-470 and up to a 50-meter shower of very intimidating white hot sparks."

The grenades come twenty-four to the case, with prices ranging from $840 to $1,080 a case.

The item that particularly attracted the attention of Marcinko and Mason was an all-plastic supersafe grenade that was not yet in production. Byers had designed it for a variety of purposes: as a burn or burst tear-gas grenade, or as a smoke, concussion, or fragmentation grenade. One of its special features was that it could be cocked and then uncocked if the user decided not to throw it.

Mason arranged for friends at SEAL Team Six to sign a document indicating the team needed the grenades. When Gormly heard what had happened, he was not amused. He figured he might be interested in testing fifty to seventy-five of the grenades, but forty-three hundred seemed like an awful lot of them. When Marcinko called to try to get his approval for the purchase, they ended up shouting at each other.

"I think he was a little angry, and I was, too, from being blindsided by this whole thing," Gormly later testified.

Officials in Washington, under pressure to prove they could acquire munitions and other equipment quickly when it was needed by the various antiterrorist units, approved the deal. RAMCO received more than $100,000 from Byers. Mason, nearing the end of his navy career, moved to Phoenix and set up the company. By the time the others involved became aware of what was happening, he had gone through all the money, spending it on fancy cars and lavish office furnishings.

Marcinko and Byers were indicted for conspiracy, even though investigators could not establish that they had ever met. On 20 October 1989, Byers was found guilty of one count of conspiracy and one count of conflict of interest. Marcinko was acquitted on one count of making a false statement. The jury failed to reach an agreement on two other counts, including conspiracy.

Marcinko was tried again in January 1990. This time, he was convicted of conspiracy, bribery, conflict of interest, and making false claims against the government. He was acquitted on another count of conflict of interest. Marcinko did not testify in his own behalf in either trial. His attorney, Yale Goldberg, advised him that, if he testified and the jury didn't believe him, he could be denied his pension on the grounds that he had made a false statement under oath.

Whether the outcome of the trial might have been different if the jury had been exposed to Marcinko's strong personality remains an unanswered question. Still, Goldberg insists, after two trials, Marcinko came "within a pimple" of winning the case.

In a statement to the court, Assistant U.S. Attorney John Klein urged a stiff sentence. Marcinko, he said, had enjoyed the privileges of a navy commander, "but he did not fulfill the responsibilities which accompany that respected office. Rather, he sold his office for personal gain. He participated in a scheme to loot the U.S. Treasury of over $100,000 in order to establish a business venture for himself following his naval retirement. He was motivated by greed and greed alone."

On 9 March 1990, Marcinko was sentenced to twenty-one months in prison and fined $10,000. He began serving his sentence at the federal penitentiary at Petersburg, Virginia, on 16 April 1990 and was released the following spring. Byers was sentenced to twenty-one months in prison and to pay restitution of $50,000.

Three years earlier, Marcinko's promotion to the rank of captain had been reviewed by the secretary of the navy, and the decision was reversed. By that time, Admiral Lyons, Marcinko's "sea daddy," had been relieved of his command in a policy dispute and had retired from the navy.

Lyons, who continues to believe that Marcinko was set up, says, "I'm sure there were people who didn't agree with the vice chief's decision who were later on in a position to do something about that. You wonder at times who the real enemy is."

In the end, Marcinko didn't win promotion, didn't get the money that was supposedly the object of the grenade scheme, and lost his freedom. The government also kept the pistol with his likeness scrimshawed on the handle.

Although Team Six has had a succession of highly regarded commanders in recent years, and its name has been changed, members are still troubled by the damage done to the unit's reputation during the Marcinko years.

The positive legacy he left to the navy was the special hostage-rescue team he created in such a remarkably short period of time. One former member of SEAL Team Six who often found himself at odds with Marcinko credits him with spurring a significant improvement in the entire SEAL organization, with more money and an expanded force. "It took men like him to put us where we are today," he says.

CHAPTER TWELVE
A TINY LITTLE ISLAND

When you go to war in a hurry, you can't think of everything. And what you don't think of can get you killed. Lt. Johnny Koenig was leading a unit from SEAL Team Six as they crept through the early morning darkness on the tiny Caribbean island of Grenada. It was 25 October 1983, and their task was to seize Government House and protect Governor-general Paul Scoon as U.S. forces launched a hastily arranged invasion.

Suddenly, the stillness was pierced by the *beep . . . beep . . . beep* of Koenig's wristwatch alarm. It was 6:15 A.M., the time he normally arose, and he had forgotten to turn off his alarm in the haste to prepare for the operation.

Moments later, the SEALs heard the sound of bullets whistling over their heads. The normal reaction would be to shoot back. But Koenig remembered his training. Perhaps this was reconnaissance by fire. The SEALs remained silent, and the shooting stopped. Under the original plan, the SEALs would have carried out their assignment well before the invasion. But due to a series of mishaps, the schedule had slipped badly. By the time they approached the mansion, it was obvious to everyone that a full-scale military operation was underway.

The assignment to protect the governor was one of four given to the SEALs during the Grenada operation.

President Reagan had ordered American forces to seize the island after a leftist coup attempt led to the execution of the island's prime minister. The turmoil seemed to threaten the lives, or at least the freedom, of hundreds of American medical students attending classes on the island. The safety of the students was a high priority at the White House. No one had forgotten the political damage President Jimmy Carter had suffered because of the long Iranian hostage crisis. But the administration had other motives as well. The United States had watched with apprehension the construction of a long runway, long enough to handle high-performance jets and bombers. This was an opportunity to remove the potential threat of a strategically located Soviet air base in the Caribbean. It was also an opportunity to send a message of the United States' willingness to use force to advance its interests.

For SEAL Team Six, Grenada was the first opportunity to show what it could do. It was also a test of the Joint Special Operations Command, to which Team Six belonged, and of how well the top commanders could use these highly trained, antiterrorist, hostage-rescue forces.

In addition to the seizure of Government House, members of SEAL Team Six were also assigned two other tasks. One was to place beacons at the Point Salines airfield, on the southwestern tip of the island, to guide troop-carrying air force transport planes. The other was to disable a large radio transmitter at Beausejour on the island's eastern shore.

SEAL Team Four, a conventional team, was given a basic old-fashioned UDT mission: to scout beaches on the northeastern coast in advance of a marine landing.

Of the four assignments, the protection of Scoon most closely fit the antiterrorist, hostage-rescue specialty of SEAL Team Six. That was why the team had been created, blessed with money and equipment, and why it had trained so intensively. This was also the most politically sensitive assignment. Grenada was a member of the British Commonwealth, and Scoon, as the Queen's representative, was the sole remaining symbol of legitimate government. The United States wanted him in a position to reestablish a government. It also needed his blessing for the invasion although, under the circumstances, that might be a while in coming.

Koenig and his men successfully entered Government House and found Scoon, his wife, and nine staff members safe and hiding in the basement. But they almost immediately found themselves in danger. Outside were several armored personnel carriers which significantly outgunned them.

In the midst of a war, there is a tendency to think that everything suddenly stops working. Actually, many things continue to work including, in this case, the telephones. Lt. Bill Davis calmly picked up the phone, called the airfield where American forces were already in control, and asked for gunship protection to hold the APCs at bay. This incident is probably the basis for one of the most persistent myths of the Grenada invasion: that an officer, frustrated by the failure of communications, had used his credit card to make a call back to the States to request assistance.

A short time after Davis had determined that the phones still worked, the phone rang and someone asked for Scoon. The SEALs heard the governor-general answer questions about the situation in the house. He assured the caller there were many Americans with big guns. Actually, there were a few Americans with little guns. But the caller apparently chose to believe the exaggerated report of the party holding the mansion. The personnel carriers patrolled past the gate but came no closer.

By the time the sun was up, Government House had become a little backwater of the war. While the governor-general and the SEALs were still potentially threatened, the area around the house was relatively calm. That was not the case at Fort Frederick, headquarters of the local defense force, below the hill on which the house stood. Koenig and John Mason, the corpsman who was later to be at the center of the illegal activities in Team Six, climbed a hill behind the house to watch as helicopters came under furious antiaircraft fire from the fort. Looking through the powerful telescope of a sniper rifle, they had a ringside seat.

But as they watched the scene in fascination, Mason noticed a man in a clearing down below looking back up at them with a telescope and then disappearing into the jungle. It seemed just a curious coincidence until an RPG (rocket-propelled grenade) was fired from the point where the man had entered the jungle. The round ricocheted off the peak of the roof of Government House and tumbled through the air just above the heads of the two men. If the man's aim had been a fraction of an inch higher, their sightseeing would have cost them their lives. Sitting out on the hillside to watch the show down below was a dumb thing to have done.

The small contingent of SEALs was able to hold Government House and protect Scoon, but they weren't strong enough to fight their way out of the house and down the hill to the American lines. It was not until the following morning that a marine company made its way to the mansion, bringing sufficient force that Scoon and the SEALs could leave. The admiral acting as the on-scene commander later complained that he had to delay the war until he had rescued the SEALs.

Politically, the SEALs' effort had been successful. Scoon agreed to sign a letter, back-dated to 24 October, requesting help from the United States and a group of Caribbean nations.

At about the same time that the SEALs set out to take Government House, another group from SEAL Team Six, headed by Lt. Donald K. ["Kim"] Erskine, was moving into position at the large radio transmitter at Beausejour. Their task was to seize the transmitter to prevent its use. But they were not to destroy it. The Americans wanted to use it for their own broadcasts. This was not a mission that required the special training or equipment of SEAL Team Six. And it was not a mission that was essential to the success of the occupation of the island. The Beausejour transmitter had been built with Soviet assistance for long-distance transmission to allow the island's leftist government to be heard throughout the Caribbean. Broadcasts from a smaller transmitter, at another location, could be heard in Grenada itself, and the Grenadan forces continued to use it and a mobile transmitter for hours after the invasion began.

Erskine and his men soon found themselves in a furious gun battle with superior Grenadan forces backed up by armored personnel carriers. They did what every SEAL does naturally when facing overwhelming force: they fought their way to the sea. Erskine was hit several times and knocked down, but continued to lead his men despite a severe wound to his elbow. After hiding out near the shore, the SEALs slipped into the ocean and swam for several hours, far out to sea, until they were finally picked up by a destroyer, the USS *Caron*. It was an episode reminiscent of Thornton's rescue of Tom Norris after he had been wounded in Vietnam.

One writer, trying to pierce the secrecy surrounding the operation, concluded that none of the SEALs at Beausejour had been seriously wounded. Otherwise, he reasoned, they could not have made the long swim to the *Caron*. Actually, Erskine's wound was so severe he almost lost his arm. He eventually recovered and continued his navy career. A fellow SEAL who thinks he is doing well in the weight room when he can press 200 pounds, says of Erskine, "He used to be able to press 420 pounds. Now he can only do 380."

Because of the secrecy that still surrounds SEAL Team Six's involvement in Grenada and the fact that Erskine immediately entered a lengthy period of hospitalization, his feat was almost forgotten until some of his men proposed him for a medal. He later received the Silver Star in a citation that does not mention Grenada or the Beausejour transmitter by name. But it gives a vivid account of the action:

> During early morning hours, Lt. Erskine successfully secured a target within an environment of dense enemy concentration. Determined to hold his position, he twice engaged the enemy and eliminated their combat effectiveness, taking 10 wounded prisoners of war without casualty to his assault element. Administering to the enemy wounded, Lt. Erskine again established a defensive perimeter. Engaged a third time by a numerically superior force, his position came under heavy automatic weapons, RPG-7, and 20mm cannon fire. With complete disregard for his personal safety, Lt. Erskine directed fire and maneuver tactics which allowed his force to take up new positions. Although painfully wounded himself and closely pursued by a large enemy force, he courageously directed his men in evasion and escape maneuvers which resulted in the safe extraction of his entire force.

After the SEALs had been driven off, planes from the USS *Independence* and gunners aboard the *Caron* attempted, unsuccessfully, to topple the tower.

According to the original plan, the SEALs and the other special operations forces would have been in and out of the island, their very involvement a closely guarded secret, by the time anyone outside Grenada knew the operation was underway. But word about the involvement of the special operations forces soon began to leak out because of an operation involving SEAL Team Six in which four men were lost at sea.

This incident occurred on the night of 23 October, a day and a half before the invasion, which included the assaults by the other two units from SEAL Team Six. The plan was for a mixed group of a dozen SEALs and four air force combat control team members to parachute into the sea off the south coast of the island, join up with small boats launched from a nearby destroyer, and then go ashore to plant radio beacons near the airfield to guide transport planes carrying army Rangers in the first wave of the invasion.

Although the drop was to have been made at dusk, it was after dark when the men stepped out into the night six hundred feet above the water. The darkness made it more difficult to land safely in the water and to find the boats and each other.

The jump was also made in weather conditions that were marginal at best. A wind of more than twenty knots was whipping the ocean to at least sea state five on the Beaufort scale. Sailors call this a fresh breeze, creating moderate waves, with many whitecaps and some spray.

When the jumpers gathered and climbed into their boat, they found that four men were missing. Exactly what happened to them will never be known. But there are two plausible theories.

One is that the men were so heavily burdened with weapons, ammunition, and other gear—adding up to perhaps four hundred pounds—that their life jackets did not provide enough buoyancy to keep them afloat, or to bring them back to the surface quickly enough after they had plunged into the rough seas. SEALs are trained not to release their parachutes until they have reached the water. For a parachutist to judge the distance from the water in the daytime is difficult; at night, it is virtually impossible. But with the wind blowing so hard, the SEALs at Grenada had a powerful incentive to shed their chutes just before hitting the water, to avoid being dragged. If they released too early, they would have plunged deep into the stormy sea and perhaps have been injured as well.

The other theory is that the jumpers were unable to get rid of their chutes after hitting the water, became tangled in the shroud lines, and drowned.

"Letting them jump out of an aircraft . . . when they could have flown to an island and walked aboard ship was unconscionable to me," says Adm. Ace Lyons, who had commanded naval forces in both the Atlantic and Pacific. "Nobody is ever held accountable."

But many SEALs, who agree that the condition of the wind and waves would have ruled out a jump in training, emphasize that, with the can-do spirit drilled into the SEALs, it is unrealistic to think they would refuse to jump. It would be almost like members of a championship football team refusing to play in the Super Bowl because of bad weather. For the members of SEAL Team Six, especially, Grenada was the Super Bowl, the chance to prove themselves after nearly three years of hard training.

Four SEALs lost their lives that night: Machinist Mate First Class Kenneth Butcher, Quartermaster First Class Kevin Lundberg, Hull Technician First Class Stephen Morris, and Senior Chief Engineman Robert Schamberger.

The surviving men headed toward shore in a Boston whaler from the USS *Clifton Sprague*. But the engine flooded out, and the men were unable to make it to shore before dawn. They called off the operation for fear that they would be discovered, thus alerting the Cuban defenders on the island to the impending invasion.

The special operations commander recommended delaying the entire operation a day, and the same attempt to infiltrate SEALs and air force technicians into the area of the airfield was attempted the next night, 24 October. Again the boat's motor flooded out and the men failed to make it to shore.

By this time, the mission of the SEALs and the other special operations forces had been dangerously compromised. These small, lightly armed units should have time to get in, do their work, and get away or go into hiding before the shooting starts. But in Grenada, time simply ran out.

Early on the morning of 25 October, C-130 transport planes carrying six hundred Rangers streamed over the airfield at five hundred feet without the help of the beacons the SEALs had hoped to place in position. They found the airport without the beacons, but it was an hour and a half before all the soldiers were on the ground. During the drop they came under heavy, but inaccurate, fire from Grenadan forces. But casualties were miraculously light. Not a single soldier was killed by enemy action, although two died in parachute accidents.

Whether it was necessary for the SEALs to parachute into the sea is still a matter of debate. One argument is that members of SEAL Team Four were available nearby at Puerto Rico and could have boarded a ship there, sailed close to Grenada, and then taken a small boat to shore without jumping out of an airplane—and that they would have been called upon if SEAL Team Six had not been so eager to show off its skills in a real war.

Others argue that the SEALs available in Puerto Rico could have been taken to Grenada by submarine and slipped ashore. But Adm. Chuck LeMoyne, one of three SEALs to reach the rank of admiral, says that would not have been practical because members of that team had not practiced leaving a submarine under water.

"Submarine skill is a very complex operation," he says. "It is akin to flight operations under water. It takes an awful lot of coordination and skill by both the sub crew and on our part. We need to work together, to rehearse. It is damn difficult, dauntingly difficult."

Many of the arguments about the Grenada operation hinge on the haste with which it was carried out. The beach survey conducted by SEAL Team Four at the northern end of the island dramatizes the come-as-you-are nature of the whole operation.

The team members were on a routine transit to the Mediterranean when the marine amphibious force with which they were traveling was ordered to change course, land on the tiny island of Grenada, and seize the Pearls airfield. For the SEALs, it was a straightforward assignment of the type that SEALs and their predecessors in the UDT had been doing for forty years. In fact, this call to action came only a few months after the navy had decided to convert its eight UDT teams into SEAL teams.

Adm. Irish Flynn, who was the leading advocate of the change, explains the reasoning: "The distinction between SEALs and UDTs had started to blur, and there was an overlap in capabilities. The amphibious force needed a force that could do both SEAL and UDT things, but there wasn't enough room on the ships for both. We saw that the UDT and SEAL portions of a mission tended to be sequential rather than concurrent. We saw that the same guys could do both things, provided we broke down the doctrinal barriers between them. We cross trained them. And then we thought, the hell with it, let's just call them all SEALs. That's what we did."

Grenada was the first test of this concept, and it worked out well. While members of Team Six, at the southern end of the island, carried out the type of commando operation in which SEALs, and especially the new Team Six, specialize, members of Team Four performed the traditional UDT mission.

Which is not to say they had an easy time. They were fifteen miles at sea when they left the USS *Fort Snelling* at about ten o'clock on the night of 24 October, and they had a long, rough ride to the beach.

Silently creeping ashore, they were able to see that the airfield was only lightly defended. But they also could see that the condition of the shoreline, with the wind and high surf, would make an amphibious landing extremely hazardous. Early in the morning, they flashed back the message "Walking track shoes," which meant only tracked landing craft could make it ashore and they would find it tough going.

Because of the warning from the SEALs, the marine commanders decided to make the assault by helicopter, rather than to make a combined helicopter-amphibious landing. The marines quickly captured both the airfield and the nearby town of Grenville. At the airfield, there was minor opposition but no casualties. At Grenville, the Americans were warmly welcomed by the citizens.

Within a few days, the U.S. forces succeeded in subduing the resistance of the Cubans and the Grenadan defense forces, locating the students, and arranging to fly them off the island. The Reagan administration, which had prevented news coverage in the critical early hours of the operation by barring reporters and photographers and preventing those who did manage to reach the island on their own from transmitting their reports, declared the operation a victory.

But soon, disquieting reports began to emerge. The public learned of the deaths of the four SEALs. Then it learned of confused communications, the loss of helicopters, and the misuse of army Special Forces. This victory-turned-sour was to have a profound effect on the Pentagon's special operations forces, especially the SEALs.

Brig. Gen. Richard A. Scholtes, commander of the Joint Special Operations Command, met with members of the Senate Armed Services Committee in a closed session. His testimony was so highly classified that it is still unavailable. But it soon became known that his account of the failure on the part of senior commanders to understand the role of the SEALs and the other special operations forces and to use them properly, came as a sobering shock to the senators who heard him.

Sam Nunn, the Democratic senator from Georgia who later became chairman of the committee, and Senator William Cohen, the Republican from Maine, took the lead in urging the creation of a new overall Special Operations Command that would include all of the special operations forces, unlike the existing Joint Special Operations Command, which included only the highly specialized units such as the army's Delta Force and the navy's SEAL Team Six.

It was obvious to the SEALs and to the navy generally that the SEALs would become a small part of an army-dominated command structure— a tiny cog in the big green machine—and they set out to fight the change.

They had some good arguments. Unlike army and air force special operations forces, which often operate independently of major army and air force units, the SEALs have a vital role to play in day-to-day fleet operations. They are essential to the amphibious force in preparation for landings on hostile shores. They can attack enemy ships in ports and other areas where surface ships, and even submarines, can't penetrate. And during the period after the Vietnam War, when many in the navy were wondering if there was still a role for SEALs, a few farsighted SEAL officers had worked hard to find ways in which they could be valuable to the fleet.

By the early 1980s, the navy had carved out a major role for itself in a war with the Soviet Union. Instead of merely protecting convoys carrying army equipment to Europe, the navy planned to take the war to the Soviets with its carriers and submarines. Part of the strategy involved disrupting Soviet operations by hitting unexpectedly on the periphery of their empire.

"The SEALs were not major actors, but we kept getting into the room, into the plans, in order to show we could do useful things in these strikes at the periphery of the Soviet Union," Flynn says. "We worked and worked and worked that, attacking the Soviets at vulnerable points, outposts. The question was, how do you take those down with the least amount of force? How do you run an economy-of-force operation while you keep the fleet out where they can come around and clobber the Soviets where it hurts them? The SEALs account for a lot of that."

The SEALs were also finding other ways to make themselves useful to the fleet. Capt. Dave Schaible, one of the early leaders of SEALs in Vietnam, called a series of long-range planning sessions in which the SEALs thought of ways to tie themselves to the fleet. The SEALs already had their traditional role with the amphibious fleet, but they found ways to make themselves useful to the carrier fleet as well.

In exercises, they went ashore and worked their way to within eyesight of a target to be hit by carrier aircraft and demonstrated that they could provide instantaneous battle-damage assessment. Within moments after an air strike, the SEALs could tell the strike force commander by radio whether he had to send in more bombers or whether he could shift his forces to hit another target. The SEALs also showed how they could get close enough to a target to mark it with a laser beam to guide the bombers, increasing the odds that the target would be destroyed on the first strike.

The result of all this effort was that, when the question arose whether to include the SEALs in the Special Operations Command or to let them remain in the navy, the SEALs had truly made themselves an indispensable part of the fleet. Top navy officials also worried that, if one vital component of the service could be taken away, what would be next to go?

The SEALs, who presumably were most strongly motivated to keep themselves out of a joint command, were given the responsibility for spearheading the issue on Capitol Hill. But they did not do a very good job of making their case.

Bill Cowan, the marine who had worked with the SEALs in Vietnam, was a member of the staff of Republican Senator Warren Rudman of New Hampshire when the issue came up. He thought the SEALs should become a part of the new joint command and warned the secretary of the navy, "If we go to war and the SEALs don't end up playing, it's going to be their fault." But he also understood why the SEALs and the navy resisted the change, and he was amazed they didn't make a better case. "They had a good argument if they had presented it," he says. "But they didn't have a plan, didn't know how to talk to the folks on the Hill."

The result was that, as a direct outgrowth of the brief operation in Grenada, the SEALs did become part of the Special Operations Command. The arrangement was, and remains, an uncomfortable one for the SEALs. Often they feel themselves submerged in a sea of army green. But they soon realized that the change was not all bad. Gen. James J. Lindsay, the soldier who became the first commander of USSOC, was a veteran Green Beret. He had a feel for what the SEALs could do, and he gave them his strong support, in men, money, and equipment.

By the mideighties, the money was beginning to flow. Capt. Maynard Weyers recalls a session with a top aide to the secretary of the navy in about 1986. Funds available for research were abruptly increased from about $6 million a year to $23 million.

"In the old days, we were really sucking hind tit," Weyers says. "Since that time, it has been a new world as far as money is concerned."

The number of SEAL platoons was rapidly expanded. At the beginning of the 1980s, there were twenty platoons of SEALs, with one team on each coast, plus SEAL Team Six with its specialized mission.

By the end of the decade the naval special warfare community was completing its expansion to more than two thousand SEALs and sixty platoons—more than double the size of the SEAL force in Vietnam—with three conventional SEAL teams and one swimmer delivery vehicle (SDV) team on each coast. The teams were also much bigger than the original SEAL units. At full strength, they numbered 30 officers and 180 enlisted men, compared with the 10 officers and 50 enlisted men in the first two teams in 1962.

It was in the final days of the decade that the Special Operations Command and the expanded SEAL community got their next test in combat, a test that would cause the SEALs once again to reexamine their proper role.

CHAPTER THIRTEEN
TARGET: MANUEL NORIEGA

For a military planner, Grenada and Panama were similar. Both are small countries easily accessible from the water. Both had small military forces that were no match for the firepower of the United States but were still capable of inflicting heavy casualties. In both cases, there was a strong motive to cause as little damage as possible to the lives and property of the overwhelmingly friendly citizens.

But there was one major difference between Urgent Fury, the invasion of Grenada in 1983, and Just Cause, the invasion of Panama in December 1989.

In Grenada, the emphasis was on the word *urgent*. The entire operation was a spur-of-the-moment action, with no time to gather intelligence, no time to plan in detail, no time to rehearse.

In the case of Panama, American military men actually visited the targets they were assigned and gathered their own intelligence. Platoons from SEAL Team Four rotated in and out of Panama so members of the team were intimately familiar with potential targets. All of the special operations forces had been brought together under a single Special Operations Command. Careful planning began more than a year before the actual invasion, and elaborate rehearsals of many aspects of the operation were held in conditions as similar to those in Panama as possible. The planning for Panama was given the code name of Blue Spoon.

Planning was already well advanced when Comdr. Norm Carley, by then commander of SEAL Team Two, one of the East Coast teams based at Little Creek, was asked if some of his men could take part in the operation. Up until that point, the major responsibility for the SEALs' involvement in the action rested with Team Four, which is also based in Little Creek but focuses most of its attention on the Caribbean and Latin America. Team Two, in contrast, trains primarily for work in Northern Europe, operating out of a base at Machrihanish, in the north of Scotland.

Carley promptly agreed to lend his support to the Panama operation. But he laid down some strict conditions. He would not put his men under the command of another team. He insisted that, if they took part, they would be given their own piece of the action and that they would plan and carry it out with their own officers and men. Carley understood that the SEALs all have the same basic training and doctrine. But he also was well aware that the teams had developed their own slightly different methods of operation, and he felt it would be dangerous to mix platoons from two teams on a mission.

Team Two was thus given its own assignment: to put out of action as many as three Panama Defense Force gunboats in the hours immediately before the invasion began. This left Team Four free to concentrate its planning and rehearsals on what was emerging as an increasingly difficult assignment at Paitilla Airfield. Both jobs involved targets in or near Panama City, at the southern, or Pacific, end of the canal.

When Carley took over Team Two's piece of the action, he looked over the preliminary planning that had already been done. What he saw caused him some serious concern. He began adapting the plans to take advantage of the special skills of the SEALs and minimize the dangers to his men. In effect, he said: Tell me what you want done but don't tell me how to do it; let me find the best way.

One alternative in the early plans called for the SEALs to board the vessels, kill or capture the crew members, and take over the boats. Carley told the army officers in overall charge of planning for the operation that he could do that, but it could get some of his men killed or wounded. A better plan, he said, was to send swimmers in to attach explosives under the boats and blow them up. He emphasized something that those who are not combat swimmers find hard to grasp: his men would be safer underwater.

The army action officers, hopeful of avoiding damage to the boats so they could be used by the new Panamanian government, came up with a variation. Instead of blowing up the boats, they suggested, why not have the swimmers wrap cables around their propeller shafts and thus disable them without damage?

Carley agreed that that, too, was feasible. But he pointed out that troop aircraft carrying thousands of men would be passing over that very point during the invasion. Disabling the vessels in that way would do nothing to prevent the crews from firing at the troop transports as they passed overhead.

By this time, Carley was dealing with senior officers and they quickly agreed that the boats should be destroyed, not just disabled. The issue never got to the point of a direct confrontation, as it did with Lt. Tom Coulter when he resisted taking his SEALs onto the beach at Tang Island behind a white flag at the time of the seizure of the *Mayaguez* by the Cambodians.

Thus, several months before Just Cause was set in motion, members of SEAL Team Two began rehearsing for a classic ship-attack operation in which SEALs would approach stealthily underwater, attach explosives to the boats, and swim off while the crew members remained blissfully unaware of their impending doom. It was a tactic that the SEALs, and the UDTs before them, had often practiced but seldom had the chance to carry out.

As planning progressed, this seemed a textbook case of a limpet attack. In this type of attack, the swimmer wears a harness with a sheet of metal attached. A circular limpet mine is secured to the metal by a strong magnet. When the swimmer gets to the ship, his swim buddy jerks the mine free and slaps it up against the side of the ship, where the magnet holds it tight. In this case, however, the patrol boats, built in Louisiana by Swiftships, Inc., had hulls made of aluminum. The magnet wouldn't stick to the aluminum hull. Limpets can also be attached with epoxy, but that is not always reliable. And they can be attached by a special gun that shoots a fastener into the hull. That makes noise and could alert the crew.

To attack the Panamanian boats, the SEALs went back to the Hagensen pack, the same kind of haversack used in World War II to destroy underwater obstacles. The plan called for four swimmers, each pair carrying a twenty-pound pack of C-4 plastic explosive, to attack each boat, strapping their packs of explosive in front of the V struts that support the two propeller shafts. That way, even if the boat moved, the packs would remain in place.

Carley worried about the standard mechanical clock that would normally be used to set off the explosive. He had heard it was sometimes unreliable. He wanted a very accurate clock. He didn't want the blast to go off prematurely, while the swimmers were nearby. And he didn't want it delayed, giving the ship's crew time to shoot at the aircraft overhead. He found a prototype clock that had been developed for another mission and adapted it to set off the explosives under the boats.

Meanwhile, in a neighboring building at Little Creek, members of SEAL Team Four, under Comdr. Tom McGrath, concentrated on the Paitilla operation. McGrath was the same officer who had been involved in the ill-fated attempt to rescue prisoners of war from Vietnam nearly two decades earlier.

Originally, when the military began to give serious thought to a takeover in Panama, more than two years before the actual operation, army planners thought in conventional terms. Mortars and artillery would lay down a barrage on the field and helicopter gunships would swoop in to knock out any defenders who survived. Then would come the assault by parachutists or soldiers in helicopters. As more men poured in, they would create an "expanding doughnut" that would eventually encompass the entire airfield. Such an assault would involve at least three hundred soldiers; in Grenada, twice that number were used.

But such a large-scale operation would create a violent military firestorm in a heavily populated part of the city, endangering the lives and property of thousands of Panamanians, with whom the United States had no quarrel. Wasn't it possible to have a small unit sneak in and take the airfield by surprise? Since the south end of the field juts out into the Bay of Panama, it seemed a logical assignment for the SEALs.

Over the months, officers and men came and went, and platoons rotated in and out of Little Creek. And the plans for Team Four's part of Blue Spoon changed constantly. Looking back, one participant viewed the many different plans as "hilarious."

Throughout, the precise purpose of the operation remained blurry. Was it to seize and hold the airfield? Was it simply to prevent its use by General Noriega, the Panamanian ruler, to escape the country? Could the SEALs shoot down a jet or helicopter carrying Noriega, or would they have to disable his aircraft and capture him unharmed?

A month after the invasion of Panama, General Lindsay, head of the Special Operations Command, reflected the uncertainty about just what the SEALs were supposed to do. He said, "The . . . mission was to seize Paitilla . . . not seize . . . to prevent anyone from taking off or landing at Paitilla—that's where Noriega's aircraft was based—and to disable his aircraft."

Under one proposal the SEALs considered, they would not actually enter the field. Instead, a platoon or more of snipers—perhaps twenty shooters—would take down the defense from a distance. Another plan was almost the opposite: CQB (close-quarter battle) teams would go in and clear out every hangar. Another plan considered—and this is the one most SEALs instinctively favor when they tell how they would have carried out the assignment at Paitilla—was to station a sniper in one of the tall buildings overlooking the field. He would be armed with a powerful .50-cal. sniper rifle firing an explosive bullet The shell, known as a rufus round, could easily disable Noriega's Lear jet by putting a hole through an engine.

The SEALs found themselves under increasingly restrictive rules of engagement that seemed to be based almost entirely on a desire to avoid so-called collateral damage to residents of Panama. Firing by long-distance snipers was ruled out for this reason. One rumor heard often after the operation was that the planners were anxious to avoid damage to Noriega's expensive jet, that the rules of engagement were set for economic reasons. Actually, that rumor was probably a distortion of what had happened during rehearsals for the operation. McGrath, the team commander, owned a small plane, and the men used it to practice approaching and moving an aircraft, in case they had to do that. McGrath constantly urged them to be careful. He was worrying a lot more about his plane than the safety of Noriega's jet.

As the plans evolved, it became apparent that the SEALs would not be permitted to control the airfield by firing from a distance, that they would not be allowed to use naval gunfire to soften up the target, and that they would actually have to set foot on the airfield, approach and disable Noriega's jet, and remain in position to prevent him from using the field to escape by helicopter. Although SEALs have never thought of their mission as the seizure of airfields, that was what these SEALs found themselves preparing to do.

Intelligence reports said the SEALs would find twenty to thirty defenders. In an assault, the attackers should have a three-to-one advantage. That meant a force of at least sixty SEALs. Except for a few occasions in Vietnam, where several platoons combined to attack suspected prisoner of war camps, SEALs have never gone into combat in such large numbers. Neither their officers nor their men are trained for multiplatoon tactics.

Chosen to lead this assault force as the on-scene commander was Lt. Pat Tuohy. Like many SEALs, he had served as an enlisted man before qualifying as an officer. He did not have experience in leading men in actual combat, although he had been involved in the ill-fated parachute drop during the Grenada operation. But he did have one advantage that prepared him for this assignment. He had served in SEAL Team Six, where the officers are trained to command units of forty men or more.

During the planning, a good deal of thought was given to the best way to approach the airfield. Although the SEALs had been brought into the act because of their expertise in using a water approach, serious consideration was given to a land approach. Perhaps the SEALs could simply dash down one of the city streets that dead-ends at the airfield fence, cut through the fence, and suddenly emerge on the field. But this was ruled out for fear of running into one of the Panamanian units known to be roaming the city. The SEALs could find themselves in a firefight before they ever reached the field.

The conclusion was that the SEALs would approach the field from the water in rubber boats and creep ashore. One platoon would take the lead, advancing up the runway toward the hangar area. The SEALs would then shoot into the hangar to disable the jet. Two platoons would move up on the flanks, trailing the lead platoon. A headquarters platoon would form a defensive perimeter about halfway up the runway. From there, Tuohy would command the operation. He had a mortar squad in case fire support was needed. And he had two air force communications experts to keep in touch with an AC-130 gunship circling overhead.

When the individual teams had completed the plans, they went to Capt. John Sandoz, the commodore of Naval Special Warfare Group Two, for review. In hindsight, it appears that this is the point at which questions should have been raised. Had the SEALs, as they adapted to the very restrictive rules of engagement, gotten themselves into an impossible situation, preparing to assault an airfield with sixty men— a task to which the army would have assigned three hundred? But by that time, whatever the individual misgivings, the SEALs were eager to participate in the operation. As one of them said, "We all pray for peace, but if there is a war, we want a piece." Sandoz signed off on the plans.

Sandoz prepared to command the overall naval special warfare phase of the operation from Rodman Naval Station, site of a permanent SEAL base, on the western side of the canal near Panama City. McGrath would remain in a boat offshore, backing up Tuohy from there. In the other major SEAL involvement in Just Cause, Carley would insert his swimmers and then stand by in his boat, prepared to pick them up when they emerged after planting the explosives. This arrangement contrasts with the myth of the fearless commander leading his troops in combat. Sound military doctrine calls for the commander to remain in a position where he can react to events or call in reinforcements rather than getting himself tied down in a firefight.

All was in readiness, and yet none of the SEALs believed they would actually be sent into action. They had been planning and rehearsing for months, and there had been one false alarm after another.

In mid-December 1989, a major rehearsal of the special operations forces part of the attack—which would involve some 4,100 troops and 71 special operations aircraft, plus another 103 aircraft in support— was held in the United States. General Lindsay, commander of the Special Operations Command, had been concerned about the complexity of the assault, especially controlling the air traffic as planes slipped in with the special operations forces in the hours before the full-scale offensive began. He was so pleased with the results of the rehearsal that he declared his men ready to go.

In the following week, Noriega's government declared a state of war with the United States, and Panamanian forces killed a U.S. Marine and brutalized a navy officer and his wife. President Bush gave the go-ahead for Operation Just Cause, with the SEALs and the other special operations forces slated to pave the way. H hour was set for early on the morning of 20 December.

As they boarded the plane for the flight to Panama, Carley and his men received disturbing news. None of the three Panamanian patrol boats targeted by the team was in Balboa Harbor. Perhaps they would have to sit this war out.

When they arrived in Panama, the news had changed. The *Presidente Porras,* one of the three gunboats, was tied up at a floating concrete dock perpendicular to Pier 18, the main pier jutting into Balboa Harbor. Next to the boat was a docking area for boats of the Panama Canal Control Commission.

Carley and his men set out from Rodman, across the canal from their target, in two rubber boats powered by outboard motors. In addition to Carley there were four swimmers, two in each boat, along with a coxswain and an M-60 machine gunner. Chances of detection would have been decreased if the swimmers had crossed the canal on their own. But if a canal lock had been opened during the transit, they would have been swept away in the twelve-knot current.

The two boats moved as slowly as possible so as to avoid leaving a wake. It was only a mile across the canal, but they zigzagged constantly so they would not be spotted by the crew members of control commission craft. One radio report of "something funny out here" could blow the whole thing. Their goal was a mangrove swamp just north of Pier 18. For half an hour, the frogmen hid in their gently rocking boats in the swamp. Swarms of mosquitoes were a nuisance, despite the protection provided by their camouflage paint and insect repellent.

By the time they had reached the mangroves, the engine on one of the boats had quit because it was not designed to run so slowly. They had brought along a spare, but Carley elected not to change engines because of the noise associated with getting the new one going.

When time came to get started, he took two swimmers in one boat and moved to within about 150 yards of Pier 18. That was closer than he had planned, but he saw no one on the pier, and there was no backlight from the swamp, so he considered it a reasonable risk. The swimmers slipped into the water, and Carley then returned to the other boat and towed it, with its two swimmers, out to join the first pair.

Carley returned to the swamp to try once more to get the motor going, without success. So he set off across the canal, with one boat in tow, to Rodman to replace the ailing motor.

The two pairs of swimmers—Engineman Third Class Timothy K. Eppley, Photographer's Mate Second Class Christopher Dye, Lt. Edward Coughlin and Chief Electronics Technician Randy L. Beausoleil—swam underwater to Pier 18, dragging the twenty-pound haversacks of explosive. Surfacing under the pier, they worked their way through the pilings to the other side and then submerged again. Their Draeger rebreathing units gave off no bubbles, but the swimmers had to watch their depth gauges carefully to avoid oxygen poisoning.

As they neared the *Presidente Porras,* they did what the frogmen call a shallow-water peek. Coming almost to the surface, they could see well enough in the ambient light to identify the sixty-five-foot-long target. It would not do to set their explosives on one of the control commission craft or a tuna boat tied up nearby.

As the swimmers reached the patrol boat and moved in to place their charges, the engines suddenly started up. Explosions in the water nearby hammered at their ear drums. They were sure their presence had been detected. But they carefully attached the two packs with their forty pounds of explosives, set the timers for forty-five minutes, and swam away. They were able to come to the surface under a nearby pier and work their way out into the canal, using the pilings to shield themselves from the explosion of grenades in the water.

Although the swimmers assumed they were the center of all this attention, they almost certainly remained undetected. Instead, an American unit had become engaged in a firefight with the Panamanians on the shore near the pier, and grenades and rockets from that fight were falling into the water.

By the time the explosives attached to the boat went off, the swimmers were far enough away to be safe, but they were still shaken by the powerful blast. To be on the safe side, Carley had used at least twice as much C-4 as was needed for the job. When divers took a look at the sunken craft after the fighting stopped, they found that both of the boat's 1,020-horsepower diesel engines had been hurled completely out of the boat.

The swimmers' next task was to swim a dogleg—to "box out," using their compasses—around a string of piers. As they swam out into the canal, they sensed the powerful engines of an approaching ship. They dove toward the bottom, chancing oxygen sickness, as the ship churned by overhead.

Once clear of the ship and the piers, they swam southward, aided by a strong current, toward the pickup point, a fuel pier near the Bridge of the Americas. Carley and the two boats were waiting there, as promised. But the swimmers were not pleased, when they reached what they thought was a safe haven, to stick their heads out of the water and see tracer bullets flashing overhead from a nearby firefight.

The four men were uninjured, but they were exhausted. One reason, in addition to the strenuous job they had just completed, was that they were overheated because they had elected to wear wet suits. The water in the canal was warm enough that they could have done without the suits. But they had worn them in rehearsal, and they felt that, the closer the real thing was to the rehearsal, the greater the chance of success.

In contrast, the men of Team Four, after all their planning and rehearsals for the assault on the Paitilla Airfield, were to find their plans changed at the last moment.

When they left Little Creek, they assumed Murphy's Law would be in full sway: if anything could go wrong, it would go wrong. So they allowed extra time at each stage: time for the flight, time to get the boats out of the plane and into the water, time to make sure all the engines started. But almost everything went perfectly. By nine P.M., they were in the water, with H hour not scheduled until one A.M.

The SEALs, bobbing around in sixteen boats, sat out there for more than three hours. Even for men who train constantly for combat, it was a strange sensation. Little more than twenty-four hours before, they had been at home, having dinner with their wives, helping their children with the homework. And now here they were, sitting in the darkness preparing to go to war.

About midnight, the radio traffic picked up, and Tuohy began moving around from one boat to another, passing on a change in orders he had just received from a command plane. There were two changes: H hour was moved up to 12:45 A.M., and more important, the method for dealing with Noriega's jet was changed. Instead of moving up to the hangar and using their night-vision scopes to aim at the plane's nose gear and fuel tanks, the new order required the SEALs to enter the hangar and disable the plane by slashing its tires. As one of the participants says, "That was a major change in the rules of engagement. A little pickup basketball. Not a real good time to tell your troops."

With so little time left before the carefully coordinated invasion was to begin, it is probably unrealistic to expect any of the SEAL commanders—Sandoz back at Rodman, or McGrath or Tuohy in their boats—to have successfully resisted this change in plans, as Coulter had resisted orders he knew would get him and his men killed. Within minutes, the SEALs landed and established a half-moon–shaped beachhead on the runway.

Normally, two or three men would have been sent ahead to scout out the situation. But they felt a sense of urgency. Radio intercepts indicated Noriega might be heading for Paitilla. The Americans interpreted this as meaning he was going to the airfield. Actually, he was on his way to the Paitilla section of the city, where he later turned up, rather than to the airfield with the same name.

As planned, Golf Platoon, divided into squads code named Golf One and Golf Two, led the way up the runway. They had about twelve hundred to fourteen hundred yards to go, roughly three-quarters of a mile. Following about two hundred yards behind were two other platoons, Bravo on the left and Delta on the right. When the lead platoon was only about a quarter of the way up the runway, the war suddenly erupted. The SEALs could see tracers arcing all over the city. All chance of surprise was gone, and they felt terribly exposed. Up ahead, outlined against the lights of the city, they could see men running. But because of the curvature of the land, they could only see the figures from the waist up. It was impossible to tell whether they were carrying weapons. Under the rules of engagement, the SEALs did not have to wait to be fired upon. If they were opposed by men with weapons, they could shoot. But they couldn't be sure whether the men were armed, so they held their fire and continued up the runway.

Golf One and Two stopped just in front of the hangar containing Noriega's jet. Golf One, commanded by Lt. Tom Casey, was on the right. Golf Two, commanded by Lt. (jg) Mike Phillips, was on the left. The plan was for Casey's squad to remain in position while Phillips and his men dashed into the hangar and disabled the plane by slashing its tires.

But as the SEALs peered into the dark interior of the hangar, that plan was abruptly abandoned. With their night-vision scopes, they could see a number of armed men in the building, hiding behind barrels and heavy metal doors. They had walked into a deadly ambush.

The SEALs opened fire. But their bullets bounced off the barrels and doors of the hangar. For them, there was no protection as the Panamanians responded. SEALs with long combat experience shudder when they picture the scene: the Americans caught in the open at a range of only thirty yards from a well-protected foe.

Casey shouted that he had heavy wounded. Phillips switched the aim of his squad to provide a curtain of fire in front of Golf One. At that point, standard procedure called for the SEALs to pull back, carrying their wounded and dead with them. But there was no way the few men remaining uninjured could cover their withdrawal and carry their stricken colleagues. Phillips radioed for backup from Bravo Platoon, about two hundred yards to his left rear.

He also sent two of his men over to help Casey. They groped from one man to another in the dark, finding one after another wounded or dead. Of the nine men in the squad, Casey was the only one not hit and still able to shoot. They set about dragging the wounded men behind Golf Two's position so the men still firing could protect the wounded with their own bodies. It was a hellish experience. The rescuers couldn't see where the men were wounded or how badly. All of the SEALs were still weighted down by many pounds of gear, so it was hard work just to drag the wounded. And the bullets continued to fly. As he dragged one of the injured men, Chief Petty Officer Donald L. McFaul, one of the most experienced men in the platoon, was hit in the head and killed. There were now two SEALs dead and a number hit so badly they were out of action.

In the midst of the firefight, Lt. Connors and his squad from Bravo Platoon stormed up the runway to take up a position between the two squads of the lead platoon. By rights, Connors should not have been there. He had been under treatment for a tropical disease at Walter Reed Army Medical Center in Washington when he heard his unit had been ordered to Panama. He talked his way out of the hospital and reported in at Little Creek just in time to board the plane for Panama.

As the squad from Bravo Platoon came on the scene, Connors and one of his men were hit, but not badly wounded. The original rules of engagement limited the SEALs to small-arms fire, but the bullets from their 5.56mm and 7.62mm weapons were bouncing off the hiding places of the Panamanians. They decided to shoot back with 40mm grenades. The so-called forty mike-mike grenades can be fired from an adapter attached to an M-16 rifle. As Connors raised up to fire a grenade, he was hit once more and killed.

Tuohy had set up his command position partway up the runway. An officer listening in on the satellite communications back at Fort Bragg was amazed how calm Tuohy sounded as he talked to an army general circling overhead.

"I could hear everything Pat Tuohy said," he recalled. "I could hear he said he had two KIA [killed in action], three KIA. Seven WIA. Need a helicopter. Just as calm as he could be. The general asked if he wanted to withdraw over the beach to the water. He said, 'Sir, my orders were to seize the airfield and hold it until relieved and those remain my intentions, over.' Just as calm. . . . Pat Tuohy is a guy who excites a lot of emotion. . . . But what I heard in those radio transmissions bespoke a very brave man."

As the firefight continued, Tuohy moved all of the remaining SEALs forward and formed a large circle, with the wounded and dead in the center and all guns pointing outward. With the arrival of the additional SEALs, the firing, which had gone on for about fifteen minutes, finally stopped.

During the entire fight, the men on the ground could hear a four-engined air force AC-130 gunship, with its awesome arsenal, including a 105mm gun, circling overhead. The SEALs had even brought two air force combat control team technicians with them to make sure they could call for instant help if they needed it. But throughout the fight, the technicians got no response from the fliers. They finally radioed back to Howard Air Force Base and asked for a new plane with a radio that worked. But by that time, it was too late.

Whether additional firepower from the AC-130 would have made a major difference is doubtful, since the bulk of the SEAL casualties occurred in the first few moments of the firefight.

The medevac helicopters were also too late to save the life of one of the badly wounded SEALs. Although the helicopters were only five minutes' flying time away, there was a mixup in orders, and it was an hour before they arrived. By that time, a fourth man had bled to death.

In the original plan, the team was to have been relieved at dawn by soldiers of the 82d Airborne Division. The SEALs pulled back down the runway, formed a new perimeter, and waited. But the soldiers didn't arrive. The SEALs ended up remaining on the airfield for some thirty-seven hours, through the day after the battle, through the next night, and into the following day.

At dawn, it became apparent that the Panamanian defenders had fled during the night, probably immediately after the firefight, taking their dead and wounded with them. The SEALs heard a few shots that may have been from snipers, but they had no further contact with Panamanian forces.

Finally, a 250-man force of army Rangers descended in their helicopters to relieve the navy men. During the long wait, the SEALs had only MREs (meals, ready-to-eat). As it became clear that there were no hostile forces in the vicinity, they began moving about the airfield.

They eyed a candy machine in one of the hangars and hesitated, aware of the rules against causing damage. Finally, they broke it open and helped themselves to the candy. Their hesitation seemed almost ludicrous when the army's big troop-carrying helicopters landed and the hurricanelike wind from their rotors flipped over every plane still standing on the airfield.

Even long after the shooting stopped, the SEALs remained unsure how many Panamanians were involved in the ambush. During the fight, the SEALs counted what appeared to be four bodies in the hangar and estimated they may have been opposed by ten to twenty men. If that estimate is correct, the intelligence on which the SEALs had based their planning—that they would probably face some twenty defenders—was pretty close to the mark.

What apparently happened was that the Panamanians detected the SEALs either coming ashore or advancing up the runway and had time to pull back into the hangar to set up a hastily arranged ambush. Probably only two or three sharpshooters, firing from the protection of fifty-five–gallon barrels filled with cement, stuck it out through the entire firefight. And they were the ones who probably accounted for all, or most, of the American casualties. The heavy SEAL losses led to a report, repeated in an official analysis by the House Armed Services Committee, that the frogmen had been overpowered by armored personnel carriers that happened on the scene. But that was not true; they were never attacked by APCs.

When the SEALs counted their losses, there were four men dead and nine wounded, more than they had ever lost in a single engagement in the nearly three decades of their existence. The dead were Connors, McFaul, and Petty Officers Christian Tilghman and Isaac G. Rodriguez. Rodriguez might have survived if the medevac helicopters had arrived during the "Golden Hour" after he was wounded.

Word of the losses at Paitilla sent a wave of sorrow and anger through the SEAL community. It was clear that something had gone badly wrong. But because details of the action remained classified, it was not clear exactly what had gone wrong or who was responsible. Was it unrealistic rules of engagement that came from the army, or perhaps even from the Department of State? Was it the failure of senior SEALs to insist that the mission be tailored to their style of warfare? Was it the fact that more than three platoons were involved? Or was it just the vagaries of war? Admiral LeMoyne, who by that time was on the staff of the Special Operations Command, took that position.

"My reading of Panama," LeMoyne says, "is that we had a mission that was appropriate to us, we trained, prepared to do it, and we went in and did it. We performed it. I would like to have done it without suffering those casualties. We were not able to do that. I attribute that to the vagaries, the uncertainties of warfare. After the SEALs got hit, hit very hard, the end result was they stayed right on the target, they overcame the opposition, they accomplished what they were sent there to do and did that very well."

But Comdr. Gary Stubblefield, former commander of SEAL Team Three, a West Coast team that was not involved in Panama, took a much more critical view. A Vietnam veteran and a respected combat "operator," Stubblefield was within days of retirement. He wrote a stinging letter addressed to his superiors through the chain of command on 7 January 1990. Titled "Accountability in the Field," it said:

Throughout the history of Naval Special Warfare, the community personnel have gained a well-deserved reputation for being able to enter a unique niche in combat environments, do a respectable job and walk away from the situation with little or no friendly casualties. In the eyes of many, Panama has shattered that record by creating more casualties per capita than typical ground troops by a multithousand factor. Most tend to blame this upon the infusion of "army green mentality" being forced upon our navy doctrine and further enhanced by the belief that "special operations forces" are typically given the toughest job in today's combat scenarios.

This is simply not correct. From the earliest days of training, up through actual operational scenarios, we have always been taught that we plan and operate "to win." The old adages that we live to fight another day and that we are not trained to charge bunkers has always been part of our heritage. However, there appears to be a new philosophy developing within our own ranks, particularly among those leaders who have never actually been involved in many special operations or combat situations. It is that we have become an expendable force; that we are tougher, better trained and therefore take on the worst combat scenarios which we don't send common soldiers against. Quite the opposite is true. Because we are better trained and more conditioned to react positively under difficult situations, it is precisely the reason we plan and execute our missions more carefully to preserve these "high value personnel."

Review of the airfield operation, even to the most casual observer, without the benefit of back-briefs, reveals that our leadership delivered the SEALs on the ground into an unfair role and created a situation which, under the conditions given, could only create casualties. The objective, no matter how stated, was to prevent General Noriega from using the airfield for evacuating the country. This could easily have been accomplished with a small number of SEALs using some of the advanced weapons and technology we have been spending large amounts of money to develop and procure over the past two decades.

Instead, our leaders sent too many troops, who are not accustomed to working in larger numbers, against the defended position when it was absolutely unnecessary in order to achieve our objective. These leaders must be held accountable and not allowed to lead our fine young SEALs into such unwarranted and costly scenarios again rather than given praise for a job well done.

Finally, we must learn from these costly mistakes and design into future training and preparation of all special warfare personnel that most objectives have the ability to be accomplished without loss of life if the planning and execution are based on firm common sense and then weighed against the value of our personnel whom we have spent so many hours and dollars preparing to carry out Naval Special Warfare operations.

Stubblefield's immediate superior, Capt. Raymond C. Smith, Jr., commodore of Naval Special Warfare Group One, thought the letter made a lot of sense. He gave it a positive endorsement and sent it along to Admiral Worthington, commander of the Naval Special Warfare Command in Coronado, and thus the senior SEAL commander.

By that time, Stubblefield had retired, but Worthington called him in anyway.

"I get awfully tired of arguing with some of the old SEALs that weren't there," Worthington says. "I brought one of the retirees [Stubblefield] in, sat him down and told him, 'you don't know anything about the intelligence that went into this, yet you're writing letters to everybody saying how fouled up it was.' Now I got a case of the ass about that. The op was good. SEALs weren't the only people killed. More people on the other side died than SEALs died."

But wasn't the multiplatoon nature of the operation a departure from SEAL doctrine?

"My answer to that is, so what?" Worthington says. "They were given a military job, they were Americans, they were trained, the most healthy group of people down there. Why can't they do that? Not a single SEAL, even in planning, stood up and said, 'that's not our doctrine.' Well, change the doctrine."

One suspicion among many SEALs is that the Paitilla action was permitted to become so large because it gave many SEALs the opportunity to participate in combat and win a medal. When Just Cause was over, medals—more than forty of them—were lavishly bestowed upon the SEALs involved.

One veteran SEAL officer expressed his concern over the temptation to involve more men than are actually needed: "We tend to want to get everyone involved, whether or not their help is needed. It gives them 'experience'—experience dying, being wounded, being scared shitless, being shot at. SEALs get mad if they are left out. I say, 'I don't give a shit if you never get shot at. If I don't need you, you can stay at the base camp.'"

After the Paitilla operation, this same officer was sent off on another mission with strict orders from Sandoz, the overall SEAL commander in Panama: "Don't get another SEAL killed!"

SEALs carried out a number of other small, specialized actions both before and after the main event in Panama. Members of SEAL Team Six were among the special operations forces who went in early in an unsuccessful effort to find and seize Noriega. And members of Carley's SEAL Team Two, along with other SEALs, checked out a series of islands where Panamanian forces could have been hiding out. These operations were conducted without running into opposition.

For the special operations forces involved, Panama was a larger, far better coordinated, and more successful operation than their participation in the Grenada invasion six years earlier. In addition to about 500 navy men, including the SEALs, there were some 2,850 soldiers and 800 air force personnel. Two and two-thirds battalions of Rangers jumped into the Rio Hato area, and another battalion jumped in at the Torrijos Tucanmen airfield. The army's antiterrorist Delta Force stormed a prison just before the major attack was launched and rescued an American who reportedly worked for the Central Intelligence Agency.

The dangerous nature of the assignments given to the special operations forces is indicated by their heavy casualties: 11 killed and 129 wounded.

The overall invasion was so successful that army Lt. Gen. Carl Stiner, the commander, boasted that there had been no lessons to be learned. To many SEALs, it seemed obvious that there were lessons that should be learned. Whether the SEALs were capable of learning those lessons was another question. Although it could not be foreseen at the time, another test for the Special Operations Command—and for the SEALs—was just over the horizon.

CHAPTER FOURTEEN
TO THE PERSIAN GULF—AND BEYOND

S addam Hussein's Iraqi forces invaded Kuwait on 2 August 1990. Nine days later, a contingent of 105 West Coast SEALs and support personnel were on the ground in Saudi Arabia, setting up a base on the coast south of Dhahran.

Between the SEALs and the Iraqi army were two hundred miles of sand—and not much else. It would be weeks before sizable marine and army airborne units arrived to begin a buildup of forces powerful enough to prevent the Iraqis from sweeping south into Saudi Arabia.

In those first dangerous weeks, the SEALs were virtually the only American fighting men standing between Saddam Hussein and further conquest. Desert Shield at that time was a very fragile defensive array, indeed. For the SEALs, the first order of business was not to plan how to resist an Iraqi drive to the south. SEALs don't throw themselves in the path of columns of armor or massed infantry. Their first priority was to plan how to get away if the assault continued.

As it turned out, four SEALs, manning an observation post in a cavelike bunker on the coast just south of the Kuwait border, suddenly found themselves involved in the first ground combat of the war on the night of 31 January. By this time, the great air assault on Iraq had been underway for nearly two weeks, but action on the ground had been limited to sporadic artillery duels.

The early evening was almost eerily quiet—too quiet. And then about ten o'clock, the men heard the ominous sounds of heavy machinery—tanks—moving toward them just above the border.

Suddenly the desert, already bright with moonlight, lit up under the glare of a series of illumination grenades, one right over their heads. A tank rolled up onto the berm 150 yards away and opened fire. The Iraqis knew the Americans were there, but they didn't know exactly where. The SEALs wisely decided not to help the enemy's aim by opening fire. The SEALs had heavy machine guns and 40mm grenades, but they were no match for the guns of a tank.

Their first thought—natural to SEALs—was to head for the water. But when they saw a marine vehicle pass by safely, they decided to make a run for it south across the desert in their jeeplike HMMWV. They were the last Americans to leave the border area. Until the last minute, when they took down the antenna for their satellite communications system, they radioed reports on the movement of the Iraqi forces. As they sped south toward Khafji, they saw air force antitank planes attack. "The A-10s just ate them up," said one of the SEALs.

The SEALs paused in Khafji to make sure all the U.S. units had been able to pull back from the border, and then sped on south to their main base on the coast.

After a fierce fight, Saudi forces, assisted by U.S. Marines and allied aircraft, drove the surviving members of the invading force back across the border.

For Capt. Ray Smith, commodore of Naval Special Warfare Group One, the assignment as commander of Naval Special Warfare Task Group, Central, in Saudi Arabia, was both a special opportunity and a special challenge. A 1967 graduate of Annapolis, Smith had commanded an Underwater Demolition Team platoon, but he had missed the opportunity to command a SEAL platoon in combat during the Vietnam War. In the Persian Gulf War, he was on-scene commander of a multiplatoon task force, the first such unit to be sent overseas in the history of the SEALs, and the largest deployment of SEALs since the Vietnam War.

It was also the first time the SEALs had been called upon to serve as an integral part of a much larger force involved in a major conventional war, and this would pose special challenges for Smith.

In their introduction to combat, in Vietnam, the SEALs had, to a considerable degree, fought their own little war, largely independent of the bigger operations going on around them. In Grenada, they had been part of a hasty, relatively small-scale operation involving poorly coordinated army, navy, air force, and marine units. Panama had been a major special operations forces action in which the SEALs played out specific, long-planned parts. None of these provided a clear guide to what the SEALs should be expected to do in the Gulf or precisely how they should do it in coordination with the much larger forces involved.

The decisions Smith made, and the performance of his SEALs, would help define the future course of naval special warfare. The challenge facing him was to demonstrate that his very small and very specialized force, trained primarily for low-intensity, unconventional warfare, could make a difference in a big, conventional war.

When the Iraqi forces crossed the border, Smith was given seventy-two hours to pick his force, select his equipment, load everyone and everything in three C-5 and three C-141 aircraft, and take off for the war zone.

By any measure, the force under Smith's command was a tiny part of the overall effort. At the peak, the American force in the Gulf area totalled more than 540,000 troops, of whom some 9,000 were part of the Special Operations Command. Smith's force numbered a scant 260, including special boat units and support personnel. Of these, only 60 men—four platoons—wore the SEAL insignia. Four more SEAL platoons were afloat with the navy-marine amphibious force—two platoons in the Persian Gulf and two more in the Mediterranean and, later, the Red Sea. SEALs routinely accompany the amphibious force, and these four platoons were not part of Smith's special task group.

The naval special warfare contingent was small even in comparison with the SEAL community of some two thousand men. Understandably, many of the SEALs who remained at home—especially those on the East Coast, who played little part in the operation—were unhappy at being left behind.

The East Coast SEALs thought Gen. Norman Schwarzkopf, the overall commander, was to blame. Gossip had it that Schwarzkopf didn't like any special operations forces, especially the SEALs. According to the good news–bad news story circulating in Little Creek, the army Special Forces arrived in Saudi Arabia and told Schwarzkopf, "The bad news is, we're here. The good news is, we didn't bring the SEALs."

Members of Smith's small contingent got no hint from the army high command that they were unwelcome. They were called in early, which is essential if special operations forces are to be most effective. And they were favored with their choice of shore bases, first at a recreation area known as Half Moon Bay, just south of Dhahran, and later at Ras al-Mishab, a short distance south of the Kuwaiti border. Smith established his headquarters at Ras al-Gar, near Jubail, about seventy-five miles to the north of Dhahran. If they were not welcome, they could have found themselves in tents out in the desert, with plenty of sand but no water.

Smith could have made himself popular by fielding a significantly larger force. But both the rules by which he guided his operations and the nature of the war itself placed a limit on the number of SEALs involved.

Smith laid out five guidelines, which he called his concepts of employment:

1. High probability of success.
2. Maritime environment.
3. In support of commander-in-chief, central command components.
4. Contribute to overall effort.
5. Single-platoon/squad-level operations.

Perhaps the most significant, in view of the SEALs' experience in Panama, was the last. In this war, the SEALs went back to their traditional small-unit role. There would be none of the multiplatoon operations of the kind that had led to disaster at Paitilla.

"I wanted to do what we do well, and I wanted to make sure my boss knew what we could do," Smith says. When the SEALs arrived, no one, including Smith, knew quite how the SEALs would fit into this big conventional war. Smith looked for ways to be useful—as a maritime force, in support primarily of the navy and marines, and in small-unit operations.

Perhaps surprisingly, the SEALs found themselves focusing on tasks that would have been familiar to the Underwater Demolition Teams of the 1950s, or even of World War II. Left off the agenda were some of the most important skills they had practiced from the midseventies on in an effort to make themselves useful, not just in amphibious operations, but to the fleet as a whole.

For years, SEALs have practiced sneaking ashore in hostile territory to place beacons to guide bombers to their targets, or to actually mark the targets with laser beams. They have also put a good deal of effort into working their way close enough to enemy targets so they could radio back reports on bomb damage within minutes after bombs had fallen and the planes had streaked away.

Another of their specialties is to attack enemy targets directly, leaving their calling card, in the form of a packet of explosives and a timer, on the bottom of a ship, the base of a bridge, or a key component of a power plant.

In the Gulf War, the SEALs did not get the opportunity to try out any of these specialties.

A major reason was the revolution in technology that has transformed the battlefield. Tomahawk cruise missiles and highly accurate bombers were able to destroy targets that, in earlier days, might have been assigned to the SEALs. And satellites and the cameras of reconnaissance planes, in many cases, provided fast, accurate reports on bomb damage, making it less important for SEALs to go in and eyeball the target.

Another reason not to send SEALs on these specialized missions was the intense concentration of enemy forces along the Kuwaiti coastline, the maritime environment where the SEALs, rather than other special operations units, would be expected to operate. By one estimate, Saddam Hussein had clustered sixty thousand troops along a twenty-five-mile stretch near the coast. One officer who considered the possibilities concluded it would have been "lunatic" to send SEALs into such an intensely hostile environment.

Offshore, the SEALs provided a host of valuable services. They jumped from helicopters to attach explosives or towing lines to enemy mines and destroyed twenty-five of them. They flew daily on helicopters assigned to rescue allied fliers and, on one occasion, they arrived within minutes after an air force F-16 pilot splashed into the sea and helped him to safety.

They captured an oil platform being used by the Iraqis as a military base and took twenty-three prisoners of war. They also seized Qarah Island, the first Kuwaiti land to be recaptured by the allied forces.

Working with the special boat units, they spent hours patrolling the gulf in search of Iraqi patrol craft. Later, operating at night in their little rubber Zodiac boats, they slowly cruised off the coast of Kuwait, watching for any sign of Iraqi naval activity. Lying low in the water and moving so slowly that they made no wake, they were virtually invisible. On a number of occasions, they spotted Iraqi patrol boats, radioed their position, and then moved away. If the frogmen in their vulnerable rubber boats had been spotted, a few bullets would have ended the war for them. But they were never detected, at least partially because the Iraqi crews were so busy searching the sky for allied planes rather than looking down at the dark waters.

All of these operations were useful, but in the overall scheme of things they were hardly of the type to make any real difference in the outcome of the war.

As the ground war was about to begin, however, the SEALs were given the opportunity to demonstrate how a handful of well-trained men can have an impact on larger events totally out of proportion to their numbers.

As part of the buildup, the United States assembled a powerful amphibious fleet in the northern reaches of the gulf, with seventeen thousand marines poised for an amphibious landing in Kuwait. As viewed from the bunkers of Baghdad, such an operation made a good deal of sense militarily. Saddam Hussein and his commanders expected a frontal assault on their heavily fortified positions in Kuwait, rather than the end run to the west that Schwarzkopf actually carried out. If the allies had followed Hussein's game plan, an amphibious landing would have given the Iraqi forces a lot of trouble, and they had to be concerned about it.

The allies fed Hussein's fears by putting on an elaborate dress rehearsal for a landing, with the press invited to report on the preparations.

In early January, SEALs began making nightly studies of the Kuwaiti coastline, looking for the best invasion beaches. Instead of going in during the day, as their predecessors had done in World War II, they did their work at night, using night-vision devices to pierce the darkness. Each night, they spent several hours in their Zodiacs watching the shore. Then, three-man teams swam in close to the beach and floated there quietly for several more hours, studying the lay of the land, trying to pick out defensive fortifications and watching for signs of movement by the Iraqi forces.

Their reports were not encouraging. Most of the Kuwaiti shore was dotted with buildings. As soon as the marines landed, they would find themselves in a kind of urban warfare, forced to work their way between buildings. Each street or alley or gap between buildings was a potential killing zone.

Finally, the SEALs found one stretch of about a mile and a half with few buildings. Open fields lay just beyond the beach. Physically, it was a perfect site for an amphibious landing—if the Iraqis had not come to the same conclusion and equipped it with elaborate defenses.

For several nights, the SEALs concentrated on this one stretch of beach, first watching from their Zodiac boats and then swimming in closer to get a better look.

The word went back up the chain of command to Smith, then to SOCCENT (Special Operations Command, Central) and finally to Schwarzkopf's headquarters. The SEALs were let in on one of the most important secrets of the war: there would be no amphibious landing, but there would be an elaborate deception. The SEALs drew up a plan to fool the Iraqis, and then they waited. Most of them knew no more about when, or if, the ground offensive would begin than television viewers back home. Finally, they got the word. The deception operation would be carried out early on the morning of 24 February, just before the ground war began.

Lt. Tom Deitz, an Annapolis graduate who had been detached from SEAL Team Five, where he was a platoon commander, to take part in the Gulf War, was put in charge of the SEAL portion of the operation. Deitz had never heard of the Beach Jumpers—the navy men who specialized in deception operations in the years following World War II—but his plan read like a page out of their book. Late on the night of 23 February, Deitz and fourteen other members of his platoon left their base at Ras al-Mishab and sped north in two Fountain-class high-speed patrol boats.

It was about a forty-mile trip, reminiscent of the forays against the north by Vietnamese sailing out of Da Nang nearly thirty years before. Often the water was so rough that the SEALs returned from such speedboat rides black and blue. But the water was smooth and silky this night. The only danger was the possibility of collision with a mine. Everyone tried not to think about that.

For several days, the "invasion" beach had been hammered by frequent air strikes and barrages of naval gunfire. But on the night of the deception operation, the defenders were puzzled by a strange, even eery, silence. Neither guns nor bombs disturbed the stillness.

As the patrol boats idled offshore, the fifteen SEALs slid their three Zodiacs into the water and then climbed aboard and moved quietly toward the enemy beach.

At about five hundred yards from the shore, Deitz and five other men slipped into the water. Although when the SEALs first arrived in the war zone in August the water in the Gulf was a steamy ninety-two degrees—warm enough to worry about heat exhaustion—it had dropped to a chilly fifty-three degrees by February. The SEALs wore wet suits, gloves, and tight-fitting helmets to prevent the loss of heat through the head, with booties under their fins. They did without face masks because of the chance that reflected glare might give them away.

They wore no underwater breathing gear, but each man carried a three-minute SCUBA bottle in case he had to swim underwater to evade enemy gunfire.

Except for protection against the cold, they could have been mistaken for the naked warriors of World War II.

In Deitz's planning, the choice of the nine men who remained behind in the Zodiacs was as important as the five he took with him to the beach. In each boat he had a "gearhead," who could keep the engine running no matter what, and an expert communicator. Also left behind were several senior petty officers, men who could be relied on to make the right decisions if anything went wrong.

As they swam toward the beach, each of the swimmers pushed a twenty-pound haversack of C-4 explosive, fitted with a small flotation bag, in front of him. Dangerous as it might seem to swim toward an enemy beach hugging a bundle of explosives to your chest, that was not one of the SEALs' worries. The C-4 would not explode if hit by a bullet and might even provide some protection.

The men were also able to rest their weapons on top of the haversacks, making it easier to swim. Three of the frogmen were armed with HK MP-5 submachine guns and three with M-16 rifles fitted with M-203 grenade launchers. Each man had his favorite brand of knife strapped to his leg just above the ankle. Some carried the standard-issue K-bar knife. Deitz had a knife he had bought at a diving shop in San Diego. "The knife was just if we got tangled on something," Deitz says. "It was not for slitting throats. That's what you have a gun for."

The men swam toward the beach in a horizontal line, about twenty feet apart. When they reached the point where the water was about six feet deep, they floated quietly and watched the shore. Then, seeing no signs of activity, they spread out until, with about fifty yards between each of them, they covered about an eighth of a mile.

It was a dark, moonless night, and the sea was as still as a mountain lake, with the water lapping gently on the beach. The SEALs deflated the air bladders and deposited their haversacks of explosives on the sand near the water's edge. The bags were heavy enough to remain in place without being buried or fastened down. A few minutes before eleven P.M., each of the men pulled the pins on two timers attached to his haversack. The timers were set to go off at intervals beginning at one A.M.

Unlike Carley, who insisted on a special type of timer when he was planning the attack on the Panamanian patrol boat, Deitz was comfortable with the standard military-issue timer. In 1987, when doubts were raised about its reliability, he had conducted a series of tests, setting off some forty clocks at different depths. They all went off precisely on time, and Deitz felt very confident using them in a real-world operation—but not so confident that he didn't insist on placing two timers on each bag of explosives. The SEALs always want a backup. They reason that "two is one; one is none."

With the timers set, the SEALs swam back out to their Zodiacs and then rejoined their two patrol boats about seven miles offshore. Meanwhile, two more patrol boats had been lurking about two miles from the beach. At about twelve thirty A.M., they began raking the dugouts and other fortifications along the beach with fire from their .50-cal. machine guns and 40mm mortars.

Just as they broke contact, the first of the haversacks went off. But instead of making one big bang, they exploded at irregular intervals of two to ten minutes apart. The result was to give the defenders a solid half hour of excitement. The explosions on the beach seemed to mean only one thing: the demolition of beach defenses in preparation for a landing. As the Iraqis looked out to sea, they could make out two rows of buoys placed by the frogmen, seeming to mark the invasion corridor.

Hovering seven miles offshore and storing their gear, the SEALs heard the charges go off and knew they had done their job well. What they didn't know was whether it had made any difference in the conduct of the war.

As the echo of the last explosions died away, the patrol boats sped south. When they docked at Ras al-Mishab, other SEALs excitedly gathered around and asked how it had gone. Deitz gave them an honest answer: "It was kind of boring."

Later that morning, with the ground operation underway, Chief Warrant Officer Roger Hayden, tactical operations command watch officer, received a message for Deitz from Smith:

> Tom: Please pass to your men an "extremely well done" on last night's mission. CENTCOM has passed to us that elements of two Iraqi divisions reacted and moved, based on your operation. That reaction was exactly the objective we had hoped for. Keep up the great work. Commodore sends.

"It really didn't hit home, until we got that message, that it worked," Deitz says. As the marines knifed northward through the Iraqi defenses that morning, there was no doubt that the SEALs—just six of them—had made a difference in the conduct of the war by suckering the Iraqis out of position.

Later, after the SEALs had docked at Kuwait City with elements of the Kuwaiti navy they had helped to train, Deitz and Hayden visited the site of the deception operation. They found the shoreline heavily mined and scarred by trenches and fighting pits. If the marines had gone ashore there, they would have had a rude welcome. But then they probably would have moved quickly inland.

"There was just one line of defense," Hayden says in amazement. "I've never seen anything like it."

While most of their operations focused on their traditional maritime role, the Persian Gulf War also gave the SEALs a chance to try out one of their newest pieces of equipment, the fast-attack vehicle, or FAV.

Originally developed by the army as a weapon for its light infantry in the early 1980s, the FAV is a military version of the off-road vehicles used by thrill-seekers in the western deserts. The version used by the SEALs carries a crew of three men. A driver and navigator-gunner sit side by side in two bucket seats. Mounted above the engine on the right side is a .30-cal. M-60 machine gun. The third man rides in a swivel seat above and behind the driver's compartment. He is armed with both an M-60 aimed toward the rear and a .50-cal. machine gun on a swivel covering the area to the front and sides of the vehicle.

The FAV crews found that night-vision goggles, the powerful Volkswagen engine, and large shock absorbers permitted them to sweep across the trackless Saudi desert at night at speeds of more than sixty miles an hour. They made nightly patrols along the Saudi-Kuwait border, prepared to dash in and rescue downed pilots. Beside the navigator-gunner is a large meshwork basket designed to cradle an injured pilot as the FAV streaks toward safety. The vehicle provides no armor protection for the crew or a rescued pilot. They rely instead on their three weapons to suppress enemy fire and their high speed and maneuverability to get out of harm's way.

During the war almost all the allied pilots returned safely from their missions, so the SEALs did not have an opportunity to carry out a rescue on the ground. They did, however, provide security as the United States reoccupied its embassy in Kuwait City.

One disappointment for the SEALs was the very limited use of SEAL delivery vehicles. The SDVs would have been perfectly suited for surveillance of the Kuwait shore and, especially, the harbor at Kuwait City. But even though Smith was a former commander of an SDV team and familiar with the use of the little submersibles, they were not used in the Gulf until January, only a short time before the allied offensive began—and soon ended. Although all SDV operations remain highly classified, the SEALs, who train to operate the delivery vehicles from submarines, reportedly had difficulty figuring out how to use them effectively in waters so shallow that it was difficult for large submarines to operate.

Smith and his task group returned to Coronado on 11 March 1991. During their seven months in the war zone they had achieved one of Smith's most important, but unwritten, goals. He brought all the members of his task group home safely, without a single casualty. The returning SEALs also brought home positive answers to many questions about the ability of the SEALs to work effectively with other forces in a major conventional conflict and, despite their small numbers, to make a meaningful difference on the battlefield.

The most important lesson of the war for the SEALs, Smith says, is that they proved they can "fit into a major force fighting a major war." But they also learned, he said, that they can be most useful if they concentrate on the things they do well, and "stay within the bounds of our capabilities."

Since his return from the Gulf, Smith has been chosen for appointment as a rear admiral. This places him in a key position to draw on the lessons he learned as commander of the task group in Desert Shield to shape future development of the SEALs.

In the past, however, the SEALs have not been very good at learning from their experiences, especially when things went wrong, and applying those lessons to plans for the future. The failure of UDT Sixteen during World War II at Okinawa is never spoken of. Neither is the SDV operation in 1972 in which Spence Dry lost his life. The SEALs took part in Urgent Fury in Grenada in 1983, but it was not until 1989, six years later, that three officers who served in that operation met with SEALs, other than their colleagues in Team Six, and shared their experiences. A meeting devoted to the SEAL participation in Just Cause, the invasion of Panama, was held shortly after the operation. But most of the SEALs present found the briefing unsatisfactory, and a few were so disturbed that they walked out.

Many of the lessons the veterans of Desert Storm have to pass along involve the fine-tuning of tactics, techniques, and equipment that all worked pretty well. Still to be answered are the broader, more doctrinal questions about the place of the SEALs in the future, in both war and peace, and there is reason for concern that these issues are not being adequately faced.

A number of the most experienced SEALs, including several whom their colleagues had looked to as future leaders, have recently retired. While each had his own reasons, ranging from a desire to spend more time at home to plans for a second career, many were also motivated at least in part by a feeling that the SEAL community was drifting, without a clear vision of its future.

One particularly pointed question from the Gulf War was raised by the performance of the Tomahawk cruise missiles and the smart bombs dropped by the F-117 Stealth fighter-bomber and other planes. If a ship or submarine, firing from hundreds of miles away, can send a Tomahawk through the door of a power plant or a bunker, why should SEALs risk their lives to penetrate enemy territory to attack such targets?

The experience of Desert Storm undoubtedly demonstrated that there are occasions when the new weapons are a better, less risky way to knock out key enemy targets. But the SEALs are convinced that the same skills that permit them to attack such targets can still be highly useful.

The SEALs are a perfect choice if the United States wants to neutralize something, or send a message, without acknowledging U.S. responsibility, says Capt. Thomas N. Lawson, deputy commander of the Naval Special Warfare Command.

"Let's say, before the shooting in Iraq, if the Iraqis had a ship in port and we made the ship sink. The Iraqis would say, 'I can't prove it was the U.S., but I know it was the U.S., and they're sending me a signal. This is an indication of things to come. How bad do I want to stay down here on the Saudi border?' For that kind of thing, we provide an option," Lawson says.

The SEALs also have the capability to send a message by causing only limited damage. A missile can be very precise, but it is also very destructive. As another option, a couple of pounds of C-4, slipped into place by a SEAL, are enough to bend the shaft of a ship and prevent it from moving without sinking or destroying the vessel. The message may be more subtle, but it is just as clear.

Lawson also sees a significant shift in emphasis as a result of the change in relations with the Soviet Union. In the past, the SEALs focused much of their attention on direct action, such as blowing up a bridge or a power station, and on strategic reconnaissance, both related to a major superpower conflict. Now the spotlight is swinging more toward foreign internal defense—helping other nations to deal with internal problems, both military and social. A few SEALs, sent in to help in training, bridge-building, or medical service, may often be more acceptable to a foreign country than a carrier offshore or a larger military contingent.

A major shortcoming of the Special Operations Command as a whole that was exposed by the Gulf War was the shortage of soldiers and sailors who could speak the languages of the region. Language training will receive more emphasis in the future, but a force as small as the SEALs will always have difficulty training enough men to speak the right languages for any future emergency.

The leaders of naval special warfare will have to walk a narrow line between training the SEALs to speak other languages and help people of other countries—the hearts-and-minds kind of thing—and still making sure that they keep their sharp edge as the world's best fighting men. Traditionally, the SEALs have focused primarily on their ability to influence events by violence in contrast to the army's Special Forces, with their stress on working with foreign nationals.

One form of violence that SEALs talk about among themselves is the possibility of capturing or killing terrorist leaders or even foreign heads of state. One of the frustrations of their involvement in Desert Shield and Desert Storm was that Saddam Hussein remained off-limits. Attempting to take out Hussein would have been an assignment tailor-made for the specially trained antiterrorist experts of SEAL Team Six. In fact, one former member of the team, while at the Naval Postgraduate School, wrote a study of how the team might be used to carry out clandestine assassination attempts. His thesis remains highly classified.

U.S. policy, set by the White House, forbids assassinations. A number of officials of both the Reagan and Bush administrations have argued unsuccessfully that that policy be changed so that leaders of terrorist groups could be targeted. If the policy is ever changed, the SEALs might well be called upon to carry out such operations. They might also be used, in international waters, to capture persons wanted for violations of U.S. laws. The United States has, on several occasions, seized persons wanted for such crimes as terrorism, murder, and dealing in drugs, either in foreign countries or on the high seas, so there is a precedent for such operations.

Another serious question raised by Desert Storm is whether SEALs will be needed in the future to mark targets for the bombers or assess bomb damage. The current assumption is that they may well be called upon to carry out such operations in future conflicts. This would be especially true in circumstances where the United States does not have supremacy in the air, as it had over Kuwait and Iraq. In such a case, sending in SEALs to mark targets and check on bomb damage might be the best, or perhaps the only, way to carry out offensive air operations without unacceptable losses of planes and pilots.

Even though operations in the Gulf War were limited to squad or platoon size, debate continues over whether the SEALs should plan for more multiplatoon operations, such as the one at Paitilla, or whether they should concentrate on platoon- or squad-sized operations. There are a number of reasons to think that, even if multiplatoon operations are not ruled out, they will be rare events.

SEALs, particularly on the East Coast, who have had experience with the larger assault forces of SEAL Team Six, still argue that there is a place for multiplatoon operations. But there is a growing realization that SEAL Team Six can safely conduct such operations because its hostage-rescue assaults would almost always be carried out in circumstances where the area surrounding the building or aircraft where the hostages are held captive would be firmly in friendly control. Operating in circumstances where the enemy controls the area, a multiplatoon SEAL unit might, as in Paitilla, be both too large for surprise and too small to dominate the situation.

Although top SEAL leaders defend the multiplatoon Paitilla operation as a proper one and say that, given time to plan and train, they might carry out such relatively large-scale tactics in the future, most SEALs consider Paitilla flawed, an unfortunate aberration from the kinds of things SEALs should do rather than a portent of things to come.

Even if the SEALs should decide that there is a place in their repertoire for larger-scale operations, the number of men they can put into action in the future will be limited in many circumstances by decisions that have already been made on important pieces of equipment.

Just coming into use is a new vessel, a 170-foot PC (patrol ship, coastal) so large that it carries a crew of twenty-eight and is a commissioned navy ship, unlike the smaller boats that have long been a familiar part of SEAL life. Despite its size, the new vessel was designed to carry only a single eight-man squad and two Zodiac boats, limiting the size of unit the SEALs can send on an operation.

The new PC is one of the mixed blessings of the incorporation of the SEALs into the Special Operations Command. On the positive side, they are getting a new vessel, something that might not have happened if they had not had access to the relatively deep pockets of the joint command. The ship has a range of two thousand nautical miles and a speed of thirty-five knots, and it will be more seaworthy and much more comfortable than the little boats in which SEALs are used to being battered about.

It is not, however, the vessel the SEALs would have chosen if they had had a free choice. When commanders of the SEAL teams and special boat squadrons saw plans for the PC, they complained that it was too big, too heavy, too slow, and improperly armed. They would have been happier with a modified version of the 110-foot Island-class Coast Guard cutter. But the Pentagon's Southern Command, which can be called upon to patrol along the lengthy coasts of Central and South America, wanted a vessel with a good, long range, big enough to travel comfortably over long distances. The result was a compromise: a ship big enough to patrol Latin America, but also capable of carrying SEALs. Thirteen of the nine-million-dollar ships have been ordered for use by naval special warfare forces.

Although the experience in the Gulf demonstrated once again that the older boats available to the SEALs are inadequate in their original design and tired from years of use, it will be several years, at best, before new boats, smaller than the coastal patrol ship, are available.

The size of future SEAL operations will also be limited by the size of the ASDS (advanced SEAL delivery system) and the submarines from which it will operate. The ASDS, which has been under consideration since the early 1980s and will not come into service until later in this decade, will be a small submarine in which the crew members will be protected from the cold and darkness of the sea. But it, too, will carry only a single squad of eight men.

The ASDS is being designed to operate from the deck of a modified Sturgeon-class attack submarine. The hope is to make relatively minor modifications to the sub so the ASDS can take off from the submarine and then return and lock onto the sub. Theoretically, this will make it possible to eliminate the dry-deck shelters required by the "wet" submersibles now in use. But that may not prove to be an advantage, because the navy also intends to continue to use the older SDVs, and they need a shelter from which to operate.

Theoretically, the SEAL force could be expanded beyond a squad by sending more than one submarine on a mission or taking along other SEALs who would lock out and swim or ride their Zodiac boats to the target. Practically, that is unlikely to happen because the Sturgeon-class subs are too small to carry a large number of frogmen and, in the near future at least, there will be only two subs, one on each coast.

While the SEALs have debated among themselves whether multiplatoon operations are too big, little thought seems to have been given to the question at the other end of the scale: Is a single squad operation too small? If an eight-man squad suffers even a single casualty, the need to care for an injured man or retrieve the body of one who is killed drastically reduces the unit's ability to carry out its mission. In Vietnam, the SEALs often felt most comfortable operating in squad-sized or smaller units. But they could almost always call in artillery fire and helicopters to pluck them to safety if they got in trouble. In the future, there may be many circumstances where SEALs will be completely on their own, with no hope of help or rescue.

In the case of both the new patrol ship and the ASDS–Sturgeon-class submarine combination, with their one-squad limit, decisions about the future of the SEALs seem to have been made without a great deal of long-range planning about the circumstances in which SEALs might be called on to fight. And to some extent, these decisions have been shaped by forces outside the small naval special warfare community.

Officers at the NSW headquarters in Coronado insist that, once they have their new equipment, the SEALs will make good use of it, and that is certainly true. The SEALs have made a habit, almost a virtue, of making do with what they have, innovating whenever necessary, and getting the job done against all odds.

The very adaptability of the SEALs is one of the reasons they have been spared, so far, from the budget-cutting afflicting most of the rest of the military. With all the uncertainty about the future of the U.S. military, there seems to be a feeling in the Pentagon and in Congress that the SEALs will remain a good investment. Even with a force larger than ever in the past, and with relatively expensive new ships and minisubs in its future, naval special warfare consumes less than half a billion dollars a year, a fraction of one percent of the Pentagon budget and half the cost of a single new destroyer. Most of the NSW budget goes to pay the SEALs and the two-thousand–odd men and women in the support forces.

Central to the great strength of the SEALs, of course, are the men themselves. They are smart, incredibly strong physically, and superbly trained.

Two senior SEALs—Rear Adm. Irish Flynn and Master Chief Boatswain's Mate Rudolph E. Boesch, both now retired—described the effects of the SEAL training course in a letter to the editor of the *Proceedings* of the U.S. Naval Institute in September 1989:

> We have not found another training course in the armed ser-
> vices that produces men ready to reconnoiter and clear beaches
> when walls of surf plunge repeatedly in a quarter-mile zone of
> white water over a reef-studded nearshore. No other course se-
> lects those who endure the hours in almost complete darkness during
> the swimmer delivery vehicle's transit, shuddering constantly as
> the surrounding water and compressed gas they breathe suck body
> heat from them, while still ahead loom struggles with claustro-
> phobia and real perils under a ship. Then—much later, when
> everyone is at the limit of strain and hypothermia—an underwa-
> ter rendezvous and reentry with a submarine. Compared to the
> water-associated work, the SEALs' other responsibilities—para-
> chuting, explosive demolition, land operations, close-quarter battle—
> seem safe, almost carefree endeavors.

And yet there are two different, and even somewhat contradictory, concerns about the BUDS (basic underwater demolition/SEAL) course, the crucible in which SEALs are formed.

One concern is the perception of many veteran SEALs that the course has been dangerously softened in recent years under pressure to in-crease the number of SEAL platoons. In the past, the trainee who found the course too tough or not to his liking simply rang the bell or said, "I DOR (drop on request)," and he was gone. Now there is no longer a bell to ring, and the trainee who wants to quit is counseled by a series of noncommissioned and commissioned officers and encouraged to remain in training. Whether this change is producing a group of SEALs who are not as good as they should be, or who will quit when the going gets tough, no one knows. Although a number of studies have been done of men in training, there have been no solid follow-up studies to measure how well men perform once they have pinned on the SEALs' "Budweiser" badge.

The other concern is that the SEALs tend to believe that, if a man has successfully made it through BUDS, and through the additional training in his first team, he can then be relied on under all circumstances. That is not always true, as the SEALs learned early in the Vietnam War, when a number of men quit when the dying started. And even if a man can be relied on not to run away, that does not mean he will think well under pressure. And it doesn't mean that, even if he performs well in combat, he can be relied on to plan a successful operation.

Coupled with this is the worry that some SEALs, having proved themselves in BUDS, think they are so good they don't have to plan and rehearse for an operation and that they can even play fair in combat. Gary Stubblefield puts it this way:

A lot of guys get what I would call a gunfighter mentality. They think it's like in the movies. They think you can stand off and trade equal and fair shots and, because you're a better shooter, you're going to win. It's not that way.

Did you ever see *Water Hole No. 3,* that old movie [1967] with James Coburn? A gunfighter out in the street calls Coburn out of the saloon. The guy is standing out there, his feet spread apart, waiting for Coburn to walk toward him, and he would begin walking. Coburn comes out, walks over to his horse, pulls his rifle out of his scabbard, puts it across his saddle, gets a good bench sight, shoots the guy dead, puts the thing back in his scabbard, walks back in and has a drink.

That's perfect intelligence. To me, there's nothing wrong with that. To me, that's the way war should be conducted. You don't fight a war to trade bodies. You fight a war to win. And if it means you stand two blocks away and shoot the guy with a rifle, and he only has a pistol, I think that's perfectly intelligent. A lot of our people don't have that attitude. They have the attitude that we're tougher and we shoot better, we don't get hurt as easily and we can go in and square off with these guys and we'll win.

It is clear from these important questions that SEALs continue to debate among themselves and that they are still involved in the process of trying to define exactly what it is that they do, how they fit in militarily in a changing world.

Just as the SEALs grew out of the UDTs and created such new and specialized units as Det Bravo, working with the Provincial Reconnaissance Units in Vietnam, and SEAL Team Six, with its focus on antiterrorism, they may well find new and unforeseen ways to use their skills in the future. As long as they keep asking themselves, "Who are we?" they will continue to find an important role to play in the nation's defense. If they ever find their niche and sink comfortably into it, their usefulness will be at an end.

BIBLIOGRAPHY

1. WHO ARE WE?

This account of the battle at Panama's Paitilla Airfield, in which SEAL losses were the heaviest in their history, is based on interviews with SEALs who were on the ground at Paitilla, were involved in the operation in a support role, or were men with extensive combat experience who later familiarized themselves with the operation.

Unfortunately, at this writing, the after-action reports that might provide a more detailed, and perhaps more revealing, account of what happened at Paitilla have not been made available to the public. And some publicly released information is misleading. A report by the House Armed Services Committee, released on 12 January 1990, *Operation Just Cause: Lessons and Warnings in the Future Use of Military Force,* erroneously reports, for example, that the SEAL losses at Paitilla were the result of a chance encounter with armored cars.

A detailed account of the Paitilla operation is contained in Bill Salisbury, "When SEALs Die," *San Diego Reader,* 4 October 1990. Another account of the battle, focusing on the death of Lt. John Connors, is contained in Malcolm McConnell, "Measure of a Man," *Reader's Digest,* October 1990.

The critical letter referred to in this chapter is quoted in full in chapter 13. Gary Stubblefield, the writer, declined to provide me with the letter, but it was widely circulated in the SEAL community and I managed to obtain a copy.

2. BLOODY WATERS—TARAWA AND NORMANDY

The terrible loss of life when the marines landed on Tarawa in November of 1943 added great urgency to the formation and training of the Underwater Demolition Teams, which are the direct antecedents of today's SEALs. That battle is described in Comdr. Francis Douglas Fane and Don Moore, *The Naked Warriors,* New York: Appleton-Century, 1956; John Costello, *The Pacific War,* New York: Rawson, Wade, 1981; and Rear Adm. Edwin T. Layton, *And I Was There: Pearl Harbor and Midway—Breaking the Secrets,* New York: Morrow, 1985.

Details of the doomed landing at Gallipoli came from Richard Hough, *The Great War at Sea, 1914–1918,* Oxford: Oxford University Press, 1983; and Robert Rhodes James, *Gallipoli: The History of a Noble Blunder,* New York: MacMillan, 1965.

The story of the British Combined Operations Pilotage Parties (COPPs) is told in Bill Strutton and Michael Pearson, *The Secret Invaders,* New York: British Book Centre, 1959.

Most of the information about the career of Phil H. Bucklew is drawn from his oral history interviews conducted in 1980 by John T. Mason, Jr., of the Naval Institute, which I read at the Navy Library in Washington, D.C. His description of his work with the British in the landings in Sicily and Italy corresponds to the accounts in Strutton and Pearson, cited above. Even though Bucklew was involved in various aspects of naval special warfare for more than two decades, he was never a member of an Underwater Demolition or SEAL team, and at least partially for that reason, he remains a controversial figure among some members of the community.

The account of the first naval demolition effort of World War II near the Vichy French port of Lyautey in North Africa is drawn from *The Naked Warriors.*

My account of the extraordinary career of Draper L. Kauffman comes largely from the oral history interview with him conducted by Mason in 1978 and 1979. It, too, was examined at the Navy Library. His son, Draper Kauffman, Jr., granted me permission to quote from that interview. *The Naked Warriors* also contains a good deal of information about Kauffman, his involvement in the formation of the Underwater Demolition Teams, and their role in the Pacific War.

The account of the preparations for the Normandy landing and the landing itself are drawn from Bucklew's oral history, *The Naked Warriors,* and Cornelius Ryan, *The Longest Day: June 6, 1944,* New York: Simon and Schuster, 1959. Although there have been differing estimates of the casualty rate among the gap-assault teams during the Normandy invasion, I have relied on the figures contained in *The Naked Warriors,* which show that by far the heaviest losses were sustained at Omaha Beach, where 52 percent of the navy men involved in clearing obstacles from the beach were killed or injured.

These figures correspond to a roster of the dead, wounded, and unwounded participants in the Omaha Beach landing that was distributed at a Navy Day Recognition Service on 27 October 1944 at the Naval

Amphibious Training Base at Fort Pierce. That roster was made available to me by James Robert Chittum, of Las Vegas, Nevada, who served in UDT Three in the Pacific.

3. FROM SAIPAN TO TOKYO BAY

Rear Adm. Cathal L. ("Irish") Flynn, now retired, gave me a good overview of the history of the Underwater Demolition Teams and their evolution into the SEALs. Even though he had spent a long and often dangerous career as a SEAL, there was a note of awe in his voice as he spoke, during an interview, of the "breathtakingly courageous things" done by the Underwater Demolition Teams in the Pacific in World War II.

Many details of those operations are contained in the Kauffman interview cited above and in *The Naked Warriors*. A great wealth of material is contained in the official histories of the UDTs written at the end of World War II. They are available on microfilm at the Navy Library. The UDT histories, as well as the overview provided in the *History of Commander, Underwater Demolition Teams and Underwater Demolition Flotilla, Amphibious Forces, Pacific,* are contained on one roll of microfilm, NRS II-490-511, available in the Operational Archives, Naval Historical Center, Washington Navy Yard. The anonymous authors of the histories of UDT Seven, which took part in many of the Pacific operations and also trained a number of the other teams, and UDT Eleven, provided detailed information on the operations in which they took part as well as very candid comments on some of the problems encountered, such as sand in the food.

Little has been written about the failure of UDT Sixteen to carry out its assignment of destroying the Japanese obstacles at Okinawa. Kauffman refers to the incident briefly, and the history of UDT Eleven tells how the team was sent back in the following day to blow up the obstacles left standing by UDT Sixteen. A detailed first-person account of the incident is contained in Edward T. Higgins, *Webfooted Warriors,* New York: Exposition Press, 1955. Higgins was a member of UDT Eleven, the team assigned "to finish the job they loused up." The history of UDT Sixteen makes no mention of the team's failure to carry out its assignment. The wonder is not that there was such a breakdown but that, considering the hurried training and the great danger and physical demands of UDT work, there were not more such failures.

Irish Flynn first called my attention to the extraordinary career of

Frank Kaine, "MacArthur's frogman." Kaine described his career in a series of oral history interviews with Comdr. Etta-Belle Kitchen of the Naval Institute in 1981. I examined that interview at the SEAL/ UDT Museum in Fort Pierce, Florida.

Lt. Tom Westerlin, "Birth of the Figure 8 Rope," *All Hands,* October 1978, describes the method used to retrieve swimmers from the water.

4. A DIFFERENT BREED—COMMANDOS FROM THE SEA

Much of the material for this chapter came from an interview with Dr. Christian J. Lambertsen, M.D., at his office at the Institute for Environmental Medicine, of which he is the founding director, at the University of Pennsylvania Medical School in Philadelphia.

The list of his accomplishments during World War II is drawn largely from a memo to the director of the Office of Strategic Services on 26 September 1945 from Comdr. H. G. A. Woolley of the Royal Navy. Woolley met Lambertsen in October of 1942 when the British officer was in charge of maritime activities for the OSS.

The commendation of Lambertsen by Lt. Comdr. Derek A. Lee, RNVR, was written 16 April 1945.

The information related to the history of combat swimming comes primarily from Howard E. Larson, *A History of Self-Contained Diving and Underwater Swimming,* Washington, D.C.: National Academy of Sciences National Research Council, 1959, which was provided to me by Dr. Lambertsen.

Most of the material relating to U.S. Navy operations in China during World War II is drawn from Vice Adm. Milton E. Miles, as prepared by Hawthorne Daniel from the original manuscript, *A Different Kind of War: The Little-Known Story of the Combined Guerrilla Forces Created in China by the U.S. Navy and the Chinese During World War II,* Garden City, N.Y.: Doubleday & Co., 1967. Miles does not mention Bucklew's visit to China, which is drawn from Bucklew's own reminiscences, cited above.

5. NEW HORIZONS—AND WAR IN KOREA

The account of Francis Douglas Fane's career in underwater work comes from *The Naked Warriors* and an interview with Fane, who now lives in retirement in Fort Lauderdale, Florida. Still lively and combative in his eighties, Fane gave a vivid description of his long career in the navy and his innovative work in the period immediately after World War II.

Material about the careers of Kaine and Bucklew is drawn from their oral histories, cited above.

Details of the training in the use of underwater breathing apparatuses are from interviews conducted at the SEALs' training center in Coronado. *The Draeger Student Guide* (locally prepared), used by students in training, lists the depth limits for a diver breathing pure oxygen.

Lambertsen's recollections were obtained in an interview with him, cited above.

Descriptions of some of the navy's early attempts to make it easier for combat swimmers to get from one place to another were provided by W. T. ("Tom") Odum, of the Naval Coastal Systems Center in Panama City, Florida. Kaine also referred to a number of these in his oral history.

Robert E. Fulton, Jr., described the development of his sky hook and other inventions during an interview at his home factory in a rural area near Newtown, Connecticut.

The fatal accident involving Photographer's Mate Third Class James Earl Fox was described to me by Admiral LeMoyne, who was in charge of the operation. The accident and the subsequent investigation are also described in detail in the official accident report provided to me by the Office of the Navy Judge Advocate General.

The night pickup off the California coast was described to me by Maynard Weyers, one of the four men plucked from their rubber boats that night, and by Fulton, who was present for the test.

John Raynolds told me of his experiences in the UDT during the Korean War in an interview at his office in Greenwich, Connecticut. Retired Capt. William Hamilton, Jr., also told of his experiences during that period in a series of interviews.

The attempt to destroy the North Korean fishing industry is described in James Berry, "Operation Fishnet," U.S. Naval Institute *Proceedings,* December 1990, and Anon., "Frogmen in Korea," *Colliers,* February 21, 1953.

6. BIRTH OF THE SEALs
Hamilton, cited above, told me of his work in Washington in the fall of 1961 that led to the formation of the SEALs in January of the following year.

Other details of that period are contained in Edward J. Marolda and

Oscar P. Fitzgerald, *The United States Navy and the Vietnam Conflict.* Vol. 2, *From Military Assistance to Combat,* 1959–1965, Washington, D.C.: Naval Historical Center, 1986.

The formation of the two original SEAL teams was described to me in interviews by David Del Giudice, first commander of Team One, at his office in Burbank, California, and Roy Boehm, first commander of Team Two, at his home in Punta Gorda, Florida. J. H. ("Hoot") Andrews also told me of the early days in Team Two, of which he was storekeeper, during an interview in Las Vegas.

Henry S. Thrift described his early experiences with UDT Twenty-one and SEAL Team Two in an interview at his home in Lake Wales, Florida. William N. Bruhmuller was interviewed at his home in Panama City, Florida.

Pierre Ponson, a veteran member of the Chuting Stars, told me of his experience as a SEAL and parachute expert in an interview in Little Creek, Virginia.

My description of SEAL training is based on a visit to the training center at Coronado and the SEAL base on San Clemente Island. Lt. Scott Flinn, who monitors the health of the men in training, was interviewed at Coronado.

Warrant Officer George Hudak was interviewed during my visit to San Clemente.

My description of the way SEALs use explosives is based on a visit to Little Creek, where I accompanied a group of SEALs going through requalification in this skill.

Capt. Theodore Grabowsky told me the anecdote about the possible shark-sighting off San Clemente during an interview in his Washington office.

Albert W. Winter, a retired SEAL, told me of his brush with death from hypothermia during an interview at his home in San Diego.

The death of Hospital Corpsman Third Class John Joseph Tomlinson from hypothermia is described in the official accident report obtained from the Office of the Navy Judge Advocate General.

Winter, cited above, described to me the development of the large SEAL "Budweiser" badge.

I interviewed Dr. Thomas J. Doubt of the Hyperbaric Medicine Program Center at the Naval Medical Research Institute, at his office in Bethesda, Maryland.

The outline of the basic underwater demolition/SEAL (BUDS) training in Coronado is contained in "A Guide to Naval Special Warfare," a navy brochure provided to prospective trainees.

The tests that showed changes in SEALs as a result of their training are described in D. G. McDonald, J. P. Norton, and J. A. Hodgdon, "Determinants and Effects of Training Success in U.S. Navy Special Forces," Naval Health Research Center, report No. 88–34, 8 August 1988.

Other studies of SEALs consulted were: Lt. Comdr. Richard H. Rahe and Comdr. Ransom J. Arthur, "Stressful Underwater Demolition Training: Serum Urate and Cholesterol Viability," *The Journal of the American Medical Association,* 11 December 1967; James A. Hodgdon, Harold W. Goforth, Jr., and Richard L. Hilderbrand, "Carbohydrate Loading as a Means of Extending Endurance Performance," *Proceedings,* 21st Annual Conference of the Military Testing Association, San Diego, 15–19 October 1979; M. B. Beckett, H. W. Goforth and J. A. Hodgdon, "Physical Fitness of U.S. Navy Special Forces Team Members and Trainees," Naval Health Research Center, report No. 89–29, 7 July 1989; J. A. Hodgdon and M. B. Beckett, "Prediction of Percent Body Fat for U.S. Navy Men From Body Circumferences and Height," Naval Health Research Center, report No. 84–11, March 1984; Eric Gunderson, R. H. Rahe and R. J. Arthur, "Prediction of Performance in Stressful Underwater Demolition Training," *Journal of Applied Psychology,* Vol. 56, No. 5, 1972; Lt. Comdr. Robert J. Biersner, David H. Ryman, and Capt. Richard H. Rahe, "Physical, Psychological, Blood Serum, and Mood Predictors of Success in Preliminary Underwater Demolition Team Training," *Military Medicine,* March 1977; and Lindsay Carter and Richard H. Rahe, "Effects of Stressful Underwater Demolition Training on Body Structure," *Medicine and Science in Sports,* August 1975.

The account of the involvement of the early SEAL teams in operations on the Cuban shore and during the Cuban missile crisis of 1962 is drawn from interviews with Roy Boehm, William T. Cannon, George Walsh, and David Del Giudice and the oral history of Frank Kaine, cited above.

The dates for the harrowing survey of the Havana harbor are fixed by unclassified citations issued to those who participated by Adm. Alfred G. Ward, then commander, Amphibious Force, Atlantic Fleet.

The citations do not mention the nature of the "special operations" involved. But an article in the Norfolk *Ledger-Star,* written by Jack Kestner, the newspaper's military writer, shortly after the missile crisis, speculated accurately that the navy's frogmen "undoubtedly know more about the beaches and off-shore waters of Cuba than Castro does himself." The article was based, at least in part, on an interview with the skipper of one of the submarines that took part in those operations.

I also consulted Robert F. Kennedy, *Thirteen Days, A Memoir of the Cuban Missile Crisis,* New York: W. W. Norton, 1968.

Details of the voyage of the Mekong boat flotilla were drawn from Marolda, cited above, and an interview with Del Giudice.

7. A PLEASANT LITTLE WAR

The early involvement of the SEALs in Vietnam is described by Marolda and Fitzgerald, cited above. The situation there was also described to me by Flynn and Weyers, cited above, who served in Da Nang in those early days.

The Gulf of Tonkin incident is described in detail by Marolda and Fitzgerald and in the twelve-volume *Pentagon Papers,* more formally known as the Department of Defense's *United States–Vietnam Relations: 1945–1967,* Washington: GPO, 1971.

William Colby's doubts about the effectiveness of the raids against the north are contained in an oral history interview available at the Navy Library.

Although others told me of Del Giudice's involvement in the operations out of Da Nang, he declined to discuss that part of his career with me.

Capt. Michael L. Mulford's account of the delivery of the first Nasty class boats to Vietnam is contained in an oral history interview conducted with him by Marolda and available at the Navy Library.

Grabowsky told me, in an interview in his Washington office, of the incident in which he almost went along on a raid against North Vietnam. Although Flynn and Weyers say neither they nor any Americans working under them, to their knowledge, went on such raids, several retired enlisted men told me they did accompany the Vietnamese frogmen but did not go ashore. Later in the war, I was told, Americans participated in such operations and actually went ashore in the north.

Both Boehm and Weyers told me of their experiences during the early involvement of the SEALs in the southern area of South Vietnam, and Weyers described the firefight in which Billy Machen became the first SEAL killed in combat in Vietnam.

8. THE MEN WITH GREEN FACES
James D. Watson told me of his experiences in Vietnam when I visited the SEAL/UDT Museum in Fort Pierce, where he is the director.

Bill Bruhmuller told me of his experiences in Vietnam when I visited him at his home in Panama City, Florida.

Rodney Pastore was interviewed at Little Creek, where he was command master chief of Naval Special Warfare Group Two.

Ronald K. Bell, a retired captain, was interviewed at his home in Coronado.

The sign reporting that SEALs kill for fun and money was described in Craig R. Whitney, "Navy's 'Seals,' SuperSecret Commandos, Are Quitting Vietnam," *New York Times*, 29 November 1971.

Larry W. Bailey, also a retired captain, was interviewed at his home near Mount Vernon, Virginia.

Casualties suffered by the SEALs in Vietnam are described in T. L. Bosiljevac, *SEALs, UDT/SEAL Operations in Vietnam*, Boulder, Colorado: Paladin Press, 1990, also available in paperback, with an index, New York: Ivy Books, 1991. Bosiljevac, a SEAL officer, wrote his manuscript as part of his work toward an advanced academic degree. It provides the best detailed, overall account, from unclassified sources, of the SEALs' involvement in the Vietnam War.

Personal experiences of individual SEALs who served in Vietnam are described in Ian Padden, *U.S. Navy SEALs: From Boot Camp to the Battle Zones,* New York: Bantam, 1985; Darryl Young, *The Element of Surprise: Navy SEALs in Vietnam,* New York: Ivy Books, 1990; and Kevin Dockery, *SEALs in Action,* New York: Avon Books, 1991.

The incident in which Warrant Officer Eugene Tinnin was killed is described by Bosiljevac and by the official history of SEAL Team One for 1968, available at the Navy Library.

Command histories for SEAL Teams One and Two, parts one and two, NRS 1988–4, are available on microfilm at the Operational Archives, Naval Historical Center, Washington Navy Yard.

Bailey, cited above, told me in an interview of the similar incident in which he shot one of his own men.

The accidental deaths of members of Team One in a helicopter crash and in the explosion of a mortar shell are included in the team's official histories for 1968 and 1970.

The boats used by the SEALs in Vietnam are described by Bosiljevac.

Thomas L. Hawkins, a retired commander, and Grabowsky, cited above, told me in interviews of the feelings toward them by others in the American military.

Vice Adm. Robert S. Salzer discussed his experiences with the SEALs in an oral history interview available at the Navy Library.

The arrival of Vice Adm. Elmo R. Zumwalt and his influence on the war in the delta are described in Lt. Comdr. Thomas J. Cutler, *Brown Water, Black Berets*, New York: Pocket Books, 1989.

Charles Watson, who became a lawyer and a state prosecutor, described his experiences during the Tet offensive in an interview at his office in Colonial Heights, Virginia.

Bucklew's report on his survey trip to Vietnam is contained in "JUSMAG, Vietnam. Infiltration into South Vietnam" (Bucklew Report), NRS 397, available on microfilm at the Operational Archives, Naval Historical Center, Washington Navy Yard. Del Giudice, who accompanied Bucklew, also discussed that trip with me in an interview.

Thrift, cited above, described his experiences in the Ca Mau area in an interview.

William Cowan, who as a marine officer often worked with the SEALs in Vietnam, told me of his experiences during an interview in his office in Fredericksburg, Virginia.

The operation in which Lt. Joseph R. Kerrey won the Medal of Honor is described by Bosiljevac and by the official citation awarding the medal.

Boehm told me of his disillusionment with the war in Vietnam in an interview.

LeMoyne, cited above, and John Wilbur, now an attorney in Palm Beach, Florida, who was his predecessor as overseer of the PRU program in the delta, told me of the SEALs' participation with the PRU.

Bosiljevac describes the incident in which Tom Norris won his Medal of Honor and the action a few months later when Engineman Second Class Michael Thornton won the medal for his rescue of Norris. Both Capts. Mike Jukoski and Douglas Huth told me, in interviews, of their association with Norris. The two actions are also described in the citations accompanying award of the medals.

9. THE SUPER SEALs

The operation in which Lt. Melvin ("Spence") Dry became the last SEAL to lose his life in the Vietnam War is described in Edwin L. Towers, *Operation Thunderhead: Hope for Freedom,* La Jolla, California: Lane & Associates, 1981. According to Towers's account, he was responsible for planning the attempted rescue of the escaping American prisoners and was in the helicopter from which Dry jumped to his death. Despite the passage of some twenty years, details of the operation are still considered classified, so it was not possible to compare Towers's account with official records of the operation.

However, several SEALs, who were not present but were familiar with the incident, were able to confirm a number of details recounted by Towers.

Dry's death was reported in an official accidental injury/death report on 9 July 1972. Although the location and names of the units involved were withheld because of the classified nature of the operation, the official report of Dry's death corresponds with Towers's account, and Towers is listed as one of three witnesses interviewed. A copy of the report was obtained under the Freedom of Information Act through the navy judge advocate general.

A good summary of the history of combat swimming is contained in Howard E. Larson, *A History of Self-Contained Diving and Underwater Swimming,* Washington, D.C.: National Academy of Sciences National Research Council, 1959, which was provided to me by Dr. Lambertsen. Another overview is contained in Richard Compton-Hall, "Reemergence of the Midgets," *Military Technology,* October 1987.

Larson's history describes the Italian interest in human torpedo riders. Further information about the Italian use of this unusual form of warfare is contained in Raymond De Belot, Rear Admiral, French Navy (Ret.), *The Struggle for the Mediterranean, 1939–1945,* Princeton: Princeton University Press, 1951; William Schofield and P. J. Carisella, *Frogmen: First Battles,* Boston: Branden Publishing Co., 1987; and David Zinman, "Wartime Adventures of a Human Torpedo," *Washington Star* from Associated Press, 17 December 1961. Zinman's account is based on an interview with Lt. Luigi

Durand de la Penne, who led the Italian attack on the British fleet at Alexandria.

A detailed and fascinating account of the British efforts to sink the German battleship *Tirpitz* is contained in Leonce Peillard, *Sink the Tirpitz!,* New York: Putman's, 1968.

The U.S. Navy's efforts, during the 1950s and afterward, to develop its own small submersibles were described to me by W. T. ("Tom") Odum, head of the ocean engineering department of the Naval Coastal Systems Center in Panama City, Florida, and by Parks, cited above. Current efforts in the development of submersibles and underwater breathing apparatus were described to me by Odum and Parks, as well as Walter W. Howard, head, naval special warfare systems development branch, and Robert H. Banks, director of the diving and salvage division, in Panama City.

Hawkins, cited above, is one of the navy's most enthusiastic supporters of the SDV concept. He described their development and use in an interview, even though what he could discuss was restricted by the classified nature of much of the information about SDVs. He also described the use of SDVs in an article, "SDVs: Underwater Transit for a Chosen Few," *Faceplate,* Spring 1975.

In testimony before the House Armed Services Committee in the spring of 1983, a navy witness told how the Mark 37 torpedo had been adapted so that two of them could be carried by the Mark 9 SDV. "And with that," he told the committee, "the special warfare people can get in close to the beach and take under attack shipping that might be in the harbor from some reasonable range so that they don't hazard themselves in close." He described the system as operational in both fleets.

I toured the SDV hangar at Coronado with Chief Quartermaster Nick North and the similar facility at Little Creek with Comdr. Doug Lowe, executive officer of SDV Team Two, and Command Master Chief Herbert Haskin. Haskin later described, in an interview, his long experience in SDV operations.

Submarine operations by frogmen are described in detail in John Dwyer, "Surface Action: Submarine Support Special Ops," *Soldier of Fortune,* May 1987.

These operations are also described in the command histories for UDTs Eleven and Thirteen for 1970.

The physiological challenges faced by SDV operators were described to me in interviews by Dr. Doubt, cited above, and Capt. Edward Thalman, of the Navy Diving Center in Bethesda.

10. THE LIEUTENANT (JG) SAYS NO
Comdr. D. T. ("Tom") Coulter told me of his part in the *Mayaguez* affair during an interview in Little Creek, where he is executive officer of Naval Special Warfare Group Two.

I consulted files of the *New York Times* for details of the capture of the *Mayaguez* and her crew and the subsequent rescue attempts, as well as for official statements issued in Washington at that time.

The involvement of the SEALs in the U.S. intervention in the Dominican Republic was described to me by Bailey, cited above.

The special obligation of SEAL officers to protect their men was described by Steve Elson in an interview.

11. THE MARCH OF THE JEDI
The creation of special military hostage-rescue units after the failure at Desert One has been described in a number of newspaper and magazine articles. Among those consulted were: Jeff Gerth and Philip Taubman, "U.S. Military Creates Secret Units for Use in Sensitive Tasks Abroad," *New York Times,* 8 June 1984; David C. Morrison, "The 'Shadow War,' " *National Journal,* 10 May 1986; Norman Black, from Associated Press, "Navy Aiming to Expand Commandos," *Washington Post,* 21 February 1987; Norman Polmar, "SOF—The Navy's Perspective," U.S. Naval Institute *Proceedings,* August 1987.

The navy's 1986 "Special Warfare Master Plan" details plans for growth of the SEALs and refers to a special atomic demolition munition and to SEAL Team Six.

The role of SEAL Team Six is also mentioned in Jim Stewart, "U.S. Special Forces Play Large but Little Known Role in Persian Gulf," *Atlanta Journal & Constitution,* 1 November 1987; and John Collins, "United States and Soviet Special Operations," a study by the Congressional Research Service, Library of Congress, 1987.

Richard Marcinko, who was in prison at the time, responded to my questions with a lengthy letter. Quotations attributed to him are from that letter.

The anecdote about Marcinko and Lon Non was related to me by Rear Adm. George Worthington.

Comdr. Norman J. Carley, now retired, told me in an interview of the period in the late 1970s when the foundations were laid for the creation of SEAL Team Six, and Lt. Theodore Macklin, also now retired, told me of his recruitment into the team.

Comdr. Thomas Mountz, who spent five years as clinical psychologist with SEAL Team Six, told me in an interview at his office at the Naval Investigative Service in Washington of his service with the team.

The involvement of the SEALs in the *Achille Lauro* affair was confirmed in a press conference by Adm. James D. Watkins, then chief of naval operations, in Norfolk, Virginia, on 11 October 1985. His remarks were reported in "If F-14s Failed, Special Forces Were Ready," *Army Times,* 21 October 1985.

The quotation from Bell is from an interview with him, cited above. The quotation from Hawkins, cited above, is from an interview with him at his office in northern Virginia.

The troubles with Team Six were the subject of a number of newspaper articles. Among those consulted were: Charles R. Babcock, "Finances of Secret Navy Team Probed," *Washington Post,* undated 1987; Ted Bush, "September Federal Trial Set for Former SEAL," *Navy Times,* 10 August 1987; Ted Bush, "SEALs Lawyer: Creative Financing Got Supplies," *Navy Times,* 11 September 1987; Charles R. Babcock, "Ex-Member of Elite Navy Team Pleads Guilty," *Washington Post,* 17 September 1987 (refers to guilty plea by John Mason); Charles R. Babcock, "U.S. Widens Corruption Probe of Navy Hostage Rescue Team," *Washington Post,* 18 December 1987; David Martin, "Navy Anti-Terrorism Team," CBS "Evening News," 14 April 1988; Robert F. Howe, "Grenade Maker Guilty in Kickback," *Washington Post,* 22 October 1989.

Details of the charges against Marcinko and Charles M. Byers are taken from the indictment issued by a grand jury in the U.S. District Court for the Eastern District of Virginia in the July 1989 term.

Further details revealed by the Naval Investigative Service investigation are contained in a series of fact sheets issued by the NIS and the U.S. attorney's office between July 1989 and 9 March 1990, when Marcinko was sentenced.

Quotations from Hamilton, Mason, and Captain Robert Gormly are taken from the transcript of the trial of Marcinko and Byers.

The investigation was also described to me in an interview by Clifford R. Simmen, who headed the probe.

Comdr. Jack Schropp, who is retired, described his concern about

SEAL Team Six in a telephone interview from his home in Petaluma, California.

Weyers, cited above, told me during an interview of his problems with Team Six.

Vice Adm. J. A. Lyons, now retired, was interviewed at his home in northern Virginia.

Capt. George Vercessi, now retired, told me of his involvement with Red Cell and Marcinko during an interview in his Washington office.

The officer whose call to the office of the inspector general that apparently kicked off the probe of Marcinko and SEAL Team Six requested that his name not be used because he feared that if his name were printed, it would create needless turmoil in the SEAL community.

John Mason acknowledged, while being questioned during the trial of Marcinko and Byers, that he had been removed from the rifle team because he had falsified his score.

The catalogue describing the various types of grenades made by Byers's Accuracy Systems was included in the evidence obtained during the investigation and was found stored in the federal courthouse in Alexandria, Virginia.

12. A TINY LITTLE ISLAND
The best overall account of the Grenada operation is contained in Maj. Mark Adkins, *Urgent Fury: The Battle for Grenada,* Lexington, Massachusetts: D. C. Heath, Lexington Books, 1989. Despite the secrecy surrounding the use of SEALs and other special operations forces in Grenada, Adkins provides a remarkably detailed description of the battle.

I have relied on his account of the operation but supplemented that with interviews with SEALs who were either on the ground in Grenada or were familiar with the conflict from their conversations with SEALs who were involved. For many years, even most SEALs were kept in the dark about their organization's involvement. Finally, in 1989, six years later, a briefing for SEAL officers was conducted at Coronado by three officers who had participated as members of SEAL Team Six.

Beginning at the time of the battle, and continuing for a number of years, there were newspaper and magazine articles and broadcast news reports about various aspects of the operation. Among those consulted were: John G. Fialka, "In Battle for Grenada, Commando Missions Didn't Go as Planned," *Wall Street Journal,* 15 November 1983; Anon., "New Barracks at Norfolk Named in Memory of SEAL Schamberger," *Navy Times,* 3 September 1984; Frank Greve, "A Report of U.S. Military Ineptness in Grenada," *Philadelphia Inquirer,* 21 October 1984; Charles Mohr, "U.S. Concealed Grenada Losses, Report Charges," *New York Times,* 22 October 1984; Tom Brokaw and Fred Francis, "U.S. Casualties in Grenada," NBC "Nightly News," 22 October 1984; Walter Andrews, "Weinberger Refutes Claim of Unreported Deaths in Grenada," *Washington Times,* 24 October 1984; Robert C. Toth, "U.S. Elite Troops Lack a Mission, Experts Charge," *Los Angeles Times,* 18 November 1984; Richard Whitmire, "Elite Force's Grenada Role at Issue," *USA Today,* 26 October 1984; Deborah G. Meyer and Benjamin F. Schemmer, Interview with Noel C. Koch, *Armed Forces Journal International,* March 1985; Charles Mohr, "Commando Squad Is Trained to Kill With Full 'Surprise, Speed, Success,'" *New York Times,* 21 June 1985; Tom Diaz, "Parachutes Blamed in Divers' Drowning," *Washington Times,* 11 July 1985; Lt. Col. Gary L. Bounds and Maj. Scott R. McMichael, "Elite Forces," *ARMY,* November 1985; Sen. William S. Cohen (R-Me), "Fix for an SOF Capability That Is Most Assuredly Broken," *Armed Forces Journal International,* January 1986; John Dancy, "Move to Streamline Special Operations Forces," NBC's "Today" show, 15 May 1986; David C. Morrison, "The 'Shadow War,'" *National Journal,* 10 May 1986; "Navy Seals: Special Warriors," *All Hands,* December 1987; Christopher K. Mellon, "The Low Frontier: Congress and Unconventional Warfare," remarks at the National War College, 11 January 1988; James M. Perry and John J. Fialka, "As Panama Outcome Is Praised, Details Emerge of Bungling During the 1983 Grenada Invasion," *Wall Street Journal,* 15 January 1990; Bill Salisbury, "War Beneath the Waves—You Know Ken," *San Diego's Weekly Reader,* 5 October 1990.

13. TARGET: MANUEL NORIEGA

This chapter, an expansion of chapter 1 describing the attack on the Paitilla Airfield in Panama, relies on the same basic sources and additional information.

A number of newspaper and magazine articles reported on the involvement of the SEALs in the Panama operation. Because of the secrecy surrounding much of what occurred during Operation Just Cause, many of these reports lack important details or, in some cases, are simply wrong.

In this account I have relied primarily on interviews with SEALs who were either involved in the Panama operations or are familiar with them from sources within the SEAL community. This basic information was backed up, in a number of instances, by the citations for the many medals issued after the attack.

Carley, cited above, gave me a good description, in an interview, of the sinking of the *Presidente Porras* by four combat swimmers under his command.

Among the articles consulted were: Charles W. Corddry, "SEALs Reportedly Hunted Noriega," *Baltimore Sun,* 21 December 1989; Bill Gertz, "Assault on Paitilla Airport Costs Elite Navy Unit 4 Dead," *Washington Times,* 22 December 1989; Douglas Jehl and Bob Secter, "Invasion Was Coup for No One," *Los Angeles Times,* 27 December 1989; David Evans, "Military Experts See Flaws in Attack Plan," *Chicago Tribune,* 24 December 1989; Bernard E. Trainor, "Flaws in Panama Attack," *New York Times,* 31 December 1989; Barbara Amouyal, "F-117A Stealth Fighter Draws Fire Despite Success in Panama," *Defense News,* 1 January 1990; Bill Gertz, "Pentagon Investigates Possible Security Leak by Troops in Panama," *Washington Times,* 5 January 1990; William Branigin, "U.S. Agent Rescued from Panama Cell Minutes Before Anti-Noriega Offensive," *Washington Post,* 1 January 1990; Douglas Waller, John Barry, Christopher Dickey, and Spencer Reiss, "Inside the Invasion," *Newsweek,* 25 June 1990; James Bennet, "Mission Improbable: Why—10 years after Desert One—the U.S. Still Isn't Ready to Fight the War Against Terrorism," *Washington Monthly,* June 1990; Larry Bonko, "'Just Cause' Lives: SEALs Honored for Heroism in Panama," *Virginian Pilot and Ledger Star,* 5 January 1991.

Other information about the Panama invasion was provided by Maj. Gen. Hugh L. Cox, deputy commander in chief of the Special Operations Command, before a subcommittee of the House Armed Services Committee on 7 March 1990.

Gen. James J. Lindsay, then commander of USSCOM, discussed the operation in congressional testimony and in a meeting with the Defense Writers' Group in Washington on 31 January 1990. His description of the purpose of the SEALs' involvement at Paitilla is drawn from a transcript of that meeting with reporters.

LeMoyne and Worthington, cited above, provided their comments on the Paitilla operation in interviews.

Stubblefield's letter, as noted above, was not provided by Stubblefield, but a number of copies were circulated within the SEAL community, and one of them was made available to me by another source. Stubblefield, in an interview, confirmed the thrust of the letter. Capt. Raymond C. Smith, Jr., confirmed in a telephone interview that he had forwarded Stubblefield's letter with a favorable endorsement.

14. TO THE PERSIAN GULF—AND BEYOND

The buildup of SEAL forces and their operations in the Gulf War were described to me in an interview at Coronado by Lt. Tom Deitz and Chief Warrant Officer Roger Hayden.

Captain Smith, commander of the Naval Special Warfare Task Group, Central, in Saudi Arabia, discussed the Gulf War in a telephone interview and outlined the operations carried out under his command in a twenty-six-page summary of operations. Biographical information on Smith is contained in a biography made available during the ceremony when he left his post as commodore of Naval Special Warfare Group One in July 1991.

In an address at the change-of-command ceremony, Smith referred to the presence of a SEAL delivery vehicle unit in the Gulf but neither he nor other officials in Coronado would provide any details of its use.

Capt. Thomas N. Lawson, deputy commander of the Naval Special Warfare Command, shared his thoughts on the future role of the SEALs during an interview in Coronado.

The shortage of language specialists was pinpointed in *Conduct of the Persian Gulf Conflict: An Interim Report to Congress,* released by the Pentagon in July 1991. The report includes a seven-page section on the participation of special operations forces in Desert Storm and briefly describes the role played by naval special warfare forces.

The new 170-foot PC ship now coming into use and other new equipment were described to me by Lt. Comdr. Walter S. Pullar III, assistant chief of staff for program objectives memoranda for the Naval Special Warfare Command, in the course of two interviews in Coronado.

A number of SEALs shared with me their thoughts on whether SEALs in the future should plan for multiplatoon operations. Admiral Flynn, in an interview, raised the other question described in this chapter of whether the eight-man squad is too small a unit to operate effectively in the conflicts in which the SEALs might find themselves involved in the future.

I used the quote from Stubblefield expressing his concern about the "gunfighting mentality" because it was a colorful description of the problem. But I heard the same concern expressed by a number of other SEALs from different generations. Doug Fane, cited above, had much the same thing to say concerning his experiences in the Korean War, as did Warrant Officer George Hudak, a Vietnam veteran involved in training would-be SEALs.

INDEX